Awakening in Change

Working with Change
On the Path to Enlightenment

Merl Will-Wallace

ISBN-10:0615994695
ISBN-13:9780615994697

There comes a time
When you just have to let go
And allow what is
Lead you to a more enlightened life.

This is the Grace of Change.

DEDICATION

To the three driving forces that were the backbone in the creation of this book, William Bridges, Ernest Holmes and Adyashanti. Your clarity in understanding change has allowed me to synthesize a process for allowing change to guide myself and others along the path of enlightenment.

CONTENTS

ACKNOWLEDGMENTS

To my men's group at the Center for Spiritual Living in Colorado Springs, whose insights, encouragement and support were critical to the writing of this book. Who said men can't talk about anything other than sports? To Edward for his brilliance in editing the content within these pages. And, most important, to my lovely wife, Barbara, for her constant support, patience, wisdom and expertise in grammar that made this book readable.

Preface

Welcome. You are in the right place. Know that your intuitive sense to look beyond the cover of this book has drawn you to exactly what is needed in your life at this time. You are being driven by that quiet voice within. That knowing voice you may not even have consciously heard yet. I am firmly convinced you are meant to read these words at this time. Change is here and you are hungry to understand what it means for you now and in the future.

You most likely picked up this book because the title struck a small chord in your mind and maybe your heart. Probably the word that stands out for you is *change*. We are engaged in a millennium of ever accelerating change. How we look at life, interact with others and respond to a rapidly changing environment, culture and way of living requires greater skill and understanding if we are to keep up. Constant change *is* the new reality.

We have seen an explosion of knowledge, which has lead to both good and bad outcomes. We have also seen the pace of life accelerate along with the rate of change. What has seemed like a fairly constant and stable life for our ancestors is now transient and constantly shifting. The certainty of life has transformed into mystery. We are less certain as to what will happen next; and all we know is that life, as we know it, is rapidly transforming into something new.

Look around. Our environment and the well being of the planet as a whole are now in jeopardy. The independence of our economies no longer exists. Nations are rapidly changing in leadership and structure in an effort to meet the needs of their people. Employment is uncertain, and there are very few life-long jobs any more. Personal relationships are rapidly changing. Divorce is becoming more of the norm, and we seem to be changing partners as quickly as we change jobs. More people are marrying later in life or just choosing to stay single.

Most important, we are rapidly changing who we are. Individual identity is illusive and uncertain as we attempt to adapt to all of the change going on around us. We are less confident, and more fearful that who we think we are will fail in the face of our mounting challenges from life. The whole idea of a separate self seems smaller, weaker, and more vulnerable, so we look for a new definition of *who* and *what* we are. We seek to find a greater understanding in which we possess greater power and ability than we currently have at our command. We sense a greater power within, but are having trouble tapping in to this power. Our lives are in a seeming constant state of flux.

The predictions for our future have a common theme: learn to change or perish. At first blush not a very cheery thought. If we can learn, however, to embrace change and to enter into the rapid waters of life firmly grounded in the present moment and with a sense of adventure, then, maybe these predictions are not as scary. Maybe we are on the brink of new levels of consciousness, new ways of interacting with others, and gaining a greater perspective of our connection with all we experience. Change, then, is the catalyst of our evolution.

In titling this book "Awakening in Change" I am acknowledging that change is our greatest teacher.

- ➢ Change is the energy to wake us up from the stories that make up the waking dream of our life, and allows us to experience the reality of the present.
- ➢ Change challenges us to see the truth.
- ➢ Change teaches us about impermanence and its effect on our ability to control our life.
- ➢ Change reminds us constantly that life is flowing and not stagnant.

In the swirling confusion that change can create, we awaken to our true nature and just *be*. In these and many other ways change is not our enemy but a form of Grace.

It is my desire through this book to help you understand the paradigm shifts needed to fully embrace change in your life. It will require not only a better understanding of the process for managing change, but it will also require that you take a serious look at *what* you really are. If this seems like a strange question don't worry, it will be explained in part one of the book. I consider this a survival book for the new age we are birthing into. Don't be afraid. This new age has a lot to offer as long as you're willing to change.

I would hedge a bet that you have change going on in your life right now, and it is causing you some discomfort, or out-and-out suffering. If this is true, then you are in the right place.

I have been there and done that. Through my own struggles I have come to learn that change doesn't have to equal suffering. Change, whether it starts slowly from inside or abruptly from outside, is the single greatest blessing you can receive. Now you're saying, "He's crazy. Change is difficult and painful." I understand that feeling. I used to feel the same way; and sometimes, when change starts, I am initially grabbed by a sense of pain and resistance.

What I have come to realize is that the source of my suffering is my resistance to change and not change itself. It has been a long journey to get to this realization and I have stumbled frequently on this path of learning. The struggle with change, however, has taught me much. There is an inherent awakening that is going on within us when change occurs. *Change is not a random event in our lives. It is the next step in our search for 'what' we really are.*

Consciously or unconsciously, we are no longer content with who we are and what we are doing with our life. Change provides the opportunity to reinvent who we are. Like the butterfly, we are transforming from 'who we have been' to 'who we want to be'. The problem is, the 'old self' is still around and wants to hang on. For us to transform 'what' we are, there needs to be a literal death of the 'old self'. In accepting change we are awakening to a Force within us that is the destroyer of our 'old self' and creator of the 'new self'.

We can get stuck in this transformation of the self. The 'old self' is comfortable and familiar and will resist going gently into this good night. Or maybe we have become so disgusted with the 'old self' that we rush to reinvent ourselves only to find our 'new self' ungrounded, lost and disoriented. Frequently we just retreat back into the 'old self' to seek safety and comfort. You know . . . when old habits seem to return and we end up feeling weak and defeated. So our resistance to change, based in a fear of loosing or keeping the 'old self', either holds us from evolving, or scatters us to the wind in an ungrounded flurry of a reinvented 'new self'.

ENGAGING IN A PROCESS FOR CHANGE

Three discoveries came to me during my journey through change that totally altered my orientation. My first discovery was that there is a structured process that can guide us through three steps for managing change in an effective and positive way. I have a deep sense of gratitude for the work of William Bridges in developing a process for change that, I believe, is transferrable to understanding and effectively dealing with all of our major issues. How do I know? I have worked with it through many small and extensive changes in my life, and it has not failed me to date. I have also worked with Bridges model with others over the years as a manager, a coach and a counselor. I have found it instrumental in helping others understand and accept what has happened, where they are, and what they need to do to move forward. Bridges model is a systematic approach to change, which, if followed, will help to make change easier and more meaningful. This process also provides a greater assurance of being successful with change. This model has become the core of my current work with others.

I have built on Bridges model over the years to take it deeper into my overall model for counseling. As I began to expand on Bridges work I began to see connections to a wide variety of other therapy models, which could be integrated into a more comprehensive process for change. This is where the next two discoveries became critical.

Reorienting to the Higher Self

When I first started to use this process I was able to create an understanding of what was really happening, but I still struggled. Change was still hard. It wasn't until I connected this process with my Buddhist teachings related to self, that I came to understand that the missing element in finding the blessing in change was my orientation to 'what' I really am. Not who - but what.

Through the teaching of the Zen master, Adyashanti, I have come to see that the real Self is much larger than the 'little me' that I have been so attached to. This realization, or 'spiritual awakening' as Adyashanti would call it, is the key to removing the resistance and suffering related to change. If this 'old self' is just a small part of who we really are then all is not lost when we trade the 'old self' for a 'new self'. Both are part of our Higher Self; it is just that the 'old self' no longer serves us and can be set-aside for the 'new self'. We can thank it for what it has revealed to us and gracefully let it go. The awakening to our Higher Self provides a core constant to the impermanence of life. The Higher Self accepts change, external and internal, as natural. The Higher Self within us has no fear of change, consequently, It has no need to resist.

It was the awakening to the Higher Self that was a significant factor in reducing my struggles and suffering related to change. While we can manage change without awakening, this awareness removes much of the fear and resistance that most of us experience as a natural byproduct of change. In making this shift there were some sacrifices. I had to give up the illusion of who and what I am, and I also had to give up the illusion of control over my life. My need for control when I was focused in my 'little me' was paramount. As I moved away from an orientation on the 'little me' I came to accept that my needs to defend my self-perception and to control my external experience were small sacrifices to make when compared to becoming awake to the power and consistent presence of the Higher Self within and around me.

I have found that this reorientation to the Higher Self is absolutely critical in gaining the full benefits that change presents to us. The glue that holds us together is our Higher Self. There is nothing to fear in shedding the 'old self' as we are just in the process of creating the 'new self'. There really is a resurrection that follows death.

Awakening to the Higher Self is very subtle. It happens spontaneously, but it may take us months or years to actually realize our consciousness has made the leap from a virtual dream state to the truth of life. This is where the third discovery came in. I came across the teachings of Ernest Holmes and Science of Mind. This New Thought philosophy has combined key, common precepts from all the major religions and philosophies.

FINDING OUR CONNECTION THROUGH CHANGE

One of the common precepts that is critical to my process of awakening in my Higher Self was the concept of Oneness. In *The Science of Mind* Ernest Holmes defines this Oneness:

> "There is a Universal Mind, Spirit, Intelligence, that is the origin of everything: It is First Cause. It is God. This Universal Life and Energy finds an outlet in and through all that is energized, and through everything that lives. There is One Life back of everything that lives. There is One Energy back of all that is energized. This energy is in everything. There is One Spirit back of all expression. That is the meaning of that mystical saying: "In Him we live, and move, and have our being." (Acts 17:28)"

It was this conscious awareness that we are One with the Infinite that became my mental guidepost in my spiritual awakening process, and it offered the glue to reunite the fragments that change had created in my life.

I also gained a working understanding of how powerful the mind is in creating our reality. Awareness of our thoughts and how they directly impact what is attracted to and created in our life added new meaning to my Buddhist practice of mindfulness. I also learned the power of positive affirmations and spiritual mind treatment can be an effective tool in supporting positive change. I will discuss these principles in greater detail later but I will just say now the mantra, *"Change your thinking and change your life."* became real to me as I demonstrated its power within my own change processes over the years.

In combining the works of William Bridges, Ernest Holmes and the teachings of Adyashanti, I have come to understand a broader, more effective method for managing change. With this mastery of change, I gained a greater understanding of how to stay in the flow of life, reducing the turbulence along the way. Applying these principles, constructed to facilitate change, has made me a much more effective as a coach and counselor. I have found that the therapeutic process is accelerated, saving my clients money and suffering. In mastering change, I gained a greater love for all aspects of my life; hence my tag line, *"Master change and love your life."*

The psychotherapeutic approaches and practices I integrated into my change model for working with people are centered in Jungian, Emotionally-Focused, and Contemplative psychotherapy. All of these approaches start with an awareness of the Higher Self and Its central nature of health. This awareness opens a space for Self-directed auto correction of the basic misunderstandings intrinsic in the mind that create our perception of suffering. These approaches are not based, as is most other forms of psychology, in pathology, but in dissolving misconceptions and illusions, which keep us from understanding our unlimited connection and potential through an individual expression of the Universal One. As our understanding expands it will take us beyond the limited self to an unlimited potential found in an awaking to the reality of Universe.

I have divided the book into three sections. Part I is a reorientation to our understanding of who you are. Awakening to the fact that we are more than the separate self we have thought we were, gives us the power and courage to face change. I have also provided in this part of the book important qualities, which are discovered as we awaken to our greater being. These qualities, when accepted and engaged, provide us with a new orientation, which facilitates future change in our lives. Some concepts presented reflect an inward orientation to reduce our barriers to and set the stage for effective change. Other concepts are outward practices that will open the doorway to change and assist in moving forward.

Part II goes through the process of change. It provides an understanding that <u>all</u> steps in the change process are necessary to create a permanent change. This understanding sets the stage for us to maintain a positive mind-set on our path to our 'new self'. I will explain why each process is absolutely essential to positive, permanent change, and that skipping one of the processes can send us down a circuitous path that will lead us right back to where we were before we started. Change is never so painful as when we are struggling to move forward, only to find ourselves right back at where we started. Understanding the process of change reduces our potential to fall backwards and provides the energy required to sustain the effort needed to assure our successful transformation through change.

Part III covers personal and professional experiences with change management. I will look at how the change model is useful in working through the accelerated frequency of change in our future; and I will conclude with a discussion on how managing change during our life prepares us for the ultimate change, transition from this life to the next.

Throughout this book I have included small examples of the work I have done with others. I have put it in a counseling prospective and have changed some of the information as to not reveal specific identities. My work presented in this book has been as a manager, a professional coach, a counselor and, most importantly, as a friend.

In the pages of this book I hope to share with you what I have learned, knowing that it will provide for you a useful process for change. I will hopefully uncover for you a new paradigm for change that will help you navigate the future. May it provide you with a peaceful mind and a joyful heart as you embrace the continuous flow of change in your life.

PART ONE

SIX CONCEPTS TO EMBRACING CHANGE

When starting to build a house you can't start without a vision of how the house will come together. The same is true with change. You need to assemble the mental, emotional and physical concepts required to build a successful change process.

In this section we will explore some critical concepts that I have discovered in assisting people with change as well as managing my own change in life. Each one has a synergistic effect on the others. Combined together, these concepts provide an effective approach to managing even the most difficult changes you will face.

It begins with a reorientation to what you are, expanding into a broader, more connected concept of being. We look at how to dive deep into the lessons of life and to gain all that we need from each one. We then investigate how to get closer to change, rather than running from it. Finally, we look at how to stop resisting life and begin to partner with life during the change process.

This section may seem fairly esoteric, but I assure you that each concept is extremely practical in managing change. It's all about application. Take the time to learn how to use these concepts before you start to build your successful method for change. Process (covered in Part Two) is important but is also more manageable with the right orientation and vision.

CHAPTER ONE

REORIENTING TO SELF

The experience of awakening differs from person to person. . . But in that instant, the whole sense of "self" disappears. The way they perceive the world suddenly changes, and they find themselves without any sense of separation between themselves and the rest of the world.

Adyashanti, *The End of Your World*

We should have faith that there is but One Mind. This Mind is both the Mind of man and the Mind of God. We use the Mind of God since there is but One Mind. This Mind is the essence of creativeness and the essence of goodness.

Ernest Holmes, *The Science of Mind*

For the last 2,400 years mankind has not been able to picture himself/herself beyond this 'little self' we call ego. Our total identity has been confined to this body and mind, seeing nothing beyond. The teachings of the masters have been a mystery and there was no vision of a connected, Higher Self within each of us. There was Spirit or God and then there was us. Never the one will truly know the greater. Yet there has always been a sense, a longing for something greater that we could claim to be a part of.

Then something wonderful happened in the collective consciousness. It became aware of Itself to such an extent that It could consciously recognize Itself <u>within</u> the individual. With this change we all became able to identify this Higher Self within us. God finally became personal and intimate. Suddenly the teachings that seemed incomplete in our study of religion, whatever form, took on a new level of understanding when viewed from the lens of a unified consciousness.

Of course the great-enlightened masters have known this and kept it alive in their teachings, but few of us could really understand this broader way of being until now. When Jesus said, "My Father and I are one." he knew all about his connection to the Higher Self; but we just couldn't get it. When the Buddha awoke under the Bodhi tree he said, "We are awake." Buddha got it and his awareness started one of the great religions, yet most of us just scratched our heads. The masters held the keys to the eternal wisdom, but our consciousness was not ready to receive this wisdom. Change, however, brought about a great awakening.

Today more and more people are awakening to their 'Higher Self', and frequently the catalyst to this awakening is change. In prior lives when we were faced with change, we could only go so far. We could only change external things and situations in a way that continued to support the limited concept of what we were. If change meant that we would have to give up our 'little self', we would resist and literally fight to the death. Consequently, change was very difficult, and the only way to transform from the 'old me' to the 'new me' was by dying and then being reborn. No wonder we fought so many wars! Our spiritual awakening allows our internal and external changes to occur without the fears of and resistance to change.

As we become more aware, consciously or unconsciously, of this Higher Self within, we can literally let go of the 'old self' and create a 'new self' without having to experience physical death. As a result, change has accelerated dramatically during the last two hundred years. The big variable was to what degree we were consciously aware of the Higher Self. The more conscious we were and are of the Higher Self within, then the easier change was and is.

FINDING MY SPECIAL PLACE

I would like to share with you my own experience with spiritual awakening. I first found meditation as a technique to greater awareness in 1974 through the teachings of Paramahansa Yogananda. In the years that followed I tried a variety of meditation techniques to get in touch with my real nature. Some techniques were very structured and others just required me to set and observe. All the while I was attempting to contact the 'greater me'.

Frequently I would enter into stillness, a place of presence and peace, grounded in the present moment. It is for me a place without a dependence on the mind and thought. In this place beyond thought is an expanded awareness that encompasses and transcends the mind. This expanded awareness brings on a feeling of connection with everything. There is a sensation of timelessness and a feeling of love without boundaries. I feel empty, without identity, but fully awake. I feel a great potential for creativity and good. I have called this my 'special place'. My 'special place' is, in fact, where I connect with God, the Infinite, Spirit, whatever name you are comfortable with. This stillness is empty, and in the emptiness it is infinitely full. In truth, I did not find this place. It has always been there. I just woke up to Its presence.

Initially this experience would last for only a moment and then the mind would start up again. Sometimes I would sit and not be able to stop my constant thoughts. Over the years, however, the process of finding and settling into this 'special place' became easier, and the time I can rest there has steadily increased. At first I tried a variety of techniques to force myself into this space. Spiritual teachers abound with their own techniques and are willing to share. I found, however, that struggling was not the way. I needed to relax, release and fall into this awareness. It is like falling asleep, but, instead, I fall awake. With an intuitive knowledge of how to enter my 'special place' I can quickly dive in, no matter where I am. I just stop, take a deep breath and let my mind go, trusting in what is beyond.

For many years I thought this was nice, but I had an expectation that spiritual awakening was some constant state of higher consciousness that required tremendous discipline and practice. After all, wasn't this what all of the great masters did? Living lives of extreme austerity, giving up all for this higher state of being? So, in a way, I discounted my 'special place' as just a nice place to go.

It wasn't until I came upon the teachings of Adyashanti that I became aware that this 'special place' was really an abiding with my Higher Self. In his teachings from *Spiritual Awakening* I learned that if I just looked back I could see that I was the observer, looking at that self I called me. But who was this observer? It has no definition, no identity, It just is. It has no judgments or expectations, It just knows. I became aware that this is the Higher Self, the Universal Identity, my connection to God.

I have yet to be able to stay in this 'special place' all the time, or in what Adyashanti would call "abiding awakening". There will come a day when I believe this Higher Self will just stay central to my consciousness and never step aside, but not just yet. What I have discovered is that when my ego is out of control and I am starting to battle with life, if I just stop and go to my 'special place'; balance returns. Spiritual awakening is a gift from God and cannot be forced or derived through logic. It can come at anytime, whether we are seeking or not; and when it comes we may not even be fully aware. There is no grand fanfare or fireworks. When It comes, It is quiet, calm, and silent. To enter we must be empty, not full of self.

I have also come to realize that spiritual awakening is not something special for just a few. Yes, two hundred years ago it was, but that was before the Collective Conscious reached a point of recognition of Itself. As we move forward over the next two hundred years, spiritual awakening will be as natural as being born. In the meantime, it is available to everyone who is willing to look. No need to go live in a cave anymore. You can live your everyday life and still be spiritually awake.

As I expand my time in the Higher Self I find that this 'special place' is a great place to go when change starts to occur in my life. Change is no longer good or bad, but an experience in this thing I call life. This is the catalyst to reducing and eliminating the pain and suffering of change.

AN INTRODUCTION TO OUR 'HIGHER SELF'

Let's stop a minute and take the opportunity to go within. Sit comfortably in your chair and close your eyes. Ask yourself "What am I?" (note: the term 'who' infers a personality. 'What' goes beyond the concept of ego and personality.) Check in with what you experience when you ask this question. Don't expect anything, just sit with the question. Let your mind stop its constant chatter and just rest. Don't struggle with the mind. If it interrupts, just take note and let it go. Relax, fall awake. Take five minutes and then come back to the book.

What did you experience? Were you able to park the 'little self' for even a moment? In the silence of that moment were you awake, aware, present? If your answer is yes, great, welcome to a conscious awareness of your Higher Self. If not, if you couldn't quiet the busy mind, don't worry. Your Higher Self is still there but your ego (little self) just didn't want to get out of the way. Ponder that. Realize that there is something in you behind the ego, which is the creator/manager of this 'little self'. Continue to sit and just see if the mind will become quiet as you ask, "What am I?" Look deeply within. Look behind what your mind is telling you what you are. Sooner or later the ego will step aside to the Higher Self, to awaken into your true nature. It is really that simple.

Once you have become conscious of this simple truth you will never be the same again. Most people think that achieving a higher consciousness is going into some altered state. They couldn't be more wrong. Becoming conscious of your Higher Self is so simple that it seems like a non-event. It is actually the most important event of your life, but it feels initially like, "OK, so what?"

Breaking Free

The 'so what?' is that you are finally have a foothold within an orientation that will free you of the shackles of the ego. A larger you is now awake, aware and taking charge. You no longer have to fear that change will alter who you are. Altering who you are is a natural process that you have been resisting for many lifetimes. By the way, if you don't buy into reincarnation, then just think of it as overcoming the genetic, inherited traits of your ancestors. Same difference. Just know that you have taken a significant step in becoming free from the suffering experienced by the cycle of life. Whether you call it karma, fate, destiny or any of the other myriad of names, you have broken the chains of bondage.

The degree that we remain conscious of our Higher Self will vary from person to person. It will be constant in some people and fleeting in others. Yet once we have gone there, we can always go back. Just stop, and reconnect. This is critical as we initially face change in our life. Change has a tendency to pull us back into our 'little self' as we sense some insecurity with the beginning of change. If we can reorient our awareness to the Higher Self within, then change becomes less fearful and more interesting. You see, change cannot alter the Higher Self. The Higher Self exists only in the realm of the Infinite.

There is now a sense of anticipation. You know that Higher Self is behind all of this; It wants to change, to continue to experience in a new and different way. The question is then, into what. What is next? This is where the process for change and transition comes into play. I will cover the process in later chapters but realize now your definition of what you are needs to be flexible to get into the flow of change. Anticipate that change is a good thing for our continued evolution.

Releasing the Shackles of Old Religious Thought

There is part of us that might be saying that this sense of the Higher Self within is somehow sacrilegious. This concept may smack right in the face of our entire religious upbringing. God and I are supposed to be separate. That is what the scriptures say. Well they don't really. Whether you look at the teachings of Jesus, Buddha or Mohammed, you will find the message that all is one. After thirty plus years of studying all the religions, from Pagan to Christian, nowhere are there any original spiritual teachings where it is sacrilegious to awaken to our connection to the Infinite.

Consider this, for the last 2,400 years, man's mind could not comprehend this connection with the Infinite without severe spiritual austerities. Only a few really got it. To perpetuate some connection, God the master – student relationship was taught to the masses. With the awakening of the Higher Self everything has changed. Like the prodigal son, we can return home to the loving arms of the One. It just so happens that this in an internal and not an external journey. It's suddenly a lot shorter trip.

If all of this puts too much of a strain on your belief systems, that's

OK. I would just encourage you to sit quietly and see what is behind the mind and its creator, the ego. What is in the quiet space when thought is gone but you are not. Finding this quiet place is the only way that you can take the fear out of change. It takes the fear out of moving forward as there is no right or wrong, there is only our own path forward. If we are really connected to the Higher Self, how can we make a mistake? Judgment then is replaced by the opportunity for greater awareness.

Connecting to our Higher Self allows for a greater resilience to what life presents. We come to see the good and the bad as 'what is' rather than 'what we want' and/or 'what we don't want'. The Higher Self embraces life in all its forms, while the ego seeks only what it considers as in its own self-interest. The Higher Self is accepting and inclusive, the ego is separate and resistant. The Higher Self wants to dive deeper into the river of life, while the ego struggles to escape.

In his book, *Bounce: Living the Resilient Life*, Robert Wicks speaks of resilience and its importance to managing change: "If we become the most resilient person we can be, new positive realities and perspectives arise and flourish in the most surprising ways. Amid life's stress and suffering, maybe even because of it, when we have the tools to enhance resilience and can strengthen the sense of meaning in our lives, we better appreciate both the welcome and the unwelcome aspects of stress."

With greater resilience we can make lemonade out of lemons, and in the process find greater meaning in our life. The search for greater meaning is what the Higher Self is all about. Maslow coined the term 'self-actualization' to describe this process. Adyashanti would call it 'waking up to your true nature of being'. I like Adyashanti's perspective as it moves beyond the ego and the restricted concept of self.

EGO'S RESISTANCE TO CHANGE

One of the biggest sources of suffering in our life is the need of the ego to avoid change. The ego thrives on consistency to hold its form. Without consistency of thought and action it cannot define itself. The problem is that life is always changing. In fact, the impermanence of life is the only true constant. This places the ego constantly at odds with life, unless life just happens to conform for a time to the illusion of stability and constancy created by ego. When life challenges the attempts of ego to maintain a constant the ego resists. The ego tries every trick it knows: avoidance, fear, hate, drugs and more, to resist life, but life always has the upper hand. Life will always win out as life represents the Whole, the Higher Self, what we really are. The ego tries to manage suffering without loosing control, but it is this very control that is the root of suffering. Accepting change is the solution to suffering, not the cause.

For almost thirty years of my life I held tightly to an egotistic illusion that I was the perfect husband, perfect father, perfect provider. In actuality I was none of these things, but I resisted changes in my life to hold onto this illusion. I suffered often, but was unwilling to let go. When I came to realize I was none of these things, and just let go, change flooded my life. All that I held back was thrust to the fore. The dam had broken wide open.

The next few years were painful, but I suffered less. Change was constant, and I had nothing to grab onto. Yet in the midst of all this change I expanded my connection to my Higher Self. I gained a broader perspective of the flow of life and how I was a part of this big river. Resistance to change continued to slip away and as I remained open to change I found that there was always a positive direction to where change was taking me. I wasn't always aware of what it was at the start, but, with patience, the truth shown through. Even the perceived pain of change went away.

Accepting Change as Part of Life

In this process of accepting change as an integral part of my life I had to give up all of the illusions I held about others and myself. At first this seemed like a loss, but it was just an illusion. It wasn't real; it wasn't grounded in anything that is true. Deep inquiry helped me to understand that nothing was actually lost, since my illusions were not real.

Change constantly challenged my identity, as defined by my ego; but I found that my identity could not be lost, just transformed. I am not without an identity. It is just that my identity is grounded in the present moment, and I am aware that it will change as the present moment changes.

I am no longer attached to my identity, relying on it to give me a sense of being. That sense of being comes through my connection with the Higher Self. I now have a *resilient* identity.

This is our dilemma. If we are only identified with the ego, we will always resist and eventually loose out to life. If we connect with our Higher Self we are an integral part of the flow of life. Our issue is to recognize the Higher Self. Until we make this shift, we cannot see anything beyond what the ego has created. We are limited, confined to the mental creations of ego, and we are constantly distressed when it changes.

Once, however, we awaken to the Higher Self, we see that we are more than the ego. At this point, like Dorothy in the Wizard of Oz, we pour water on the wicked witch and she melts away. Once this happens we are free to return home; home to what we really are, an integrated, aware, eternal part of the One. This is what the great masters mean when they say, "We awaken to our God-Self." Dorothy always was wearing the ruby slippers while in Oz. It was only when she realized they would transport her home that she was able to make the journey. Our Higher Self is our ruby slippers.

Once we make this shift, our perspective of change will forever be altered from resistance to acceptance. Acceptance allows change to flow. It may not always appear easy at the start, but we will have an intuitive sense that change is always for the better, always for the greater good. This applies to us as individuals, groups, societies, our entire planet, our entire universe. To understand this you just need the perspective that the Higher Self provides.

From the perspective of the Higher Self we can see that life is a circle of creation, expansion, contraction, deterioration and transformation. Ego attempts to ignore all of these aspects of life, especially transformation, because it doesn't want to change. So ego only sees change as something it must resist. The Higher Self recognizes that the impermanence of life, and its associated change, leads to transformation. There is no end, just change.

THE ART OF STAYING AWAKE

I wish I could tell you that once you awaken to the Higher Self the battle with the ego is over. For most of us this is not true. Ego has been with us for a long time, and it will not give up its job easily. No one wants to be out of work. So we go through periods where the ego is submissive until it can remake itself into an image that will lure your awareness back to it. It will define a new you, hoping you like it and will return to the illusion of permanence. It's hard to not fall back into the dream from time to time. Yet once you awaken to the Higher Self, the ego can no longer assume total control. You just intuitively know better.

We have a safety valve once we have awakened to the Higher Self. Whenever we want we can remember that we are more. We can reconnect with the Infinite in that quiet moment beyond body and mind. This is where change is such a blessing. Change literally shakes us awake from the dream. Change pushes our impermanence right in front of our face, and when this happens, we wake up again. Sooner or later we come to realize that things are constantly changing, every moment. When we come to this realization we are grounded in the present and we remain awake to and with life. Being grounded in the present is one of the indications as to whether we are dreaming with ego or awake with the Higher Self. The awareness of being present is the key to being awake.

Ego is always interested in the story of our life. Our story gives a false sense of permanence to our life. The ego focuses on the past and future to support this sense of permanence. The Higher Self is only interested in the present moment and sees no value in the past, the future, the story. The past and the future do not exist. What is real is only the present moment in which we are alive and awake. So it is not very hard to tell whether we are dreaming or awake. Just look at where our thoughts are focused and we will know. If we are in the present moment and not in our story we are awake.

Being awake means that we are engaged in life. In fact we are more engaged because our attention is only on the present moment. In the present moment we can still plan and act. It is actually easier to plan and act because we are no long afraid of the changes that might occur. We know that we will deal with these changes when they arise and not until then. This provides an unbelievable freedom to work with change in our life. It provides a greater resilience.

Releasing Attachments

Another way to look at whether you are dreaming or awake is to look at our attachments. Attachment is a function of the ego to create permanence. The more we are attached to things, places and people, the deeper we are in ego's dream. The problem with attachment is that the things we are attached to are constantly changing. Now attachment leaves us only with three choices; loose our attachment, try to undo the change to regain a sense of permanence, or modify our attachment to reject the old image and accept the new. In all three cases there is no recognition that change is continuous, it is only an adjustment to a new level of perceived permanence. Under this scenario change is resisted or accepted in small 'spits and spurts'.

Being awake to the Higher Self you accept that all things are changing. There is a natural tendency to let go, to not grasp and hold. We accept things, places, people as they are in this moment. Don't get me wrong, it doesn't mean that we aren't engaged or caring. It just means that we no longer hold an expectation that life must 'conform' to the image that the ego wants to put forward. We allow life to unfold freely, naturally as it is meant to, without restrictions.

When we live our life without attachments we redefine and broaden our concept of love. We move to a love without limitations, a love that is free, without restrictions. The affect of this shift is life altering. We loose the selfishness, the need to possess, that the ego so desperately wants in order to create a sense of permanence. All of our interactions become easier. Judgments shift to acceptance, and life can unfold as it was supposed to. We come to love our life.

A last perspective on dreaming or being awake is the intensity of life. When we are resisting change, life continues to flow. Our resistance becomes a dam that holds back temporarily the waters of life. The problem is that life cannot be stopped. It will continue to ramp up until the resistance is gone. Small changes now become overwhelming events, and it is easy to get swept away. Life will always turn up the intensity until it gets its way.

Redefining Who Is in Charge

The Higher Self will not attach and resist. Life continues to flow, and we find change to be steady and constant. We loose the drama, trauma and chaos that is an integral part of attachment and resistance. This is what is called the 'middle way' in Buddhism.

So our orientation to self is critical to how we manage change in our life. We can make our way through change without knowledge of the Higher Self, but it will be more painful and difficult. This is why I started with an understanding of the orientation to Self. Awakening to and aligning with the Higher Self is a tremendous tool in working with change. The ego is still around but we now use it consciously to accomplish our tasks in life. It is not a case of one or the other. It is a case of which is the master craftsman and which is the tool. We can craft change much more effectively when the Higher Self is the master craftsman.

As we move forward in this new millennium there is a need for greater adaptability and acceptance of the impermanence of life. This will require a greater level of understanding of the world, life, and our own connection with both. This level of understanding is only available through the Higher Self. The ego based, separate self is not powerful enough and lacks the depth for managing this level of change.

We will need to be able to see the connection in rapid/random changes that we will be bombarded with as the world adapts to a new way of being. Understanding our connection with people, animals, plants, the earth itself, is only possible by an awakened Higher Self. This is not just a mental exercise. It is a visceral connection that goes beyond logic and our standard senses. The Higher Self lives in a state of *being*. The separate self can only hope to briefly experience it before retreating. Adapting to change is much easier from a state of *being*.

Beyond the Separate

Reacting in a positive way to change will come from a deep understanding of how everything is connected. This is a altered view of life, from our logic-based way of thinking that we have used to this point. Our logical mind operates by comparison, which requires some definition of separateness. It has been a useful way of dealing with life up to this point because a level of separation seems to provide meaning. But, as I mentioned at the beginning, our world is rapidly compressing and becoming more and more interdependent. What seemed like separate in the past no longer exists in the present or future.

If we are unwilling to go beyond our view of separation, to see the underlying connections, then we are doomed to resisting rather than adapting to our new world. Resistance creates ignorance, and, as history has shown us, ignorance can be catastrophic. This is never more evident than our resistance and ignorance today related to global warming. When we allow ourselves to see how everything we are doing has an effect of this planet, when we see the interconnectedness between our actions and our planet's temperature, then we can truly embrace positive change before it is too late.

So change requires that we first discover what we really are. That is why we started with this question, "What am I?" Once we come to a deep understanding of this 'what' as our Higher Self we are connected, in the flow. Change is our friend and not our enemy. We accept change with open arms, rather than resisting it.

I cannot overstate the importance of this reorientation to the Higher Self. As our world accelerates it means the difference between living our lives in an ever-growing state of fear or with a sense of excitement and wonder. Our world changes, but with an orientation to our Higher Self our ability to adapt is dramatically altered.

CHAPTER TWO

TAPPING YOUR INTUITION

The intuitive mind is a sacred gift and the rational mind is a faithful servant. We have created a society that honors the servant and has forgotten the gift.

Albert Einstein

Intuition is God in man, revealing to him the Realities of Being; and just as instinct guides the animal, so would intuition guide man, if he would allow it to do so.

Ernest Holmes, <u>The Science of Mind</u>

In all phases of the change process there is a need to get beyond your current perception of how things have been, how things are and where things are going. This preoccupation with the past, present and future as one entity is the basis for our stories. Our story reflects conditioned thinking, influenced by past experiences, which we believe are still true in the present. When we are seeking a way to maintain our current self, our current way of being, we rely on our conditioned thinking. When change occurs we have to think 'outside of the box', moving beyond our conditioned thinking. This is where intuition becomes a critical tool for managing change.

Change creates a whole new playing field. Whether we sense this internally or externally, the way we view our self and the world is starting to fall apart. Our current world is no longer working, and our first reaction is to attempt to pull our life back into alignment with our old story, our old perceptions of self. This attempt to stick with the status quo can create a temporary halt to change, but it will not stop how life is working to move us beyond our current perceptions of self and the world. It's like trying to play soccer in a hockey rink. You are going to just slip and fall a lot. Change will demand new paradigms as to how we view and deal with life. Intuition is our guide to the new paradigms required to effectively navigate into the future.

Intuitions Role in Change

Change becomes the mechanism by which life takes control of our world. If we don't adapt, if we don't seek a new orientation to self and the world, then life will just ramp up change to the point that all resistance is futile. Why? As I mentioned in the previous chapter, this Higher Self is always looking at the bigger picture that life presents and is in alignment with life's enfoldment. When our ego resists change in an attempt to keep life and self constant, the Higher Self is cheering on change. The Higher Self intuitively understands the impermanence of life and knows that nothing will every stay the same. Quite simply, ego can never win over life. Life is in control.

Accepting that life is in control and learning to move with it is a loose definition of destiny. There is something within us all that is perfectly aligned with life's enfoldment, so in a way we are meant to move as life directs us. Some call this God's will. This statement is not entirely true as it infers separation with God. I see the Higher Self as a natural connection with, and an extension of, God. Therefore we are here to co-create with God, not just accept what God chooses for us. Our lives are not predetermined, without choice. We are just meant to continue to evolve, awaken, expand to the next, higher iteration of who we are. We all have the free will to co-create with God. We just can't retreat to a static state of our world or self. As hard as we try, we cannot stop life from expanding, we cannot stop change. We can, however, participate in the change and offer our desires. There are no guarantees but our desires can nudge us in the direction we vision. So destiny is influencing life, without having control.

Sooner or later change shakes us loose from our ego self. All of the paradigms that have worked for us up to this point in time are no longer effective in maintaining the status quo. We have all hit the wall many times during change. You know, when you are disoriented and have a sense of helplessness. It is at this time that we start to let go of our resistances to change or we double down our efforts to resist. To survive change we need new paradigms, a new perspective of life, a new perspective of self. Where do we turn to gain these new paradigms and perspectives? Intuition. Intuition is not a function of our ego self, but inspiration from our Higher Self.

What Is Intuition?

Webster's calls intuition, "Quick and ready insight. Immediate apprehension or cognition." This definition infers that intuition is something beyond our logical, deductive mind. Intuition is a portal to Higher Consciousness that will unexpectedly flash open and shut, like the aperture of a camera lens. Usually intuition is something we immediately recognize as we are caught off guard. Frequently we will say to our self, "Wow, where did that come from." Intuition is immediate, insightful and fleeting; grab hold of it while you can or it is lost.

For most of us intuition is an unplanned event. We never know exactly when it is going to arise or how long it will last. Frequently intuition is not necessarily tied to the current line of thinking. Intuition becomes an unexpected interruption for the mind. This is why it is so easy for us to discount a moment of intuition and just continue on with our prior line of thinking. Big mistake!

When Donna graduated from college she wanted to start her own business. Donna loved to bake and she thought it would be exciting to own and operate a bakery. She was engaged to be married to Steve, who already was on the fast track to success working in financial markets. He was making a comfortable income for both of them, and they were both eager to start a family. Four months after their marriage Donna became pregnant and chose the path of a stay-at-home mom. A year later Donna became pregnant again and gave birth to a second son.

Donna came to see me around the time that her youngest son

entered pre-school. She was depressed because she felt that she had given up her dream for the sake of her family. Donna loved her family and continued to bake for them as well as their church. She just felt like she had lost her opportunity to become a successful businesswoman.

We began to explore what was possible. I asked Donna to investigate smaller enterprises she might like to undertake that would not require her to choose between her family and work. Each week she would come back and we would explore ideas. I would play the devil's advocate in helping her to clarify her thoughts around a business model.

On the third week of our exploration Donna came into my office all excited. She had an inspiration. She came up with an idea to start a catering service for weddings and special events. She would make wedding cakes at home, along with a variety of other baked goods for parties. Donna felt that this was a niche business and she could control the size of her business by the orders she took. Overhead was low as they already had a large enough family vehicle to make deliveries. Donna's baked goods were already famous with her church, which had a total congregation in the thousands. She could start marketing there.

After working on some details with Donna regarding her business plan she was off and running. I didn't see Donna for seven months. When she came back in she was in a new dilemma. Her business was so successful that it was now challenging her family life. She wanted her business to continue to grow, but she didn't want to give up her time with her husband and children. Donna and I went back to brainstorming.

I asked Donna if she could become a mentor to other stay-at-home mothers to teach them how to bake and prepare items for her customers. Donna liked this idea, but who could she find to help? We turned again to her church community. There were several families, where they were struggling financially, but the mothers didn't want to return to work. We reworked her business model to include employees. Donna identified three mothers who were interested and she began providing baking classes. Two of the mothers worked out, and Donna added a delivery van and a part-time driver. This allowed Donna to double her capacity, without sacrificing her family time. Donna changed the name of her business to 'Mom's Catered Baked Goods'. She cut back on her actual baking to have more time to coordinate operations. She was now a manager.

Donna had a passion for a family and her own business. She originally saw these as competing desires, and the thought of giving up one was making her depressed. By seeking out and following her intuition Donna was able to find a common ground that let her have family and work on her terms.

If, as I propose, intuition is a direct message from Higher Consciousness, then we should be listening intently to what is being shared. In some cases intuition will appear as a vision. We get an image from nowhere, vivid and flashing. A vision can also make us stop in our tracks. We may see something that is strangely familiar, with a 'déjà vu' feel to it. Some call this synchronicity, a linking with something from the past or in the future. Intuition can also be a word we hear in our mind, or a feeling coming from the gut. However we make contact with the Higher Self we need to take advantage of it. The Higher Self has the big picture; it has something important to show us.

Loosing the Intuitive Moment

In the instant that we ignore intuition the aperture closes and what is revealed evaporates like a morning mist. This is why it is important for us to be receptive to and willing to immediately turn our full attention to intuition. This requires us to have a nimble mind; which is one outcome from accepting change. Why do we so often miss our intuitive messages? There is an inverse relationship between ego and the plasticity of the mind. The more resistant our mind it to change, the less nimble it is. The mind then tends to ignore natural adaptions during change, like an intuitive moment.

Therefore the frequency of intuitive moments is hampered by an egocentric, closed, controlling mind. When we use our mind to constantly create separation we are creating a natural barrier to intuition. Intuition holds the whole; it states the Gestalt. When the ego is working overtime to create identity, it requires separation. This is like operating in two different dimensions. There is a tendency to focus on one and miss the other. Unfortunately, intuitive moments frequently loose out.

This is the reason why intuitive thought is so fleeting. We are actually using a different awareness from the normal awareness we use with the mind during our normal thought processes. This is why it is important to stop and just listen or watch or feel intently the message that intuition is sending our way.

Capturing the Intuitive Moment

When you have a sense that you are in an intuitive moment it is time to write. I find writing the best way to capture in thought the intuitive message. Don't spend a lot of time going down one of the many branches that will naturally form from the intuitive thought; just capture the key points first. Once you have the key points now you can go back and use your mind to explore each point. It is at this time that the mind becomes a useful tool. Use it to expand your insights into your world. I would suggest during this time of capture that you suspend judgment. Judgment is just the ego trying to get in the way.

The following is a writing I composed after an intuitive moment. I think it illustrates what I am trying to convey here,

> "I found myself in one of those logical thinking conundrums the other day and felt totally lost. This is where an old pattern of thinking no longer serves the current life situation. As a result I felt lost and anxious. There were no clear answers to what was bothering me, and my old ways of dealing with what was bothering me just wasn't going to resolve my current problem.
>
> Normally I would just get anxious, put off dealing with my problem, or race to an old solution, but I instinctively knew none of that was going to get me to the real answer.
>
> It was then that I remembered something from Ernest Holmes, *"Intuition is God in man, revealing to him the Realities of Being; and just as instinct guides the animal, so would intuition guide man, if he would allow it to do so."* So . . . I decided to give myself a 'time out' to wait for intuition to show up.

There is no way to rush intuition, so what was required was patience. I decided to set aside time each day and to allow myself to think and feel my problem. Then I just parked it in my mind and opened up to intuition with no thoughts as to what would come, just a sense of anticipation.

Eventually that 'quiet, small voice' spoke to me. What It said was radical and a bit confusing. It took a few hours of serious inquiry into the message to grasp what it was telling me. It was a totally new paradigm on how to deal with my problem. Wow!"

Intuition frequently carries change with it, and the ego most likely is not going to like it, sending the message, "bad idea". This is not the time to listen to the ego. Unfortunately we usually do. The voice of the ego is so comforting and compelling. If we are ever tempted by the Devil it is from the inside not the outside. Our temptation is to discount our intuitive thoughts.

My Lesson with Intuition

In 1987 I had an intuitive moment in which I saw myself as a counselor. I was at the point where I had finished my bachelors degree in business and was deciding on my masters. I chose mental health counseling. I was continuing to work in healthcare management while I completed my masters degree. At that time I was on the fast track to advancement in homecare. When I graduated I found myself at a crossroads. My intuition told me to make the jump into counseling at that time. Unfortunately I had my ego to contend with. Power, prestige, lots of money, it all looked very logical and enticing.

I spent the next twenty years regretting the decision to stay in healthcare management. As time went on, I got further and further away from direct patient care. As a result I became more and more dissatisfied and unfulfilled with work. It was during this time that life really ramped up the pressure. I moved from one company to the next, each one being more unstable than the last. The pressures mounted, and recognition for a job well done became harder to find. Finally I broke: nervous breakdown. It took me six months to recover. During this extended time out my 'little quiet voice' returned. "You are a born counselor." It said. I finally made the leap. It has not been easy. I am a lot older and it is harder to start a private practice after such a long break from school. What I wouldn't give to have those twenty years back and have taken my intuition more seriously.

I found, however, that I hadn't forgotten anything. All of my teachings and skills came back quickly. But I still needed to find my niche. Again my intuitive self whispered, "You have been through a lot of change in your life. You know a lot about it. Make change your focus." Well . . . the message was a little more esoteric than that, but after some deep inquiry, that was what I figured out. So I began to focus on change and transition. I found the work of William Bridges, and it made perfect sense to me. I became obsessed with change. The more I read and talked about it, the more excited I became. Intuition helped me find my niche, to show me how life was conspiring for my personal evolution.

Seeking an Intuitive Replay

You are not always going to catch every idea that intuition presents. Sometimes we get an intuitive moment when we are busy and distracted. The intuitive thought is there, we get distracted, and the thought is gone. Don't put yourself down for missing it. What I found helpful is to take a 'time out', quiet my mind and ask, "Oops, I just missed that one. Universe, can you share it again?" I then open my mind to emptiness with a sense of anticipation. More often than not the intuitive thought will return and, if not at that moment, it will sometime in the near future. It may be an hour, a day, a week, a year. The thought is never really lost because it had always been there. It is held within the Higher Self, waiting for you to wake up to it again. Frustration is just giving into the ego and only delays the reawakening to the insight. Expect that an insight missed will come again.

I do suggest that you always have some way of recording intuitive thoughts. I know some people who have small, digital recorders in their pocket to speak their insight into it. Others like the more traditional way of pencil and paper. This slower technique is more comfortable to some. Find the way that works for you, but always be ready. Learn to recognize quickly when an intuitive moment is upon you and shift immediately with full attention.

Qualities of the Intuitive Moment

I have frequently been asked in seminars, "How can I tell if what I hear, see or feel is really an insight from my Higher Self?" There is no pat answer to this question as our Higher Self connects with each of us in a unique way. There are, however, some common experiences that have been reported, which may offer some clues to the intuitive moment.

Many hear intuition speaks with 'a quiet, calm voice'. Almost like a whisper. That is why it is so easy to ignore intuition when it comes. This small, quiet voice never repeats itself, so you better be listening closely.

Others receive intuition in visions or feelings that are arising spontaneously. This could be in a meditation or driving in congested traffic when boom, we are hit by the intuitive moment. The vision usually blocks out what we see in the real world for an instant. It is vivid, but fleeting - very helpful when driving. It helps sometimes to close your eyes after an intuitive vision to see if you can capture it once again and note more of the detail. The trick is not to think about it, just recall and observe.

When we suddenly feel an intuitive moment, it will be centered in our gut at the area of the third chakra, just below the ribcage in the middle of the stomach. This space has an intuitive capacity to sense the Infinite. In a way our gut is an intuitive sense organ. This place is also the center of fear created by the mind. It is where our most basic instincts have worked to keep us alive over the millenniums. When the mind is involved, the gut will hold the sense of 'fight or flight'. It will be fear based because we are in the ego and acting from a place of separation. It's us against an unforgiving world. When the gut is sensing intuitively we will feel no fear but more a sense of wonder and expansiveness. Adyashanti in an interview from *The End of Your World* described it perfectly:

> "When we look at huge expanses, often we breathe in, right? In the breathing in, we're feeling our consciousness open to that environment. We breathe into our lungs, into our heart center, into our gut. Our whole being, or whole body, is in tune with the environment. This kind of opening of the heart – when the lungs go "aah" as consciousness expands – isn't happening because we're thinking. This is happening because consciousness is interacting

with the environment. This is what I mean by pure sensation or pure feeling."

I would add intuitive feeling. So feeling the intuitive moment is one of expansion, not contraction, exhilaration, not fear. As we just 'are' in the moment the energy rises from the third to the fourth (heart) chakra. It is here that fear dissolves and wonder begins.

The intuitive moment will never respond to questioning. Frequently when we have intuition and insight our mind immediately co-opts the moment and asks questions like, "How?" or "Why?". Intuition is beyond these judgmental inquiries. There will never be an answer. Again, that is why it is so easy to overlook insights from the Higher Self. The mind/ego wants to be the source of thought so it will immediately pass judgment and try to demand clarification. In the world of the infinite there is no need for justification or explanation, it just is. This doesn't mean that when the intuitive moment is over that we can't explore it further. As I mentioned, this is when the mind becomes a useful tool and can help add some color and flavor to the insight. But during the intuitive moment there is just the knowing, nothing more.

This brings up an associated point. Intuition is never a response to questioning, but can appear within a question. Questioning is part of our logical process of the mind; ask a question, get an answer. Intuition doesn't play on that field. Inquiry and questioning can, however, trigger an insight. I have found that sometimes after I have conducted deep inquiry to the point of exhaustion an intuitive moment comes as I rest. Sometimes it will be an answer, and sometimes it will be the next area for exploration. This is not a moment that I can make happen. It happens spontaneously. Inquiry only helps to get my attention so that I am ready to receive whatever insight comes my way.

A final quality of intuitive moments is the associated feeling of expansiveness. When we contact the Infinite, it creates a sense of vast emptiness that is expansive in nature. It's like there is no end, but it seems to be getting bigger by the second. Time also temporarily looses its grip. That is why intuitive moments, no matter how long they last, seem fleeting. We have no sense of time with the intuitive experience. We do, however, sense a shift, an expansion, a sense of no boundaries.

You may experience some, all, or none of these things during your own intuitive moment. What is important is that you are anticipatory, open and alert to intuition coming your way. If you hold this consciousness from time to time, you will invite intuition into your life, and when it comes you will know it. It has already happened thousands of times already in your life. You maybe didn't give it much attention. It's never too late to change.

Intuitive thoughts don't always make sense. Sometimes we awake to or capture only part of the message. Again, don't get frustrated. Be thankful for what you have received and patiently wait for more. It will come. If what you have received doesn't make sense right now to your logical mind, wait. How this piece of the puzzle fits into the mosaic of your life will become evident as your consciousness shifts. Intuitive moments are an act of Grace from our Higher Self, and the Higher Self will never leave us incomplete and wanting.

INTUITION DURING CHANGE

We need intuition the most when we are in the throws of change. What has worked in the past is starting to fall apart. Old ways of thinking are no longer functional. Our life has become unproductive in the processes of change. The urge is to retreat, but what we need is to open up. We need to allow intuition in.

We get stuck when we choose our old way of dealing with life. Yet these old ways are not providing the answers we need. We have lost the value and meaning behind our old thoughts and actions. There can be an extreme feeling of disorientation. We can no longer buy into the paradigms of the ego. It's decision time. Things need to change, but how? All we really know is the old way is no longer working.

In this time of confusion it is easy to get lost, which will only increase our anxiety and fear. When anxiety and fear dominate there is the strong impetus to flee from the present and retreat into an illusionary past or contrived future. This is why many people will make sudden changes in their lives after years of seaming stability. They have stepped over the edge of the cliff. Yet this reaction to change comes without the direction that intuition will provide. Reflex can save our life, but it can also take us down the wrong path. We need to look past our anxiety and fear to make room for intuition.

Choosing the Path Forward

So we can go in a couple different of directions. One is to react and run. Escape can give us momentary relief from our anxiety and fear, but it isn't permanent because we really don't know where we are going. A compounding problem arises when life will not leave us alone. We have nowhere to hide, and life will just ramp up the pressure until we engage in an authentic change. This is frequently seen today in relationships where one person will initiate a break up and then immediately jump into another relationship. Because this person has not taken the time to reorient to a new paradigm of relationships, he/she will usually find a new partner almost exactly like the person from the last relationship. This new partner will most likely exhibit even greater troubling traits than the last. It's a kind of déjà vu in spades. Escape is not the answer to change.

The other direction is to stick with the anxiety and fear, allowing all feelings to come and go. As the feelings start to recede the space left open can be filled with anticipation, which will entice intuition. This is when the Grace of intuition can appear. The Higher Self has been waiting for this moment to jump in with a new paradigm for life. It is just impossible to experience this intuitive moment if we are busy running away. At some point we just need to stop and give up. This is where surrender comes into play.

Surrender is the doorway to Grace and It's gift intuition. When we give up control at the ego level then we are opening up to direction from the Higher Self. Surrender creates a portal to Higher Consciousness. The ego isn't going to like it because the ego has to relinquish control. The process of surrender has held a lot of negativity with it from our collective history. Surrender is often considered defeat. This is an egotistic view of the world, a view that has winners and losers. In the world of Higher Consciousness there are no winners or losers because all is One. So surrender is really just getting the ego out of the way and opening up to receive the gift of Higher Self. What may seem at first like defeat transforms into a new sense and way of *being*.

Adyashanti expresses this eloquently in the end of his book *Falling Into Grace,*

> "We let go into this grace. It's something we fall into, like when we fall into the arms of another, or we put our head on the pillow to go to sleep. It's a willingness to relax, even in the midst of tension. It's a willingness to stop for just a moment, to breathe, to notice that there's something else going on other than the story our mind is telling us. In this moment of grace, we see that whatever might be there in our experience, from the most difficult emotional challenges to the most causeless joy, occurs within a vast space of peace, of stillness of ultimate well-being.
>
> If we can let go for just a moment, if we can relax, if we can fall into the center of now, we can encounter directly the freedom that we've all been seeking."

It is in this freedom where intuition awaits. Intuition is our most intimate friend, always with us, always willing to help us on our path. Don't let another day go by without reacquainting yourself with your best friend.

CHAPTER THREE

REVEALING THE TRUTH USING INQUIRY AND SINCERITY

The only time we suffer is when we believe a thought that argues with what is. . . If you want reality to be different than it is, you might as well try to teach a cat to bark. You can try and try, and in the end the cat will look up at you and say, "Meow." Wanting reality to be different than it is is hopeless.

Byron Katie, *Loving What Is*

When we are willing to be present, we tap into direct experience: that is, experience that is not filtered through our thoughts, expectations, hope, and fears. Instead, we see, hear, taste, touch phenomena, and recognize thoughts and images in the mind without adding judgments or preferences.

Karen Kissel Wegela, *The Courage to be Present*

Change cracks the bubble of our perceived reality and forces us to seek a deeper truth. In turn, finding the truth is an important catalyst to effectively moving forward with the change process. Knowing what the truth is when we come upon it is a daunting challenge. The truth is often not what we think it is. It takes a lot of spadework to uncover the truth. In this chapter we will look at what is the truth and then investigate how inquiry and sincerity are effective tools for getting at the truth.

THE TRUTH ABOUT THE TRUTH

Our lives are really just a journey to find the truth, what is real. Why is it so difficult to find the truth? What makes the truth so illusive? What is the truth about truth?

When the Truth Becomes the Story

Our first major hurdle with truth is our own unwillingness to live in truth. Most of us don't really want to be totally truthful because somewhere in the past being truthful hurt. In growing up with our parents telling the truth was a difficult task, which most of us learned to avoid. When facing mistakes we had made, telling the truth to our parents did not seem to serve us. I use the correct term, mistakes, but the common phrases used were disobeying, lying, deceitful, disrespectful, and these are just the nicer phrases. Telling the truth was often associated with a painful outcome.

The answer to the perceived pain of telling the truth was to turn the reality of our experience into a story. A good story can invent justification where there is none. Rather than allowing the realization that we made a mistake we use the story to explain why our actions were not a mistake. A story offers room for imagination and rationalization, which becomes an effective tool in covering up the truth.

As the years go by we continue to refine our story telling capabilities and the truth becomes evermore illusive. We fill our reality with stories, big and small. There are times we tell a story when the absolute truth would serve us better. At some point the story telling becomes so pervasive that our ability to recognize the truth just slips away. Our awareness moves from what we really experience into a dream fabricated by stories.

So our learned propensity to create a story buries the truth, pushing it down into the subconscious. It is still there, but we don't choose to go there. We are willing to suppress the truth to produce our desired outcome. The desired outcome is usually some variance on avoiding perceived pain from telling/living the truth. The truth hasn't gone away, and what comes as a result is guilt. This leads to convoluted justifications that will help us to find a way to live with the guilt. Our mind assists in ameliorating guilt by twisting logic and facts to reinvent the past and to bolster the story. The mind is so good at this that we suddenly forget or loose sight of reality. We have slipped back into the dream state and are no longer awake. Yet the truth is still down there, in the subconscious, waiting for the opportunity to bubble up and shake our world. IT will arise again in our next change, except, this time it will be more dramatic and challenging.

The Illusion of Control

Another perceived value provided by the story is its ability to give us a level of control over our life. We believe that by manipulating reality we gain control. Control as a way of avoiding the truth and any potential pain that it may bring with it. Control through the story also allows us to fashion who and what we are. We are no longer our authentic self but a character in a fictional story. The truth is we don't really control anything in our life, but the story helps us to believe that we do. When change comes it will always challenge our perceived ability to control life. The fear of loosing control brings forth pain and suffering into our life. There is nothing real about the fear of loosing control. We have never really had it. What we fear is loosing the illusion of control. We don't want to wake up to the truth about control; there is none.

The reality is, telling the truth does not have to be painful, but we aren't willing to take a chance. Total honesty leaves us totally exposed and vulnerable. If we tell the truth then nothing is hidden anymore. We give up the fantasy and have to face the reality that we are never in control of our life. So the idea of having control by managing the truth is an illusion, and this illusion is barely sustainable until we enter into change. When change rocks our internal illusions of control we panic and move into resistance or denial. So change becomes the ultimate truth detector related to control and resistance and denial becomes the needles on the gauge.

The more resistance or denial we have to change the less truthful we are to our self and others. Count on it. In counseling others, when I find a high level of resistance or denial related to change, I immediately start to explore the truth with my client. Invariably there is some story that clouds or perverts the truth. As we look deeply into any story we come to find that it is just not true. So resistance and denial become our worst enemies on the path to our truth.

Moving Beyond Our Story

In summary, Our stories then are our chief defense mechanism in resolving our fear of loosing control. But the reality is we have never been in total control. Change destroys the story and control, leaving us with just the truth. We just need to recognize the truth revealed and appreciate the great gift that change has given us. When we give up the story we give up control. When we give up control we release the pain and suffering associated with attempting to control. We think the truth will hurt more, but it is actually quite liberating, decreasing the pain and suffering in the present moment. We can then realize that the story is not the answer to pain and suffering, but the cause.

Sharon was a 35 year-old lead in a call center. She came to me seeking answers to how she could work with her supervisor. Sharon relayed that she felt her supervisor was out to get her. She was fearful that she was going to loose her job, even though she saw her performance as above average. After asking her several questions about her and her supervisor it became apparent that Sharon's story was that her supervisor just didn't like her personally and that clouded her perception of her work performance.

I challenged Sharon on the truth of this story. What did she know right now about how her supervisor felt about Sharon and her performance. After a lengthy set of challenges to specific aspects of the story that Sharon raised, she came to the realization that she didn't really know anything for fact as to how her supervisor perceived her.

I asked Sharon to summon the courage to honestly inquire with her supervisor, being open to any input she received. Just ask the questions you have and see where she is at that moment. I also asked her to ask what changes they could make to have a better working relationship. My only requirement for Sharon was that she not invent a story to justify what she might hear, and be open to what her supervisor is experiencing related to her work and their interactions.

To Sharon's credit she accepted the challenge, even with significant doubts about the outcome. A week later she came back beaming with a real sense of accomplishment and relief. What Sharon learned was her supervisor was actually afraid of Sharon. They shared mirror perceptions of each other, seeing each other as cold, inflexible and demanding. By Sharon approaching her supervisor in an open and authentic way the supervisor softened and became open as well. As they worked through their misperceptions of each other a new working relationship was formed.

The week had continued to see improvements as Sharon's supervisor approached her with suggestions, instead of demands, and Sharon responded without perceived judgment as to the supervisor's motives. Sharon responded positively to her supervisor's suggestions and all previous tensions seemed to melt away. Her supervisor even invited Sharon to lunch on Friday and told her how much she had improved. She thanked Sharon for approaching her and being honest.

It's important to note that Sharon did not capitulate. She didn't develop a submissive persona to please her supervisor. She was just open and honest, accepting what showed up in the present moment. Since then Sharon has been promoted twice to a mid-level management position. She continues to approach difficult employee situations suspending judgment, dealing with what is and inquiring into the truth of the moment.

Standing in the Truth

If we stand in the truth we are in a state of undivided consciousness. We are awake to life as it actually is, and free from judgments of right or wrong. We are inclusive rather than exclusive; nothing is denied. Most important we are free from the confines of a story created in the imagination of our ego. This brings a greater sense of resilience. We can deal with change much more gracefully when we stand in the truth. We become conscious of an infinite connection to all reality that the truth provides.

That brings us to the question of what is the truth anyway. Doesn't it seem like you are always looking for the truth and it is just out of reach? Aren't there times when you thought you found the truth only to see it morph or evaporate right before you? Truth is illusive and there is a good reason why. Truth begs the question, "What is real?" We have no control over reality. Reality is beyond our thoughts and stories. Reality is not what we always want it to be. Reality is always changing and the truth is we can never pin reality down to a constant.

Our desire for reality is permanence, a succession of constants, something absolute. Yet, in truth, reality is not any of these things? Our world, and life in its totality, is constantly changing, evolving, manifesting into something different from what it is right now. Think about it. Name anything that has remained absolutely constant over your life experience to date. Sometimes we think we know of a constant but eventually it is disproven. Science is full of laws and axioms that have appeared to be constant for centuries and are now being disputed by new science. The truth about reality is that it is based in impermanence and change.

If we accept that reality is constantly changing then what is real, what is the truth? The *only truth* is that noting is absolutely true except what we are experiencing in the present moment. In that instant of time what is in our sphere of perception is real, is the truth. When the mind gets engaged, as an afterthought, the truth has already changed. So the truth is beyond thought; it is the experience of the present moment without any confines placed upon it. The truth is based in experience and not in our thought about the experience. The truth is fluid.

It's not that thinking and reasoning are useless exercises. They are valuable tools when the mind assists us in making decisions and moving forward. Yet we need to come to an understanding that thought and reason are not the truth. Thought and reason need to take a back seat to the experience of the present. When this happens the truth becomes empty.

It might be alarming to find that truth is empty, but what this emptiness creates is an enormous vessel for the possibilities of change. Our truth is that nothing is known so anything is possible. We have no control over what is next but we have total control of our ability to accept what is next. While our truth is empty is provides unlimited freedom. From this frame of reference change becomes easy. The truth is immediate.

The Truth Is Now!

When we give up the illusion of control we release the fixed set of thoughts, ideas and beliefs that keeps us from accepting the truth in now, and the change it is bringing in our life. If we come to realize that all things are changing, and we know nothing for sure, resistance disappears. This allows us to fall into that endless river of life and to float easily along its currents of change.

When we relax into the river of life our physical, emotional and energetic bodies soften, becoming more flexible and resilient. Our attention becomes focused on the present moment and we start to see more clearly. To really achieve this awareness we have to suspend any anticipation of what is next. There can be no sense of good or bad as that would be an anticipation of what is next, which is just a guess and not the truth. This doesn't mean that we don't have thoughts about the future. It just means we are not attached to those thoughts. We just let go of each thought, accepting in its place the truth of the present moment. The act of consciously releasing creates the softness, flexibility and resilience.

Taking the Truth into the World

Accepting that our internal thoughts, ideas, beliefs, feelings and emotions are not the truth is half of the battle. The second half is taking this same view of life out into the world. It really makes sense, but it requires additional effort as accepting the non-truth of the external world requires an even greater and overt surrender of control. Accepting fluidity to all that we encounter initially brings about greater uncertainty. Yet, if we accept the same uncertainty with regards to the external world as we did internally, then we fall in synch with life.

By accepting uncertainty we have to suspend judgment related to the external world. We have to suspend all of our preconceptions of what is next. The outcome is an even greater sense of freedom, as we are no longer confined by external circumstances. What we experience is a response, and not a reaction, to life's changes. A response is simple and based in the present moment. A reaction is using prior perceptions and beliefs based on those perceptions to mold our response. A reaction is driven by an attachment to past events that we have given some interpretation to. It just isn't real. Accepting uncertainty allows the world to just be as it is in the now.

Accepting uncertainty provides a sense of wonder and adventure to a changing world. What is next can be good or bad but we just don't know. In the not knowing we are more willing to move forward, to engage, to interact. This willingness makes us, once again, more resilient and able to manage change. The world becomes less fearful and more interesting. The more comfortable we become with uncertainty the more excited we become as to what lies ahead. We look forward to an uncertain, changing world.

Finding Truth in Relationships

Let's look at truth from the perspective of relationships. As I stated before, the truth is that we are constantly evolving, changing beings. Who we are in this moment literally changes in the next. The changes may be subtle, but over successive moments, they become more apparent. Most of the time, however, we have the expectation that a person we have a relationship with will remain constant. How that person thought and acted yesterday should be how that person thinks and acts today. The same holds true with beliefs, feelings and emotions. So we seek to create a story about our relationship, rather than experiencing and accepting the reality (truth) of our relationship.

We expected the person to be a certain way and when they aren't we become upset. We sometimes feel that the person has deceived us and we become resentful of their changes. As we become fixated in this view we are more resistant to the changes the person has made. We challenge the truth of that person's new being. We feel betrayed and lied to. The lie is that we expect the person to not change and that just is not possible. The lie is not coming from the other person but our own expectation of that person remaining constant. We can't accept the change the person has made and, more important, we can't see that we have also changed. The truth is we are not upset with the person but change, and the desire to not be a part of it.

In working with couples the major issue most commonly stated is a lack of trust. Our trust is supported by what we believe to be true about the other person. Truth and trust then is based in a need that the other person will not change, or will change in a way that we want them to (we are in control). It just doesn't work that way. So we distrust the other person because they are doing what comes natural, they change.

When I can get a couple to start to accept each other as always changing then a whole new perspective is placed on the relationship. What births is a sense of awe and excitement as to how the other person is evolving. By accepting the other person exactly as they are in that moment the relationship is always evolving and new. There is an openness, honesty and freshness that comes to the relationship. The relationship becomes more resilient and adaptive to change. This may seem simplistic but it is our most effective tool in understanding the truth about our relationships.

The difficulty with accepting this truth is that there is no longer any excuse to control, manipulate or mold the other person. You have to accept them for who they are right now. The future of the relationship is unknown. This can be very disconcerting to our ego as we have to let go of our attachment to the other person. While this might seem cold, it really isn't. By letting go of our attachment we can move from conditional to unconditional love. Our love for the other person gets bigger, not smaller. There is also a greater sense of freedom with the absence of attachment and anticipation. The relationship then becomes based on the experience in the current moment. The baggage of the past and future is set aside. When we can overcome our need to control others, and accept whatever shows up, we have a relationship based in the truth of the now. The truth of our relationship overcomes our fears.

With this truth comes the ability to be completely honest, totally transparent. With nothing to hide we are freed from the guilt of deception or withholding. We are vulnerable to the moment. The present may hold acceptance or rejection. Rejection may be painful in the moment, but it is better to experience it now, rather than be delayed for an indefinite time by deception. Deception takes a lot of energy and keeps us from finding our true self. The truth of a relationship becomes our light for personal growth.

Karen was in a relationship with Patrick for a little over two years. Six months into the relationship Patrick had a brief affair with another woman. He had confessed his infidelity and regret at the time. Karen reluctantly accepted, but now was having ongoing anxiety about another potential incident. Karen loves Patrick but is having doubts if she can stay in the relationship with her doubts.

I asked Karen to explore the truth of Patrick's current behavior.

Did she know he had been unfaithful to their relationship since the last incident? Was there any behavior that Patrick had now that caused her concern? Had she shared her ongoing anxiety with Patrick? Could she learn to just trust Patrick in the current moment?

Karen answered no to the first three questions. I asked her if she was willing to let go of the belief that Patrick was going to cheat on her again? Was she willing to see their relationship in the light of the now? Karen said that she could. I asked if she was willing to share with Patrick her anxiety and solicit his support? She did.

Over the next several weeks we met and discussed her thoughts, beliefs and behaviors with Patrick. Karen gradually released her anxiety as the relationship with Patrick became more open and intimate. Patrick expressed that he felt more trusted, which lead him to a greater level of commitment. Karen's reduced anxiety made her less demanding and controlling in her relationship. Patrick responded by being more intimate, less cautious and more spontaneous. Their relationship had a newness and playfulness that was lacking before. After six months Patrick proposed and they married eight months later.

I want to add that Karen was being realistic. We had discussed what she would do if Patrick cheated on her again. She firmly stated that she would leave Patrick, without regret. There was nothing threatening in her voice when she relayed this to Patrick. It was just a fact; Patrick heard her and knew it to be the truth. No one can say for sure if Patrick has been faithful since then, but Karen has had no indication that he has not been and she is very happy to live her experience now. If Patrick would cheat in the future and was caught, Karen knows what she will do, and so does Patrick. Karen is living the now of their relationship and is quite happy.

Living The Truth of the Present Moment

So what is the truth about the truth? First, and this is the tough one, whatever you are thinking is not true. Thinking is the afterthought regarding what is in the moment and it has missed the train. The next moment has already arrived and it is different. Being fully awake and aware in the present moment is the only real truth. Our experience of the present moment is the truth. Who we think we are is not the truth. Allowing our self to be, without any expectations and constructs, is the truth. Seeing others as they are without any expectations and constructs is also the truth. Creating an image of who that person is and how that person is supposed to act it not the truth.

If you can come to accept these axioms regarding the truth you will have taken a major step in being able to effectively manage change in your life. Even once we can grasp this truth it is not that easy to hold onto it all the time. We get sucked back into the dream by the mind and the ego. That is just the way it is. Letting go is not that easy. Yet by constantly bringing yourself back to the truth you can steadily increase the frequency of experiencing life as it really is. And if you turn to the truth when change begins then you are a step ahead in the change process.

USING INQUIRY TO FIND THE TRUTH

If we are going to get to the truth we have to discard what is not true. An important tool in uncovering the truth, while discarding what is not true, is inquiry. Inquiry is the ultimate crap detector and is a perfect use of the mind to move beyond the mind. Inquiry can be exciting and surprising as it challenges all our stories, all that we hold dear. Using inquiry to uncover the truth requires a willingness to be open, a sincere desire to find the truth, and, most of all courage.

Inquiry is a concentrated effort to focus on a single subject and to plumb its depths in an effort to discover the truth about the subject. While it is a mental function, inquiry can have an emotional and even physical affect in doing the work. Inquiry differs from normal thinking in that it requires a sustained level of attention to the subject, resisting the urge to allow the mind to wonder in other directions. In most of our daily thinking our mind is like a butterfly, flitting from place to place, moving in random directions, carried by the winds of sensory distraction. Inquiry then becomes a discipline to manage our thoughts in a way that stays focused but also open to what arises in the present moment. Inquiry moves from an uncontrolled mind, engaged in random thinking, to a sincere search for the truth, ending in the stillness of reality.

Inquiry into the Past

Inquiry requires a staunch determination to not allow the mind to start telling stories. If the mind starts to go there it is critical to shine our attention upon the story and discard it immediately, even if the story has some relevance to the subject of our inquiry. Inquiry is about the present moment, what is going on right now, inside and out. Inquiry probes the origins of our thoughts, beliefs, feelings and emotions. Nothing in our experience is left out. The only caveat is our inquiry cannot drag us into the past.

That doesn't mean that the past cannot be a subject of inquiry. It can be quite valuable, but only from its relevance to the now. If a past belief is creating some kind of suffering now, then we need to explore the true nature of our suffering and the truth of the associated, held belief. The critical point is to not take the belief at face value. Inquiry is not superficial but deep. Have a real hunger for what is the truth right now when inquiring into the past's affect on the present.

John had moderate to severe asthma since early childhood. Despite an armload of medications his asthma prevented him from participating in athletics all through his school years. John just gave up trying. When I first met John he was 32 year-old and moderately obese. He felt trapped by his asthma and blamed it for his overall poor health.

After doing a health screening with John it became apparent that he was on a wide range of medications for his asthma that were compounding his weight problem. He had also given up any hope of even moderate exercise. As I inquired into his most recent asthma attacks John described how he would feel tightness in his chest and his immediate reaction was panic, medications and rest.

I inquired further into the origins of his feelings of panic. John relayed vivid memories of childhood, when this tight feeling lead to what he perceived as life-threatening asthma attacks. I inquired even deeper into what he meant by life-threatening. John became anxious even talking about it. He told me how his mother would get upset and rush him to the doctor. Once there, his mother would proclaim, "Do something, John is going to die!" The answer was always medication and rest. John relayed that as soon as he got the medications and rested a short while he felt much better and the anxiety went away.

I asked John what role he thought anxiety contributed to his asthma. We pursued it from where he was right now. I asked him to think about a severe asthma attack and tell me if it had any effect on the tightness he was now experiencing in his chest. I didn't need John to respond as within a minute he began to hyperventilate and wheeze. John went for his inhaler but I asked him to hold off for a minute. I took John through a relaxation exercise focusing on his breathing in the present. Within five minutes John's breathing had returned to normal and his tightness was had disappeared. No drugs.

John and I spent the next couple hours of work inquiring deeper into his asthma now. John began to understand that his asthma today was actually not a severe as when he was a child, but when he thought about his asthma as a child it made his current condition worse. I asked John if it was true that he would most likely die when he had an asthma attack today. Realizing the truth of my inquiry John gave up his long-held belief connecting asthma to death. We also explored John's current knowledge related to asthma, which was extensive. This gave John greater confidence in an ability to incrementally manage his asthma attacks. We had finally reached a point where John was dealing with his asthma in the present.

I referred John to an excellent holistic medicine doctor, who backed off on many of John's medications, especially those medications causing weight problems, and started him on a diet and with a mild exercise routine. I continued to work with John on sorting out what was the present truth about his asthma and health. John lost weight, but more importantly, could exercise on a consistent basis for the first time in his life. John still has asthma attacks but they are manageable and have not kept him from continuing to lead a healthier lifestyle.

Moving Past 'Everyday Thinking'

In today's fast-paced environment we have trained our minds to multi-task, fly from subject to subject, be nimble. This can serve us in dealing with a variety of experiences at once but it also can allow us to fool ourselves into believing what is real. In particular, we have a tendency to look at a subject or person in the now but relate our experience to it based on impressions from the past. As with John, while these reflections from the past may have been relevant then, they are not necessarily relevant in the present. Our minds, however, are moving so fast that we don't take the time to challenge our clouded perception. We then act without truly understanding our subject in the now. In many situations 'everyday thinking' is an efficient way of dealing with our world. But we need to be aware that 'everyday thinking' can also get us in trouble, especially with our interactions with other people. 'everyday thinking' is superficial and lacks the understanding that inquiry can bring. More important, our 'everyday thinking' will almost always resist change and increase our distress.

Inquiry helps us to go beyond the superficial level of a perceived knowing and delve deeper into what is not known about our subject in the present moment. Accepting that we do not really know the truth about our subject we approach inquiry without any assumptions. Our subject is fresh, unencumbered by any fixed beliefs, judgments and related emotions. Our interest and focus has the energy to get beyond the surface level. Our expectation is one of discovery, rather than confirmation of past judgments. Our desire is to uncover the truth. We may find that the truth hasn't changed, but we don't really know that until we inquire in the present.

Contemplative Inquiry

A final nuance I would like to share, before getting into approaches to inquiry, has to do with the need to approach inquiry in the simplest way. Complexity is a function of the mind and ego. A higher level of inquiry is all about keeping it simple. This type of contemplative inquiry looks to get to the root question, at the most basic level, like "Is that thought really true?" It is challenging us to stay with our experience in the present moment. By keeping our inquiry centered in present experience we avoid the multitude of distractions conjured up by the mind. The present moment is where life is emerging. It is here that we can get to the bottom of what is really happening. Noting what is happening now and pausing to gain insight is a simple, but effective method of inquiry. We contemplate the current moment.

Approaches to Inquiry (step one)

Over the years I have come to greatly appreciate Byron Katie's approach to inquiry. In her book, *Loving What Is*, Byron uses four questions to drive the inquiry process. These questions are seeking the truth. Working from current thoughts, feelings and beliefs on a subject she asks:

1. Is it true?
2. Can you absolutely know that it's true?
3. How do you react when you think that thought?
4. Who would you be without that thought?

These four questions help us to look at our thoughts, feelings and beliefs in the present moment, challenging their validity in the now, and uncovering how they affect our current state of being. As Katie identifies in her book, most of what people believe to be true really isn't, when the light of inquiry is shown upon it. Our ability to know if something is 'absolutely true' is extremely limited, and I hold non-existent. These four questions burst the bubble of knowing. They are very humbling.

I provided relationship counseling with Sally and her mother regarding the increased friction and communications issues between the two. Sally was 22 years old, working as a waitress and considered herself as independent, even though she was still living at home and had financial support from her parents. Sally saw that the genesis of their difficulties was from her mother's ridged rules and conservative orientation. She felt her mother didn't listen to her and was just trying to control her through a series of demands.

Sally's mother had a totally different view of their relationship. She felt that Sally was not making good decisions and was frequently getting into financial trouble that required she and her husband to bail Sally out. Sally's father didn't want to confront Sally so left any difficult discussions up to mom. Sally's mother was quite upset about being put in this position and was angry that it had negatively impacted her and Sally's relationship.

We worked together to find out what was really true about the perceptions Sally and her mother had about each other. In testing the 'truth' of Sally's perceptions of her mother Sally discovered that her impressions did not take into account everything that was going on. Sally was unaware of her father's reluctance to get involved. As her mother shared her feelings from the present moment, Sally became aware that her mother was acting more out of concern and a sense of caring, rather than a need to control.

Sally's mother discovered that a part of her approach with Sally reflected her anger with her husband for not participating in the discussions on finances. She came to see that her feeling, that Sally was not taking responsibility for her life, was based on a similar view she held with respect to her husband.

As we discussed each one of their feelings related to the other, what surfaced was a discontent that was not based in the truth. As they each uncovered their beliefs, which were driving their feelings, they found that most were based on past impressions and were not reflecting the present. In fact, Sally had been working to get her finances under control and was planning on becoming independent by the end of the year. Her mother wanted to support Sally and stated her belief in Sally's ability to make it on her own. After diving deeper into the beliefs behind their feelings it became apparent that there was no basis for their mutual distrust and discontent with each other.

Consequently, Sally and her mother softened their positions and move towards more open feelings of love and compassion. This sense of compassion allowed both women to be more tolerant of the other. It also opened the door for more authentic exchanges of hopes, dreams, fears and doubts. Sally's mother did her work with her husband, approaching him on her issues with his non-participation. At the end of our counseling together this discussion was still a work in progress, but Sally's mom was determined to get to the bottom of her husband's reluctance to participate. Seeking the truth created a shift in feelings for Sally and her mom, allowing more room for give and take.

Approaches to Inquiry (step two)

From this point we can dive deeper into the reality of our subject in the present. To this end I would add the following questions:

5.   What is your experience right now?

6. What parts of your experience can you really control?
7. How would your experience change if you just let go?
8. What do you still not know and need to discover?

With this second set of questions we can now move forward with inquiry, absent any preconceptions, as we gain deeper insights into our connection with the subject of our attention. Looking at our current experience and how we are reacting to it provides a continuity to change. It also allows us to make constructive choices that will influence our next experience. It is much easier to manage change when we are only dealing with what is happening right now.

The goal is to continue to dive deeper and deeper until the mind is exhausted in its efforts to separate. In this quiet moment we feel complete. There is a sense of openness, honesty and awareness. We see the connection between how we react to our experience and its interconnection to our subject's experience and actions. The depth of inquiry comes from experiencing this interconnection with our subject and to see how each influences the other. Depth brings fluidity to our reality and a more direct path to the truth of the moment, as we recognize the constant changes in our subject and our self.

Mark was a 39 year-old male who came to see me for anger issues related to prolonged unemployment. His anger was making him depressed and he didn't know how to move forward. Inquiring into his anger he ranted for an hour about big business, economic inequality, the government, pretty much anything external.

I asked him what he was experiencing right at that moment. He expressed how tired he was with everything, especially his anger. I asked him how much control he thought his anger provided over all of the external concerns. He admitted, very little. I inquired how his anger was affecting his job search. Mark admitted that his anger was keeping him from actively pursuing work. Mark also shared his awareness that his anger was affecting his performance when he did get an interview. "I can't help coming off negative."

I asked him in what way was his anger serving him right now and what it would be like if he just let go of his anger. Mark was unsure. It seemed his anger was the only way he could get energized. We explored other feelings he could be experiencing right now and how he could get energized in a different way. Mark settled on anticipation. Mark decided that as he searched for a job he would start to anticipate a good outcome. Even when he was turned down for a position, Mark didn't move to anger but shifted his anticipation to other opportunities. I also worked with Mark on visualizing what type of work he wanted to do. He focused on Internet marketing and moved his job inquiries in that direction. Mark also decided that he should get more formal training in his new area of work. Within two months Mark was in school and had an entry level position with an Internet marketing firm. Mark no longer had any energy for all of the external, limiting factors he was so focused on in the past.

By inquiring into Mark's current experience through his feelings we were able to find the root of his anger. He held the belief that he was being held back by external influences. Through inquiry, Mark discovered that his belief was not true. Mark also discovered that he could not control any of the external factors so it was not necessary to give them any of his energy. His shift to anticipation took work, but with a strong will to change Mark was successful.

Through intensive inquiry we come to realize the temporal nature of life and the unlimited potential that lies beneath. What is true is relative and we relax into not knowing. Adyashanti from *Emptiness Dancing*: "Simply by resting in not knowing you know. It's a paradox. The more you rest in not knowing, which means never grasping with the mind, the more your direct experience is that you know. In comes in a flash. . . Go to the unknown, experience the unknown, be the unknown. All true knowledge awakens within the unknown."

USING SINCERITY TO FIND THE TRUTH

Real sincerity, prior to entering into deep inquiry, is a critical pre-requisite to effectively managing change. Sincerity brings openness and a willingness to explore. In change we are all explorers. To enter into the vast wilderness of change we have to be *willing* to accept what is new and to deal with it 'as it is'. In our inquiry into change sincerity has to be engaged if we are to be 'all in' for change. We won't effectively deal with change if we are only going to give it a half-hearted, qualified effort. That is just not good enough. The sincerity to be open to what life brings helps suspend distracting thoughts and makes way for focused inquiry.

Sincerity to get to the truth keeps us from leaping forward with blind anticipation. We will never grasp the full meaning of change if we are totally focused on a singular outcome. This type of restricted anticipation is an artificial constraint, creating a limited set of possibilities for change. Anticipation, in this case, is choosing before knowing. In contrast, Mark used an open form of anticipation. It was a *feeling*, which he applied to his effort. Mark did not focus on any one direction, to the exclusion of others. In this way he avoided the cul-de-sac of mental profiling. He remained sincere in his present feelings by clarifying and choosing how he wanted to feel/experience the present moment, and let that energize his life. The sincerity to know sets aside the quick fix that limited anticipation offers and suspends quick judgments related to change. The unconscious desire is replace with a conscious, chosen value in how he experienced change.

It follows then that sincerity is a visceral feeling that opens the doorway into deep inquiry. In turn, the resulting depth of inquiry provides the discoveries necessary to understand the heart of change. Sincerity and inquiry then become tools to give change our undivided attention, without any preconceived notions of outcome. Inquiry not only helps us find the truth about change, it also helps to find the truth about our self. Sincerity is the prerequisite that sets aside our ego so that we can be open and clear in performing inquiry. Sincerity is the driving engine, pulling us deeper and deeper into inquiry.

Sincerity is becoming totally honest with our self. We must be willing to see every way we are conflicted within and without and to explore these conflicts without prejudice and judgment. Sincerity and honest inquiry are qualities of our Higher Self and always available. We just need to be willing to tap into them in our search for the Truth. Sincerity and honest inquiry seek common ground in change and work to identify the underlying, unifying forces available in the present. Sincerity and honest inquiry move our perception from separation to unification. Sincerity and honest inquiry provide continuity between the inward and outward realities, harmonizing our experience in the present.

DISCERNING TRUE SINCERITY IN UNRESTRICTED INQUIRY

Sincerity is the ongoing opportunity to be totally honest with our self and others. There are two kinds of sincerity, one that is managed by the ego and the other that is coming from our Higher Self.

Sincerity that comes from ego is always qualified. It always has conditions. The ego has an *assumption* about what is, and attempts to be sincere but is most likely not willing to move easily from its assumption. The ego is willing to listen and inquire but only to a point. When the assumption it supports is challenged in any way the ego will either shut down the inquiry or attempt to direct it in a way that supports its position. When we are inquiring into change, we are going beyond the current position of the ego. So egoistic inquiry into change is flawed from the beginning.

Egoistic inquiry has a tendency to get more and more complex the longer you inquire into change. We often think we are looking at change from all angles but, in reality, we are usually just trying to justify why we don't need to change. Inquiry at this level becomes a resistance to change. Within egoistic inquiry we find many resisting emotions like anger, hurt, sadness and entropy. We look for something or someone to blame. We partition our inquiry into acceptance of what supports our thoughts and feeling and rejection of any challenges to these thoughts and feelings. In egoistic inquiry we think we are seeking the truth when it is just the opposite. Our egoistic fears rationalize 'living the lie'.

Inquiry centered in our Higher Self is free from the confines of the ego. It is the 'beginner's mind' so eloquently described by the late Zen master, Shunryu Suzuki. Inquiry at this level is without identity so it has no position from the start. I call this unrestricted sincerity and inquiry. This allows for innocence to enter the inquiry, which keeps us from excluding anything. Sincerity at this level knows that nothing is for certain and the search for the truth is without boundaries. With unrestricted sincerity and inquiry there is a heightened *interest* in all that arises, leading to an absence of judgment and a willingness to go deeper.

Unrestricted sincerity and inquiry is critical to understand what change is offering us in the present moment. This provides a nimbleness in how we respond to change and greases the wheels for the process to move forward. It also brings a higher degree of understanding to what is happening now; and greater understanding brings greater acceptance. It takes the fight out of change. Without mental restrictions change is wide open and we are willing to respond in an infinite number of ways. We gain greater maneuverability when we learn to row with the stream of life, rather than against it.

As I stated at the beginning of the book, change and transition is about what we are becoming. In this process it begs the question, "What am I, really?" What we are, internally and externally, is the center of change. Our ability to move away from a fixed concept of self and to openly explore the full range of possibilities allows us to maximize change for our expanding awareness of self. If we just let go of what we have been and earnestly seek what we are becoming we get out of the way and allow a natural enfoldment to our true nature.

If you are starting from a position of unrestricted sincerity there is always a sense that, "I don't really know anything." There is a deeper desire to want to know the truth. There is a willingness to accept whatever unfolds if it brings you closer to the truth of what you really are in this present moment. This path has a higher level of uncertainty and mystery involved, but it also brings more energy and excitement. And isn't this the real nature of change, uncertainty and mystery? What makes you turn to the next page in a book? Isn't it because there is uncertainty and mystery and you have a heightened sense to explore what comes next? Unrestricted sincerity then opens the door to uncovering uncertainty and mystery.

I was counseling Jack, who was very unhappy with his current employment. While it was providing for his needs Jack didn't like what he was doing and whom he was working with. This is a very common starting place for people looking at a career change. Jack had developed a set of one-off options for a new career but he wasn't really happy with any of them. He came to me for help in deciding which option was the best for him.

I started with the question, "Tell me what you are?" This seems to throws my clients off guard every time. Jack came back with, "Don't you mean who I am?" I explain that 'who' implies something fixed, with a specific identity. 'What' takes the perceived personality out of it and removes the restrictions that the ego would like to place on this level of inquiry. Jack didn't like it but was willing to play with me.

As we moved forward over several weeks Jack inquired into many variations of 'What I am?' What he found was that each version he came up with was fabricated by some external influence and/or his internal, egoistic perceptions. It became easier for Jack to see the external influences molding his current identity and to set them aside. The ego's version of self became subject to a greater level of sincerity and inquiry. Each week we challenged one version after another until one day Jack came in and said, "I have no idea as to what I am." Finally he was empty and in this emptiness there was unrestricted potential.

We were ready to move to the question, "What do I want to become?" The possibilities were now unlimited. Jack no longer held any preconceived thoughts and was willing to just experience what unfolded in the present moment. What came forward was his love of children and a desire to teach and mentor. Jack was connecting with the Spirit within. He found what he was through inquiry and co-creation with his Higher Self.

Within three months he had moved from business sales to a primary level educator. This involved some major financial changes and created some relationship challenges from his partner, who didn't initially share his vision. Within a year he had a permanent position as a third grade teacher. He had navigated a major career change and is very happy.

It is not uncommon when working with people who want to make a career change that they are moving from a self-centered set of ego-driven needs to a desire to serve a greater good. In the case of Jack he gave up recognition, associated with position and financial security to share his time and talents with budding young minds. None of this was an easy change, but sincere inquiry helped him make major decisions and successfully navigate a major career change. If you asked him if it was all worth it I am confident you would hear, without hesitation, "Yes it was, and I wouldn't go back for anything!" Sincere inquiry into "What I am?" provided the necessary energy for Jack to make a major, life transition.

When we are in a state of unrestricted sincerity and inquiry we are immersed in the flow of life. We are being carried by the sweet spot in the current of change. We are centered in a natural enfoldment into our true nature. What we find is that change goes much more smoothly when the ego gets a time out. When we remove the ego's ownership of life we remove the divisions inherent in ego's nature. We return to wholeness, beyond the illusions of inner and outer, right and wrong, good and bad.

THE EGO, PUTTING IT IN ITS PROPER PLACE

The ego is also a consummate storyteller and a consummate critic. Like a good friend telling an interesting story, the ego can be quite engaging and convincing but, because the ego is not directly experiencing life, it is only a story. The ego is also viewing the show and writing its review. Now if a friend tells us a story we have to decide whether we believe it or not. Unfortunately, because we so deeply identify our self with the ego, we don't use the same level of judgment when we listen to the ego's story.

This is how the ego traps us. We become dependent on it to tell us 'what is real' when, in fact, the ego doesn't have a clue. So the story becomes our reality when it is actually pure fiction. We become stuck in the past or the future and resistant to change. The ego circumvents our desire for sincere inquiry into what is, using the story as a substitute.

The ego has a deep need to be in control so it is more than willing to weigh in all the time. If we don't recognize the ego for what it is we just perceive that this afterthought in our mind is telling us the truth. We accept the whispers of the ego as our own thoughts. It's like allowing a friend to totally dominate your life. You just give up all control. To regain control we have to remove the dominance of the ego. This occurs by simply recognizing that the ego, and it's possessive nature, is not what we really are. The ego is a mythic creature of our own creation. We choose to give it life and to sustain it, or not.

What is really happening with this constant chatter from the ego is an actual blocking of our real experiences in life. The ego does this because it knows that it is a ghost, without form and substance. It is an energy field that requires a constant movement to maintain itself. The ego is an action and not a thing. If we start to ignore the ego it would evaporate like a morning mist. When we accept all thoughts, feelings and actions just as they are in this moment we are in complete alignment with life and our old friend is out of a job.

Don't get me wrong; I am not advocating a wholesale dismissal of the ego. As I have mentioned it is a tool that can be very helpful at times. What is critical is to realize that the ego is not *who* we really are. We are something much bigger.

The ego sustains itself on second hand information it receives from our senses and mind. Unfortunately the ego doesn't realize this so it believes it is always sharing the truth. The ego is just taking what we have already experienced, spins it into a story and then feeds it back to us as the truth. This can be a big problem if we are fully identified with the ego and totally relying on it to help us interact with life. Byron Katie has a great explanation in *Loving What Is*, "The truth is prior to every story. And every story, prior to investigation, prevents us from seeing what's true."

So if we are really seeking the truth we have to go it alone. We have to explore what is real without the help of our old friend. The ego has to take a time out and wait for us to call. We make that call when it is time to take action. The ego is a useful tool when taking action. It helps to keep us oriented to what we are doing. We need its persona to help guide our next actions. We just need to remember that ego is not calling the shots; what is behind the ego, our Higher Self, is the real director and producer of life.

To effectively manage change we need to give the ego a time out. It is the only way to cope effectively with change. The ego wants to separate and resist, and that will get us nowhere. I will discuss the role of the ego more when we get into the change process. Until then, you can start to explore your relationship with ego. Are you unconsciously fused as one or can you see the ego as a verb (an activity rather than a thing), trying to create separation? We need to ask, "Who is really in charge? Can we be absolutely certain that the story the ego is telling us is real? What exactly has the ego ever whispered that is the truth today? What, other than resistance, has the ego contributed to change?" These questions help to put the ego in its place. Change requires we relegate the ego to the role of a special teams player in the game of life.

So, in fact, the ego is just an idea that doesn't really exist. Yet because it is so persistent with its actions it feels like the ego is indispensible. So how do we learn to park the ego? If you allow yourself to have a thought without taking possession of it you find that there is no ego present, just an awareness of what is. If you hold that thought, without judgment, you will continue to hold the ego at bay. Nothing is lost and, in fact, everything is gained. Resistance is lost and we can face change in the current moment without limitation.

There will be a lot of resistance from the ego as it tries to re-engage, but the more you practice this technique the more skillful you become in experiencing life without ego and judgment.

DISCOVERING THE TRUTH OF CHANGE

The truth is forever present; that is, it is forever in the present moment. However, this makes the truth ever elusive; that is, when we try to fix the truth beyond the present moment it slips into illusion. The truth, like a river, is forever flowing back into the ocean of the One. As the truth flows it is constantly changing. We must seek the truth in the current moment and learn to not become fixated on any one moment of truth.

We only know the truth through the experience of the current moment. Our minds have always just missed the truth. As thoughts form the absolute truth of the moment has passed. The mind then is a shape shifter, taking the experience of the truth and making it into a story. It can be a useful story, but it is still a story, an illusion. So the mind has utility, but will always lack certainty. Certainty, truth, is only in the current moment. It is critical that we understand and maintain this orientation.

The truth and change go hand in hand. Both are alive in the current moment and illusive to the mind. The moment the mind tries to make some sense of our current experience it has already changed again. So the mind's thoughts about change are also a story, an illusion. The mind can help us to plan for action that will hopefully align us with change, but the mind can never control change. You can't control what you cannot capture. So the truth of change is only the experience of the present moment.

We can travel through life, in alignment with truth and change, when the mind remains nimble, resilient and focused on the present. We are as close as we can be when the mind is grounded in the present moment experience. As soon as the mind drifts into the past it is starting to become the storyteller. The mind is composing an intriguing form of fiction, with drama, chaos and mystery. The story may be interesting and exciting, but it is still pure fiction. We choose whether to stay as close as possible to truth and change by focusing on the current moment or to fall back into the dream of life. This is what many eastern religions refer to as 'Samsara', the cycle of illusion.

We can pull the attention of our minds out of the story and back to the present with the use of sincerity and inquiry. Inquiry helps us to awaken to the illusions of our mind's creation in the past. We challenge each thought with "Is it true?", "Do I really know it is the truth?" Inquiry on any topic will ultimately bring us to the same place, the truth is only real in the current moment. Inquiry always brings us back to our present experience. In this way inquiry restores our focus, nimbleness, resilience and alignment with change. Inquiry shakes us awake and helps us to release old stories created in the mind. Inquiry is a central tool in psychotherapy, but you can access it on your own, without a therapist or group. It is not a difficult process if you have the will to dive in.

The depth of our inquiry is aided by sincerity. Being sincere assists in releasing the hidden emotions of past stories. Sincerity also helps to release our resistance in letting go of our stories. Sincerity fuels the fire to seek the truth as it constantly changes. It is the energy to run the race, knowing you will never catch up with the truth until all the stories are dispelled.

Sincerity and inquiry are tools and operate beyond the control of the mind. They respond to the Higher Self and seek unity rather than separation. The mind and the ego are the masters of separation and will always resist sincerity and unrestricted inquiry. The ego must be realized for what it is, a tool in making choices and not an identity for making judgments, before we can effectively use sincerity and inquiry. The mind must be seen as a useful tool for reason and action, but not as the seat of truth. Otherwise our efforts to use sincerity and inquiry will become just another part of the story and a justification for the mind's creative reality. Sincerity and inquiry then use the mind, while displacing the ego, as they report to the Higher Self what is the truth. Sincerity and inquiry expose our stores for what they are and strips away illusion after illusion. Sincerity and inquiry reveal the emptiness of the truth.

To live the truth we must fully realize that it is empty; the truth is nowhere. We must also realize that the truth is all there is; the truth is everywhere. When we can live within the space between these two realities then we will experience truth, and change will take on an effortless flow.

CHAPTER FOUR

LOVING-KINDNESS: THE DOORWAY TO OPENNESS AND INTIMACY

... this love that transcends all description, when it is known as a deep connection and deep unity, this love is indiscriminate. It doesn't know how to turn itself on and off. That switch is only in the mind.

Adyashanti, *Emptiness Dancing*

Nothing real can be threatened.
Nothing unreal exists.
Herein lies the peace of God.

A Course in Miracles

This may seem like a strange topic for a book on change, but how we love is absolutely critical to managing change. I will start out with a discussion of emotions and the influence they have on our thoughts and actions. I will then discuss two types of love. One is love coming from the separate self (ego) or conditional love. The other is unconditional love, which comes through our Higher Self and is open and without limits.

Conditional love is confining, restrictive and resistant to complete openness. It is a barrier to change. Unconditional love is accepting, open to everything, without limits and embracing of change. When love is conditional it supports a restrictive view related to change, limiting our choices. Like blinders on a horse, our limited vision will provide only one direction forward. When we love unconditionally change flows easily with minimal effort and anything is possible.

EMOTIONS AND THEIR IMPACT ON THOUGHT AND ACTION

In a society that is obsessed with thought there is a new truth emerging. Our thoughts are constantly being guided and influenced by our emotions. Physiological and psychological research over the past decade has helped us to understand that the recognition of our experience starts in the heart. First the heart emits far more energy that the brain. Our heart responds to our experience *before* it ever registers in the brain, and it is the response of the heart, neuro-chemically, which has the most influence over what we will think about our experience. Finally, it is our emotions that hold our memories. When a feeling is neutral about an experience the memory of the experience fades away. So, in fact, the heart is our direct link to our experience and the custodian of our past, unresolved perceptions.

Our emotions, and the moods they create, are the vessels that hold a constellation of thoughts on a given experience. Love and fear are the two strongest emotions formed from experience. If we feel some variation of love and connection related to an experience then that experience is 'good'. If we feel fear and separation to an experience then that experience is 'bad'. Regardless of the outcome of the experience the feeling is what drives our perception of the experience. Even a positive outcome can carry forward negative energy that can color similar events in the future. Our initial impressions of new events and interactions are often colored in past feelings, which can hold little or no relevance. Yet these past feelings can greatly impact how we respond to the new event or interaction without us having any idea as to why.

Understanding Our Emotional Orientation to Change

This knowledge is critical to helping us understand how we perceive and react to change. If our emotions are love and connectedness we will embrace change. If our emotions are fear and separation then we will resist change. The fear response to change comes from the misconception that what is real can be threatened. As the quote from A Course in Miracles states, "Nothing that is real can be threatened." Put another way, we cannot loose what is *really* ours, or what we *really* are. Our Limitless Self cannot loose anything or be reduced in any way.

With this understanding in place change will not be governed by fear. If you are going to be laid off from your job, being fearful of it happening will not change the outcome; the decision has already been made. We can suffer more, however, through the resistance to being laid off. Denial, depression, entropy and anger can all be unhealthy emotional resistances to the change of being laid off. In working with many clients who have been laid off they often report back six months later that being laid off was the best thing that happened to them. They often state how unhappy or dissatisfied they were with the work they were doing and being forced to make a change was a real blessing.

If we view change from the perspective of the Higher Self then our emotional response to change will be one of love, compassion, understanding and connection. Allowing the process of change to unfold, trusting that the change is going to support our growth and evolution, we can remain relatively unattached to the immediate outcome and take a broader, more open view of the future. We can act without expectations. A common axiom in psychology is that expectations are really premeditated resentments. If we trust the process, without engaging in limiting expectations, we can assure that we will have a positive emotional response. A more productive and positive response to being laid off would be acceptance, anticipation and excitement. These emotions allow us to let go and to start to explore new possibilities immediately. Negative reactions and emotional attachments only delay recovery and forestall change. Given our current orientation to change this idea may seem ludicrous, but finding the ability to accept, anticipate and move on with positive expectations has consistently proven to have better outcomes, mentally, emotionally and physically.

If we view change from the perspective of the separate self our emotional reaction will be of fear, threat and the potential for harm. The separate self is caught in the maze of limits and scarcity. These are prerequisites for the separate self in maintaining the illusion of *its* reality. Even if we start with a positive feeling the separate self will invoke and evoke limitations and conditions. The separate self views its response as a transaction; I expect something in return for what I give. "If I give into change I expect, in return, something that will make me feel good about myself, but I am fearful that my expectations will not be met." This fear of potential loss quickly washes over all other emotions experienced by the separate self. We move from love to fear, from anticipation to expectation, from success to disaster.

Audrey was at her whit's end when it came to relationships. Over a twenty-year period she had committed to numerous relationships with men only to have them fall apart. She always tried to look at what failed in her relationships and vow to not make the same mistakes again, but there didn't seem to be a magic formula for success.

As we reviewed each of her relationships a certain pattern of emotional behavior became apparent. Audrey would start off with feelings of hope and love for the new man in her life, but with the first difficult encounters in the relationship she began to have doubts. Audrey admitted that the men frequently told her that she had become hesitant and reserved. They accused her of withholding her feelings and harboring resentments. Basically, these men were telling Audrey that she was turning away from the relationship and giving up.

I asked her if this was true. Audrey first started going into a litany of stories about how she attempted to save her relationships with various men. When she eventually ran out of stories I asked, "How did you really feel about the relationship and the man you were with?" Audrey's eyes got big and there was a long silence. I asked her to go beyond the story of what she did to save the relationships and look deeply into her feelings at the time.

Audrey took a couple of weeks to set with this question, journal her impressions and to honestly appraise her feelings and emotions. When we met again Audrey reported that she did have a tendency to get fearful and pull back at the first sign of disharmony and conflict. I praised Audrey on her willingness to take ownership of her feelings, and I asked her what impact she thought that might have on the relationship. She admitted that she was very afraid that each relationship was going to be like all the rest and she felt the need to protect herself.

With this discovery at the fore Audrey and I started to look at several of her past relationships, focusing on what actually happened and whether her reactions were based on events or negative expectations. It became apparent that Audrey had gotten into some poor relationships and she was justified in pulling back, but she also identified healthy relationships where she had just gotten scared and ran away. I then asked Audrey to dive even deeper into her feelings and ask, "Can I have a loving, lasting relationship?"

Audrey went away to ponder this question for three weeks. When we met again she told me that she felt that she was 'damaged goods' and was not able to have a loving, meaningful and lasting relationship. I responded with a simple question, "Is that really true?" Our next several visits together went deeply into this question. Audrey was persistent in her inquiry and each week we debunked each of her concepts and feelings of unworthiness. Many of these feeling stemmed from her childhood and her relationship with a stern and demanding father. At last we had reached the point where Audrey could consider herself worthy of a meaningful relationship.

I then asked another question, "Do you have the strength to express love and compassion with a man, even during hard times?" There was a long silence and finally Audrey answered, "I don't know." I then asked, "What more do you have to loose by staying in love and compassion during difficult times? Would it be any worse than what you have already experienced?" We sat in silence for over 20 minutes and finally she said, "No, it wouldn't be any worse." I told Audrey that I thought she was at a point where she could take ownership of her fears from the past and use good judgment in maintaining feelings of love and compassion, even in difficult times. I asked her if she was willing to give it a try. She said yes.

I asked Audrey if there was one man who she had been in a relationship with where she still held strong feelings. She identified David in particular where she had deep regrets in breaking up with him. She admitted that she was the one who initiated the separation and, after our exploration of the relationship, she could see that the separation was based more on her feelings than what was really going on. She was afraid and ran away. I asked Audrey if she felt she was ready to look into a reconnecting with David. To my surprise, Audrey was very excited about the possibility. I then asked her if she was willing to face the possibility of 'no' with love and compassion. Again Audrey was silent for a while. Slowly, deliberately, she finally answered, "Yes". I took her hesitancy in answering as a good sign. Audrey was gaining a deeper understanding of her feelings and how they can influence her interactions with others.

Audrey was positive when she called David to see if he would have coffee. At first he said no, but when Audrey responded with acceptance and she told him she felt responsible for their break up David reconsidered. Coffee went well and they started to see one another again. Audrey then asked me if she could bring David to one of our sessions. I agreed and we met for a few weeks to discuss their prior relationship and how they both felt about it. David confessed that Audrey's sudden pulling away confused him. He thought that she had met someone else, but was unwilling to admit it. He was surprised by what Audrey had to share regarding what had happened based on her new perspective. David was also pleased to find Audrey more open and compassionate to his feelings. He shared his own disappointments and fears when they had difficult times before their break up.

A month after our last session together Audrey and David decided to move back in together. Both felt they had a better understanding of their feelings for each other and were willing to give it another try. Audrey saw me a few times after, when her fears would sweep over her again. Each time we worked using inquiry to return to feelings of love and compassion. After about six months Audrey stopped calling. At last report she and David were still happily living together with mutual commitments to a long-term relationship.

Audrey had created a self-fulfilling outcome in her relationships with men. Each time her expectations affected feelings, which, in turn, affected her behavior and effected how the relationship would eventually break up. Learning that fear and withdrawal did not serve her future happiness was the breakthrough that Audrey needed to move into love and compassion. Audrey's success was based in her willingness to honestly use inquiry to make this discovery.

Unconditional and Conditional Love

Unconditional love sounds good but most of us struggle to find and live it. Why? It's because unconditional love requires complete openness and intimacy. Our separate self's greatest fear, however, is to be open and intimate with life and all it holds. If we are completely open and intimate with life we loose all sense for the separate self and the feelings of control that the separate self covets. There are many terms I use in the book for a sense of separateness, ego, identity, personality, separate self. They are all the same. When we feel the need to disconnect from the whole we immediately create separation and separation is the breeding ground for all of our fears related to life.

Unconditional love is the anecdote to the fears raised by the separate self. Unconditional love starts with openness, taking the chance to express honestly and with loving-kindness. It is said we can either be in expression or depression. Unconditional love is naturally expressive, creating connection. When we act with conditional love we conceal and withdraw from what seems to not love us. When we disconnect we often fall into the illusion of the separate self and become fearful and depressed.

So to learn to love change we must first learn to love life unconditionally in all its mystery and form. We have to learn to give up control and to accept life as it is. The term commonly used in the east for unconditional love is loving-kindness. Loving-kindness is this expression of unconditional love, internally and externally. We will explore the importance of loving-kindness, how it releases fear and how it creates a greater acceptance of change. First, however, we will look into the limitations of conditional love.

CONDITIONAL LOVE AND THE NEED FOR SEPARATION

Love is a mystery for most of us. We often experience it, feel it, and create the sense that it is coming and going. This is the love formed by mind/ego, which is conditional in nature. It is love by reciprocity. "If you love me enough then I will love you back," or, "I love it if it makes me feel good and it doesn't hurt." This is the love of the separate self. In this context love is a mystery because we are only willing to experience the part of love that we like. Often love is *fierce* and not something we initially appreciate. Not being able to see this aspect of love keeps love from being whole and therefore a mystery. Only by experiencing love in all ways that it manifests can we get past the illusion of conditional love.

The separate self believes it can be threatened and injured so it creates the need to protect itself at all times. It must be ready to attack or retreat at the first signs of pain and suffering. It believes that love is only about the good. It is under the illusion that love is the absence of conflict. It is totally co-dependent. Conditional love is reactive and dependent on the initial offer of 'qualified love' from another. "Love me and I will love you."

The origins of conditional love actually come from unconditional love, so unconditional love is not that much of a stranger. What happens is that the separate self co-opts unconditional love in a way that allows only partial acceptance of others and life. It places a condition on love, which is essential to support it's concept of self. The self has limits and unconditional love can run contrary to these limits. Unconditional love is about being and that is just too much for the separate self, which requires control over life for its sense of survival.

The separate self hedges its bets in love. It will be partially open and truthful as long as its needs are getting met and its limits are being respected. At the first sign that its needs and limits are being threatened it will withdraw and become deceitful as a form of protection. To the separate self conditional love is natural and logical. Preservation is the highest priority and deceit, for the sake of control, is acceptable.

Conditional Love – the Battle Ground Between the Separate and Higher Self

When we are centered in the Higher Self there is an intrinsic understanding that this Self cannot be threatened. It is an integral part of all that is. To threaten would be to want to injure Itself. It just doesn't make sense at this higher level of understanding. So the only way that the separate self can defend itself is to ignore the presence of the Higher Self and to reduce love to conditional, making way for the experience of pain and fear.

Because conditional love is based in unconditional love our real fear is not centered in believing that others don't love us, but in knowing that we really continue to love others even when it is not reciprocal. The separate self's deep fear of loving unconditionally holds a greater sway over our feelings than our actual experience. So the issue is not 'out there', it is an internal conflict between the separate self and the Higher Self. Unfortunately the separate self usually holds court over the mind so it has the louder voice. It uses the weapons of separation and perceptions of good and bad, to drive off the Higher Self and gain control over our thoughts and feelings. It provides the convincing argument that we should grasp the good and push away the bad, hence conditional love. This argument is persuasive but not based in the truth. It would be like cutting off your arm because you have a scratch on your hand that hurts.

The byproducts of conditional love are reservation and untruth. By becoming reserved we are not completely open to what is and therefore partially blind to our full experience of life. We think that we are putting on the blinders so that we can avoid the sight of what is not good and only seeing what is good. In reality we are limiting our joy. Life, fully experienced, is joyful. When we turn our back on any portion of life we are no longer in touch with reality. We miss all the possibilities to experience and love this life. We fall into the story of separateness. We take refuge in the story and accept living in a lie. Conditional love is restrictive, self-limiting, dishonest and inauthentic.

Being completely open to all that we experience is actually very peaceful and loving. This may be hard to comprehend but it is true. When we live our life completely open we come to see the interconnectedness of all things. When we experience this connection we have an immediate release from the grip of fear and find peace. We lose judgment with regard to perceptions of good and bad in others. There is no longer a need to withdraw. This view of life allows us to reconnect with unconditional love, to see the intrinsic good in all things and all situations. Seeing the intrinsic good brings love and peace into our being.

Conditional Love's Need for Certainty

A fear of being attracted to, compassionate with or even being willing to engage something the separate self considers bad is a primary barrier to change. This fear is further complicated by the fact that change has a high level of uncertainty. The separate self needs to *know* if it will experience love so it can react positively to someone or something. For the separate self how can it love what it is uncertain about? Conditional love then will lead us down the primrose path in change. If I can be sure it is good for me then I will go with change. If I am unsure then I will resist change. Conditional love in change fosters hesitation and negates the hidden opportunities that change provides us.

Beth was a 27 year-old female who came to me with a fear of dating. She felt lonely but couldn't seem to engage in the activities that explored a potential relationship with a man. Beth had tried many of the on-line programs for dating and found herself hesitating and fearful every time she got to the point of arranging a date.

In exploring her personal history Beth relayed how both of her parents, but especially her father, had been very conditional in their love for her. For Beth she was constantly walking the tightrope of parental love. One false action saw love withdrawn and it took a tremendous effort for Beth to get her parent's love back.

In high school Beth had fallen in love twice. Her first love had betrayed her for another girl. Beth's second love had just drifted away, and the more she tried to revive the relationship the further he drifted. I asked Beth if there was anyone she loved unconditionally. Beth said only her childhood teddy bear, which she still slept with at night.

I asked Beth if there was a part of her that still loved her parents and her two high school boyfriends. After some intensive exploration Beth admitted that deep down inside she still had loving memories and feelings for her parents and boyfriends. I asked her if these feelings of love were painful. While she had some sorrow Beth admitted her loving feelings were still fond memories. Her pain was in a sense of loss and denial for the loss she felt. I then asked Beth if there was any reason why she could not hold loving-kindness for her parents and boyfriends, even when it was not always reciprocated. Beth expressed a fear of being rejected. I reminded Beth that she had already experienced rejection but she still had the capacity for loving-kindness. Beth was unsure but willing to explore this idea further.

Over our subsequent sessions Beth began to separate her ability to feel loving-kindness from her fear of rejection. She got to the point where one did not negate the other. During this time I asked Beth to practice loving-kindness with her parents, even when they were not loving in return. Beth was curious now and willing to experiment. Beth discovered that she did not need to be loved by her parents to feel loving-kindness. Furthermore, she felt much better about her parents and herself when holding them in loving-kindness. Beth gained a great compassion for her parents and their inability to love unconditionally. She started to see a softening in her parents over several months and attributed the change to her ability to hold them both in loving-kindness.

During the same period Beth started to attend some singles functions at her church, while continuing to explore Match.com and Harmony.com. She eventually gave up the online exploration as it didn't seem personal and it inhibited her ability to express loving-kindness. Beth had a couple of dates through her singles group that didn't pan out. This time, however, Beth didn't take it personally and held no ill feelings for the men. Eventually Beth met Steven. Steven was shy and became attracted to Beth's ability to express loving-kindness without conditions. Beth and Steven took it slowly and developed an evolving love that seemed to be healing for both. During our last session I asked Beth about her future with Steven. She said she didn't know if it would lead to marriage or not, but that didn't really matter. What mattered was her ability to love Steven in the now and how that made her feel.

Through her understanding of loving-kindness Beth had come to accept the uncertainty of relationships and a willingness to not let this uncertainty hold her back from experiencing love. Beth also healed her relationship with her parents, without any expectations or needs from them. The changes in Beth's relationships became opportunities for her to break prior co-dependent patterns and take loving-kindness deeper at every turn. Beth became fearless with her love.

UNCONDITIONAL LOVE, THE PATH TO BEING WHOLE

When you hear the term unconditional love most of us go, "Oops, that feels like it is without limits!" In fact it is, but being without limits is not really that scary. In reality unconditional love is a deep, intimate connection with everything. When we are intimate with everything there is no room for opposition, there is no room for barriers, there is nothing to be afraid of. This is not something we have unlearned over the years and must make a concerted effort to relearn. Loving unconditionally has been a part of us for as long as we have been. We have all experienced unconditional love but have retreated from our awareness of it when the separate self became prominent in our psyche and interjected conditions into our feelings.

Perhaps the most common form of unconditional love is what a parent often feels for their children. It is without limits. If a child is in danger we automatically step into the fray without any concern for our self. It's not that we aren't frustrated, angry, upset or just done with our children from time to time. We can experience some or all of these emotions but underneath them is unconditional love. It's just there. We could no more extract unconditional love from our True Self than we could extract our heart from our body and expect to exist.

Unconditional love is a higher, more consistent feeling that is a natural part of who we really are. It is an attribute of our Universal Nature seated within our Higher Self. Conditional love is an aspect of unconditional love where the separate self, through the mind, has added a sense of isolation and limits to the equation. It is the perspective that love is something we acquire and, therefore, expect others to acquire from us. While this is a fallacy the separate self works hard to make it the truth. Conditional love does not replace unconditional love, it just blocks our view of what is always here.

We can experience conditional love at the same time we are living unconditional love. This is how love gets conflicted. The separate self can push its agenda to the forefront and totally block for a time our ability to love unconditionally. It's not gone, just hidden by a whole host of feelings the separate self can generate. Unconditional love sees past the good times and the difficult times. It holds to the intrinsic sense of connectedness and won't let go. The separate self, however, creates a sense of lack in love that creates perceived, unmet needs. We think that we need to acquire love when, in truth, we have all of the love we need. Deep down inside us we experience abundant love, so we become conflicted. It is this conflict that keeps us from allowing love to facilitate change in our lives.

When we decide to let go of the feelings associated with conditional love we enter into forgiveness; forgiveness for others and, eventually, our self. We come to forgiveness by way of compassion. Compassion offers a perspective of impermanence along with a sense of unity in something greater. Impermanence and unity are both aligned with life as it is. Life is always changing, but nothing is ever really lost. We have compassion for the changes life brings, good and bad and, when we are aware, we know deep down inside that nothing is ever lost. We have compassion for perceived suffering of others and our self, knowing that the pain created is an actually an illusion. We know that the perceived suffering will lead to change and an evolution of who and what we are. Actions, attitudes, opinions and beliefs all come and go with the end result of a movement back to the middle from extremes. Joy eventually fades and suffering eventually abates. We let go of our points of view and emotional entanglements to awaken in a sense of unity. It is not a process of giving up, it is a process of opening up. The result is a net gain, not loss.

Think back on a time that you were really angry with someone you love. What was your point of view related to how the person treated you with respect to your concept of what they should do if they really loved you? Now consider your hold on that point of view when you started to move towards forgiveness. Was it the same? I think not. As you softened you became more open, more interested in how to move back into love with that person. You became more aware of the other person's point of view and needs for love. You saw their suffering and became willing to move past your own sense of pain. Your pain became the budding flower of forgiveness, compassion and unconditional love. Anger was alchemized into love. All you had to do was to let go of your original point of view and emotional entrapments contrived by the separate self in the form of conditional love.

Frequently I have found that divorced couples, after a couple of years of reflection, become the best of friends. They have softened from the points of view that they had of each other and have moved from conditional love and towards unconditional love. They let go of the egoistic need to control the other, realizing that they could never really control their former spouse. This provides an openness that has room for compassion, understanding and acceptance of the other person just as they are. This is loving-kindness.

Harriet and Ralph's marriage ended in a horrendous custody battle for their three children during a messy divorce. All suffered, Harriet, Ralph, the children, family and friends. The award of custody to Harriet infuriated Ralph and all communications were cut. Arrangements for visitation went through intermediaries and lawyers continued to reap great benefit from ongoing financial struggles, as well as contentions of custody violations. The pain from conditional love lost was infiltrating their thoughts and emotions.

When I first met with Ralph his anger was so intense that he actually spit his emotions on me as he explained his situation. Our first task was to get past his anger and to the grief he was feeling for his perceived loss of love. Loss of custody was Ralph's biggest pain. He missed his children.

I first explored with Ralph his perceptions of Harriet as a mother. Was she a good mother? Ralph had little to complain about how Harriet was raising the children since the divorce. I asked Ralph if Harriet had ever discounted him as the children's father since the divorce. He reluctantly answered, "No." After softening Ralph's perception of Harriet as a mother, we could focus on his grief in the limits of visitation with the children. As Ralph inquired deeper into his sense of loss for the children I had him focus on his feelings of love for them. As Ralph tapped into his unconditional love for each child I asked, "Don't you want your children to experience this love and to feel the joy that unconditional love brings them?" Ralph cried for a long time.

I developed a plan with Ralph to open up communications with Harriet again to allow him to enquire more about how the children were doing. With some trepidation Ralph called Harriet. Within two weeks they were having regular conversations about the children. They discussed how to best ease the transition from one parent to the other during visitations, both focusing on the feelings of their children. Ralph's grief decreased dramatically as he found out more about the children when he was not with them. Harriet suggested that they both attend certain functions for the kids with an agreement that they would not argue or fight while in their presence. Ralph was delighted for more opportunities to see his children and quickly agreed. As time went on Harriet became more flexible with visitation, complaints through attorneys stopped and everyone was much happier. Both parents were now engaged in unconditional love for their children.

I then asked Ralph if any of the changes with the children had affected his feelings towards Harriet. He admitted that many of his negative feelings towards Harriet seemed to be unfounded. He was still certain that the divorce was the right move, but he no longer saw Harriet as evil and vicious. I asked Ralph if he would explore the potential of unconditional love for Harriet as the mother of their children. I asked Ralph if he was willing to let go of past feelings to look at his feelings in the present. This took some work, but Ralph began to see the 'divine mother' aspects of Harriet with respect to the children. Ralph was able to move to unconditional love for Harriet based on this paradigm.

Ralph's emotional shift became apparent to Harriet in their ongoing conversations with respect to the children and even other matters related to the divorce. As Ralph and Harriet shared stories about the children they even started to joke and laugh about specific events and behaviors. Most important, they became much more relaxed during events with the children and it was paying off on the mental and emotional health of the kids. Exchanges of the children were now planned by Ralph and Harriet and occurred, without incident and the need of an intermediary.

Holidays had been assigned for each year, but the last year I was working with Ralph Harriet invited him over for Thanksgiving dinner (her holiday that year). Ralph cried as he relayed to me the invitation and his sense of unconditional love from Harriet with respect to his needs for the children. At Christmas Ralph reciprocated with an invitation to Harriet. Besides having presents for the children, Ralph bought a beautiful statue of the Madonna for Harriet. She was greatly moved by his gesture.

Ralph had learned to move from his pain of conditional love to find common ground with Harriet and the children in unconditional love. In our last session Ralph expressed for the first time the desire to start to look at dating again. He relayed that his approach to finding love was going to be far different this time around. He had found compassion and strength in his ability to love unconditionally and wanted to find a relationship that was mutually supporting and interdependent. More important, he found a friend in Harriet.

Loving-kindness is being aware that we love our self and other in spite of how we think, speak and behave. That loving others is unconditional and natural. We don't need to think about it. In fact, when we don't think about it we just do it. Adyashanti makes this point in *Emptiness Dancing*:

> "True love has nothing to do with liking someone, agreeing with him or her, or being compatible. It is a love of unity, a love of seeing God wearing all the masks and recognizing itself in them all. Without it, Truth becomes an abstraction that is sort of cool and analytical, and that is not the real Truth. The Truth exposes itself in the willingness to open to this intimate connectedness with everything."

So loving-kindness operates in a world without opposites. It operates in the present moment, without a thought of the past or future. It is a love that is timeless and without boundaries. It is totally open. At the same time it does not exclude other experiences of love. Both can and do exist within us, but the Truth is we only need the loving-kindness inherent in unconditional love. When we are really immersed in loving-kindness all other experiences of love loose meaning. Again, you don't need to search for it; you just need to wake up to it. Unconditional love has always been a part of your true nature and being.

LOVING-KINDNESS AS THE PATH TO OPENNESS

Feelings and emotions are far stronger than thought. Science has discovered two important points related to the mind and the heart. First, the electromagnetic field created by the heart far exceeds that of the brain. The heart's field encompasses and affects the entire body, while the brain's field is pretty much isolated to itself. Second, science has now demonstrated that the heart reacts before the brain when we respond to external stimuli. The neurochemical response from the heart immediately influences our feelings and then the brain/mind responds with thought. The conclusion is that feelings and emotions coming from our heart center have an immediate influence on the body and the mind.

While a thought can trigger a feeling, the feelings and emotions evoked can then quickly dominate thought. The mind can become controlled and colored by our feelings. So our thoughts control the level that we are open-minded, but our feelings control the level that we are open-hearted. Our overall level of openness then is an inverse relationship to how controlling our thoughts and feelings are.

Control is a function of the separate self, so it makes sense that we are not going to truly experience true openness when our ego is in charge. The ego is always going to hold back as it cannot fathom allowing itself to be fully exposed to others and life. The ego considered total openness as not wise or safe. We have to release to the Higher Self, releasing with a lack of concern for what comes next. In her book, *Taking the Leap*, Pema Chodron writes,

> "There's a whole other way to look at one another – and that is to try dropping our fixed ideas and get curious about the possibility that nothing and no one remains always the same. This starts, of course, with getting curious and dropping the limiting stories we've created about ourselves. Then we have to stay present with whatever is happening to us. What I find helpful is to think of whatever I am experiencing – whether it's sadness, anger, or worry; pleasure, joy or delight – as simply the dynamic, fluid energy of life as it is manifesting right now. That shifts the resistance I have to my experience."

So openness is a stepping backward. Stepping out of our story, stepping out of our judgments, stepping out of our interpretation of what we are experiencing. As we step back we are stepping out of the cage of separate self, we are opening to our actual experience, which is an embodiment of the Whole. This Whole, life, cannot threaten Itself so when our awareness moves into this space there is no need to conceal, to protect. We can comfortably move to full exposure, real authenticity.

From this position of openness we can move beyond good and bad to see that whatever we experience is leading us to greater awareness and experience. Communications with others become more natural and genuine, which invites the other person to reciprocate. Judgment drops out of our speech, moving us into a form of non-violent communication. Most important, there is no longer any need to lie. We can comfortably tell the truth with a compassionate heart. Openness is the doorway to the authentic Self.

When we are centered in loving-kindness, and the openness it provides, we can then have the power to keep from falling forward into the cage of egotistic identity. Our external identity can be a clear reflection of the Authentic Self, or it can be a contrived expression of our ego. Reflected identity of the Authentic Self is consistent and inviting. Egotistic identity is constantly shifting in an effort to influence or dominate and is often seen as being threatened. Identity centered in the Authentic Self and expressing loving-kindness is a tool for interacting, not a weapon for control over our interactions or another person. We have to choose which identity we want to use, and that choice will determine our interactions and outcomes in our engagement with life.

Once we are fully aware of our Authentic Self then we can always stop and reorient when we find ourselves slipping back into our egoistic shell. When we reorient we once again become open-minded and open-hearted. We will make that deeper connection that operates without harm to others or our self. After a while, when we become more comfortable being truly open, we come to understand the total freedom this level of openness provides us. Then it is easy to see when we are closing down, retreating. At that time we can stop, turn and move back into the natural energy of our Authentic Self. We see that being inauthentic is really the source of suffering. When we step into our truth we remember our true nature.

Sean came to see me for difficulties he was experiencing with his girlfriend, Nia. After describing their relationship it became apparent that they were in the post honeymoon phase and were struggling with how to move to deeper intimacy. Sean stated that all seemed to be going well until about a month ago when he felt the relationship stopped moving forward. He stated that Nia was sending mixed messages; was warm one day and seemed distant the next. He felt that he was on a rollercoaster and wanted to find out how to fix things.

A red flag goes up for me every time a client uses the word, "fix". I see that as an indication that the ego is in control. Sean and I spent the next few weeks diving into his relationship with Nia from first meeting to the present. We spent most of our time teasing out how Sean was presenting himself to Nia. It became apparent to both Sean and I that he was constantly shape-shifting his identity with Nia to impress and influence her. After careful documentation of all the ego-personas he had brought to the stage we retreated to look at each one, where upon I asked Sean, "Is this who you really are?" More often than not Sean would answer, "Well no." and then go on to explain his rationale for presenting him self that way.

The further we went the more apparent it became that Nia had no idea who she was in a relationship with and was confused by Sean's many faces. I then asked Sean, "Why are you afraid to be who you really are?" He had a plethora of reasons but it all boiled down to a fear that Nia would not like the real Sean. He had a deep need to control his image with Nia to, in essence, control her feelings towards him; keeping him in a positive light. I asked him how well that was working for him and he admitted, "Not very well."

Sean began to discover that all the different identities he had presented to Nia were actually creating confusion and distrust. There were too many changes in how he interacted with Nia, especially when it came to expressing his feelings. Sean became aware of his attempts to control their relationship through his different identities. He also came to realize that it wasn't working and was actually impeding any progress towards greater intimacy.

We then started to explore who the real Sean was, what his true qualities were. It became apparent that the real Sean was a pretty great guy. After anchoring these qualities into Sean's awareness I asked him to just be himself with Nia and see where it lead them.

At first there was little movement, as Nia continued to expect the ever-changing Sean to shape-shift into the next version. After about a month Nia started to see a consistent Sean and expressed a desire to get to know this Sean better. In the ensuing months the relationship gained greater intimacy and sharing. Nia became more comfortable with and fell in love with the *real* Sean. At our last session Sean had proposed and Nia had joyfully accepted. When the real Sean finally came forward Nia's heart melted.

Being open to who we really are is extremely transformative. This openness then adds to our resiliency for change, keeping us from Pavlovian reactions to change. When we are no longer unconsciously reacting to change then we are able to see all of the opportunities change is presenting. When we realize that change is neither good or bad, and we don't have to immediately grasp or reject, we are able to stay with the present moment and respond with honesty and authenticity.

Openness is absolutely critical to successfully moving through the change process outlined in Part Two of the book. It assists in all three phases of the process, allowing for more choices. Openness is especially critical to the middle process of 'exploring the present'. Patience is critical as this phase unfolds and openness offers the key to patience.

LOVING-KINDNESS AND OPENNESS INVITES INTIMACY

When we are operating from loving-kindness and openness it is much easier to get very close to life. If the mind is out of the way then what our senses experience is direct, not interpreted. Our experiences take on a freshness and innocence. All the barriers are down and we have this strong sense of attraction to everything that life has to show us. There is an unobstructed intimacy. True intimacy only comes when the separate self moves out of the way. When there is nothing in the way of our experience and we are no longer limited by our perceptions, thoughts and feelings we gain a nimbleness in responding to what life has to offer. Any sense of danger is dealt with quickly and authentically, as there are no filters to get in the way. We act, not overreact.

We are drawn into the flow. We are drawn into the Whole, experiencing Itself and knowing that everything will resolve within Itself, coming back into balance. Centered in this intimate way there is a greater confidence in whatever comes next, and life is a joy. We have more energy and excitement about everything. This doesn't mean we live the perfect life or experience pain from time to time. It does mean that we are consistently excited about experiencing every aspect of what is next.

Loving-kindness and its two offspring, openness and intimacy, are the lubricants of change. They remove the resistance that seems to frequently arise when we come to see that life is impermanent and constantly changing. When we see that we are intimately integrated into this impermanent life then there is no need to tightly grasp and defend our current perception of who we are. When we are open to our impermanence then we naturally are open to what we are next. When all of this awareness is bathed in the light of loving-kindness then we realize, as my daughter always tells me, "It's all good."

CHAPTER FIVE

THE POWER OF AFFIRMATION

Regarding positive affirmation, *It is an active, conscious, aggressive mental movement and in such degree as it embodies an idea – and there is no longer anything in our minds which denies the idea – it will take form, because it now becomes a part of the law and order of the Universe in which we live.*

Ernest Holmes, *The Science of Mind*

Be the change you want to see in the world.

Mahatma Ghandi

Much of what I have discussed up to this point has been to bring about a greater understanding of 'what we are'. To know that beyond the separate self we are so much more, and how that awareness can help remove resistance to change. There is another aspect of our awareness that reflects an increased intimacy with our Higher Self, which has a positive influence on our life moving forward. This is an awareness where we can co-create through our connection to the Higher Self. This increased awareness gives us an ability to utilize the potential energy of life that is available to manifest what we want. This is not an absolute guarantee, as there are many other influences going on at the same time from others around us. Yet utilizing this connection with the Higher Self dramatically increases our chances for creating positive change.

By co-creating with life I am not saying that we assume control over what life has to offer. That would assume that we are able to control the many ways in which life manifests. While some new age thinkers firmly believe this premise of controlling life it is, in fact, fantasy. We are of God but we are not all that God is. We can, however, partner with life to move in compatible directions. Some people call this synchronicity. I will stick with co-creating. We can influence, but we cannot command. In the end God, life is the ultimate Source and Creator.

So I am not talking about the mind controlling events and our experiences. This would be returning to where the ego and mind are at the center of all our experience. That is not where I am going. As I mentioned earlier, however, the mind is a wonderful tool that can be quite useful. The mind can imagine form from the formless. In this case I consider the mind like a compass. A compass along with a good map can help us to understand where we are and also indicate what direction we need to go in to fined our desired destination. If we just walk through life and keep the compass in our pocket it doesn't provide any value in finding our path. If we pull it out from time to time and get our bearings then we can avoid moving in circles.

This is the utility of the mind in making choices during change. The mind helps us to imagine our possibilities and it gives God an indication of where we think we want to go. God, life, however, has the final say. So the mind helps us to clarify our direction, but it is our connection to the Higher Self that provides the energy to move forward. We can use this energy in a conscious or unconscious manner. If we are unconscious it is easy to go astray with any distraction that may arise. If we are conscious we can keep in mind our vision and look beyond the distractions that arise during change.

So how can we use the mind during the change process? We can use it to seek out the highest good for our self and others. Isn't that what change is all about, moving to the highest good for all? This is a point of view that holds that change has value and is constructive to our higher betterment. We open up to our potential for good and create a desire for that good to manifest. This moves us beyond the initial perception that change is good or bad. We are immediately freed from the burden of fear, which change can initially evoke. In using the mind, connected and intimate with the Higher Self, to set our intentions we create a propensity for good.

OUR RIGHT TO AFFIRM OUR LIFE

A key tool of the mind that we can call upon in change is affirmation. This is a mental process where we open to the possibilities for a positive outcome to change. We may not always know what is the exact outcome that best serves us, but we can affirm that we know that the right outcome is available to us. This is a positive start. We can either look to what we believe is next or we can just open to guidance to the nest step on the path. This mental approach is a lot better than swimming in a pool of self-pity and doubt. It requires releasing our constraints from the past so that we are free to move in the right direction for our self and others. Ernest Holmes discussed this idea in *The Science of Mind*,

> "Never limit your view of life by any past experience. The possibility of life is inherent within the capacity to imagine what life is, backed by the power to produce this imagery, or Divine Imagination. It is not a question of failing or succeeding. It is simply a question of sticking to an idea until it becomes a tangible reality."

First and foremost an affirmation recognizes that what is right now is going to change. Second, it recognizes that there are an infinite number of ways that things can change. Third, it recognizes that we are naturally drawn to what we focus on, where we focus our energy. If we focus on a negative outcome we are drawn to it. If we focus on a positive outcome we are drawn to it. The inherent energy in change is neutral. It can move in any direction. Life will, by nature, initiate change and we have the power to influence what that change will be.

So the truth is we have many options available to us. We can just dwell on our current situation and let the energy take us wherever it may. This is fatalism. We can focus on our current situation and only move in a reactive way to what is. I would call this reactive determinism. We can also affirm our life as good and look to a positive outcome to our current situation. I would call this affirmative determinism. We will get change in all three, but which would you prefer?

Helping to Co-Create Life Through Affirmation

Affirmation is about focusing our energy towards progress and growth. It is a desire to take positive action. It is an understanding that the ultimate outcome will be for the good. It is an acceptance of the fact that we are not in control, but we can point the way. When considering affirmation I am always reminded of the famous quote from Reinhold Niebuhr, "God, grant me the serenity to accept the things I cannot change, the courage to change the things I can, and the wisdom to know the difference." Affirmation is about our intrinsic wisdom to know the difference. If we accept the power of affirmation, but also recognize its limits in life, then we can accept any change without creating some judgment regarding the efficacy of affirmation.

Affirmation is also about expectancy. Expecting that the eventual outcome to change is positive. Expecting that you will understand and be able to take action on the best possible path moving forward. Expecting that you can share your ideas with the Higher Self knowing that your interconnectedness, through the Higher Self, will have an impact on how life unfolds. Expecting that your future can be positively impacted by your willingness to participate in this co-creative process with the Potential Power of the Universe, operating though our Higher Self.

If you haven't figured it out yet affirmation is a delicate balance. It is a partnership with equal ownership. We are not in charge and neither is this Potential Power of the Universe. It is the combined effort of both that can influence life. Yet even this influence is not for sure. The ultimate outcome is a collective of all interconnected affirmations expressed as a whole. It is, however, a much better course of action to make our intentions known to the Potential Power of the Universe, as opposed to doing nothing or expecting the worst. Why not jump in with both feet and see what happens? What do you have to loose?

Raphael came to see me because he was chronically depressed after being unable to find work for over two years. He went into great detail during our first session explaining all of the efforts he had made to find work and all of the perceived obstacles to being hired. After a half hour of listing all of the barriers he was imagining in his efforts in finding a job, including his Hispanic heritage, I asked Raphael, "Do you really believe that all of these obstacles are real?" Raphael's initial response was yes, but as we explored each he became aware that his attachments to these obstacles were more imagined than real. This made him less fixed on the obstacles that seemed to be holding him back.

I then asked Raphael what he was gaining from holding on to his beliefs related to these obstacles. After much discussion it boiled down to his sense that having the obstacles made him feel better about himself. His self-esteem was really low and the only way he could get the energy to keep looking for work was to blame others.

I then asked Raphael if he was willing to let go of his beliefs in these obstacles as they were getting him nowhere. I asked him to replace these beliefs with affirmations for his future. We worked on connecting Raphael with his Higher Self and in seeing that he had infinite potential available at all times. We also worked on helping Raphael to vision what his ideal work would look like. Raphael was so desperate to find any work that he had not set a clear intention and desire for what work he felt aligned with his Soul purpose.

Over the next few weeks Raphael continued to seek employment and he started to become more selective in the jobs he applied for. We discussed most of the positions and looked deeply into how they might or might not fit his deepest desire for fulfilling employment. Raphael slowly became aware that he was not getting any response to positions he really wasn't drawn to. He saw how he was wasting time and energy applying for just any open position that he felt he was qualified for.

In our subsequent time together we continued to work towards greater clarity about what Raphael want to do for work. Raphael's prior experience and skills were in general retail store management. He had, however, a real interest in Internet website design and Internet marketing. We discussed a potential career change and what that would entail. Raphael set his first intention and affirmation to go back to school for technical training on Internet skills. Money was a problem but we set an affirmation that he would be accepted to a good school and would find the funds to attend. Within three weeks Raphael was accepted to a recognized college for computer technology, with a focus on the Internet. Raphael was also able to garner a small scholarship and student aid.

A year later Raphael returned for assistance in setting his new affirmation for employment. During his absence from counseling he had continued to 'play' with affirmations in other aspects of his life. While Raphael admitted that he did not always manifest what he set his affirmation towards he did see a positive trend in the direction his life was taking. I worked with Raphael in visioning what his ideal job would look like. I warned about being too specific and to focus on the attributes of the work he desired, as opposed to a certain position with a specific company. I had Raphael create a vision board for his job and engage all of his senses in the creation of the affirmation. Within three weeks all was set in place.

Over the next two months Raphael applied for over thirty positions where the job description aligned with his affirmation. He had multiple interviews. In one case he was offered a position, which he declined. I asked Raphael his rationale and he said, "After discussing the position with them I just felt it didn't fit my vision for work." Raphael finally accepted a position as the Internet marketing manager for a large, not for profit organization that supports the rights of Hispanic Americans. Raphael is ecstatic with and totally energized by his new employment. He is a firm believer in the power of affirmation in co-creating his path through life. Raphael does not suffer from magical thinking, and is realistic in understanding that life is still the final determiner of outcome. Yet he also understands that if he puts forth the effort he has a say in his life path.

THE PROCESS OF AFFIRMATION

Before I begin this discussion on affirmation and change I need to recognize and acknowledge the teachings of Ernest Holmes and the philosophy of Science of Mind. Much of the material on affirmation is adapted from these teachings. They have had a profound impact on my life. The personal demonstrations that have come from using affirmation and affirmative prayer treatment have convinced me that these principles and related practices are an important tool in managing change. I have put my own twist on these principles and practices based on my personal experience, especially where it concerns change. For more information in this area I endorse the reading of *The Science of Mind* by Ernest Holmes or one of his many other books.

There is a process to co-creation in which affirmation can play an important role. It starts by making the connection with the Potential Power of the Universe via our Higher Self. The beginning of the affirmation process is nothing more than recognizing that you are something more than your separate self, and this something more is willing and able to co-create with you. It is a process of letting go. Letting go of the belief that we actually have control of the present moment and accepting that you are in the flow of change. This is not letting go of reality; it is letting go of the dream. It is a dream to think that we are in control of the present moment. When we allow ourselves to wake up from this dream it is very liberating and reality comes sharply into focus.

Resistance from Our Ego

This dream is a powerful creation of the ego in an effort to maintain a separate self. It is required for its existence. So letting go of the dream is going to face immediate resistance from the ego. The ego will develop within the dream its own logic. This logic is a potent way of reinforcing the dream. Of course logic, based in the confines of the dream, is not reality. It just seems that way. So in the process of letting to our Higher Self we have to recognize and gird our self to the ego's attempts to influence us with story. The litmus test comes when we notice what we are thinking. Are our thoughts grounded in the present moment or floating into the past or charging into the future? Reality is only in the present. Every other thought is a story within a dream that keeps us from connecting with the Higher self.

We are letting go to the Higher Self within; setting aside the ego and a desire for separateness. It is accepting that you are a part of something much more. It is remembering your natural way of Being. It is waking up. You can't force yourself to wake up. You just have to let go and it happens spontaneously. This is called Grace. The Higher Self is always present and available. Letting go allows space for the Higher Self to be present in our consciousness. This connection is critical to the successful initiation of the affirmation process and co-creation.

An Exercise in Birthing Your Affirmation

Take a moment from reading right now and experience this simple meditation of letting go into co-creation. Close your eyes and let you body fall deeply into where you are setting. Realize that you are in the flow of change, no matter how large or small. Watch, without thinking, your body changing. Each breath is a change. Each minor adjustment in how you are setting is a change. Let go of all thoughts of control. You know, "I need to do this or that next." There are no must dos in this meditation. Just rest in the waters of life and experience the current of change.

What will happen next? You have no idea. At first this might be a bit scary, kind of like cresting the top of a hill on a rollercoaster. Yet there is also a sense of expectation, excitement. Go with that. Keep from succumbing to the need to think about what comes next. There is no need to be fearful. Stay grounded in the present and know that the changes you are experiencing are all natural. You will come to a sense of complete freedom. Anything is possible. Go with that.

Now expand even further your sense of boundary, expanding beyond the confines of your body. Become aware of being, without limits. Note how it feels. You are now connecting with something greater, infinite, without limits. This is the Higher Self. In this feeling make the commitment to 'partner up' with your Higher Self. Join forces to explore the possibilities. Be open to the intuitive inspiration that the Higher Self will offer. Anything is possible. Be receptive to sharing and co-creating your ideas with the Higher Self. Avoid immediately locking onto one idea or another. One idea is not any better or worse than the other. Let them all just come until you are at a place of quiet, right back to where you started. Now just open your eyes, staying in this place of awareness.

Take a look at all of the ideas you co-created with the Higher Self. Capture as many of these ideas as you can on paper. Don't make any judgments of good or bad, just write down as many as you can remember. You're now ready for the next step.

Inquiry and Affirmation

Carefully look through all of the ideas you created with your Higher Self. Find the one(s) that you are drawn to and note them. You are now ready to use the tool of inquiry. Here are a few questions to get you started:

- What is drawing you to each of the ideas?
- What do they hold in common?
- What direction are these ideas taking you in?
- What is the outcome these ideas are pointing to?
- What changes can I expect if I move in this direction?
- What must I let go of to move forward?
- What risks must I take to move forward?
- What will I become as I reach my desired outcome?
- What higher purpose do these ideas serve?

Stick with it until you have exhausted all these questions and any others you might have uncovered. Discover all you need to know about your ideas. Now consider how you feel about your ideas. Are you still as passionate about them as you were before inquiry? Do you have any doubts about your ability to reach the desired outcomes you have uncovered? Do you sense that you and your Higher Self are aligned in a way that the Power of the Universe will support?

If your answer to any of these final questions is no then you are not ready to build your affirmation. You must have an absolute sense of certainty that your ideas are the right path and you know beyond a shadow of a doubt that you will reach your desired outcome. Stay with your intuitive feelings and avoid any resistance coming from the ego. This is a time when the ego will eagerly try to jump in and take over. Don't go there. If you can't reach this point of certainty then you can decide to start over or just be patient. You may need to travel further down the stream of life before you are ready to co-create a new experience in your life. This is not unusual and should not be seen as a failure. I will explain in greater detail in Part Two of the book when I discuss Exploring the Present. If your answers are all yes then you are ready for the next step.

Take in all of your desired ideas and outcomes. In this next step you are going to gain a vision of your desired outcome. This is not a 'how to' planning session. The effort here is to not get real specific. What you want to do is gain a general sense of direction, still leaving room for life to interplay in the process. Life is going to jump in anyway, so why not be accommodating.

Visioning and Affirmations

I am going to take you through a visioning exercise for your affirmation. Start by finding a quiet place and setting down with all your notes on your affirmation. Read them all carefully but avoid any thoughts of expanding on any one idea. Just look to get a whole picture in your mind. Now close your eyes and allow your mind to relax. When you are relaxed and not focusing on any one point ask yourself the following three questions:

- What is my vision for my highest good?
- What must I release to move towards my vision?
- What must I become to enable my vision?

You may see something, you may hear something, and/or you may feel something. There is no one way your vision will appear. Just mindfully note all that comes to you and don't analyze it right away. Just allow it to be. Write down or even draw what you experienced. Capture as much of the vividness of your vision as possible and take care to not filter anything out. That would be putting judgment into the vision. When you have adequately captured your vision take a short break.

Now review once again your initial ideas and then your notes from the visioning. Is there any pattern that you can uncover within all of this information? Have you gained some clarity for your path moving forward? If not, the cake is not fully baked. Let it go for a day and come back to everything you have discovered so far. Note anything additional that comes to you. Continue to be open to more information until things become clear. Keep a method for recording any ah-ha's that come your way as they may appear in a fleeting moment at the most inopportune times. They can come at any time; that is why this process is so spontaneous.

Working with an Affirmation

When the path is clear it is time to formulate the affirmation. An affirmation is a statement of fact. There are no might's or maybe's in an affirmation. It is a visioned outcome that has already been achieved. It is not in your current perception of reality but it is still there. This means that your affirmation needs to be stated in the present tense. You must suspend any focus on how things appear right now. Remember we are not dealing with linear time. Creation is not a function of time and space. We cannot choose a time and a place for creation to manifest. What we are experiencing and what we are affirming will eventually occupy the same space. We just have no control over the when. Anything is possible in writing your affirmation because you are creating with the Universe and It's nature is infinite.

Write down your affirmation and repeat it twenty times to yourself out load. How does it feel? You may need to tweak a word here or there. Once you are comfortable with your affirmation copy it so that and place it strategically everywhere to remind you. Put it on the bathroom mirror, the refrigerator, the dash of the car, as your screen saver. Every time you think of your affirmation say it out load. Don't make this exercise drudgery. Repeat the affirmation when you can feel it. Make it fresh with each repetition, like you are saying it for the first time. Feel the excitement of knowing it is here.

Keep your affirmation to yourself. This is part of your reality, not someone else's. You have worked to know its truth. Don't expect anyone else to be at the same place. I am not saying that you can't talk about an affirmation with others. Just don't specifically state your affirmation to them. This provides an opportunity for them to pass judgment on you affirmation. Neither accept or reject the input from others. Just set with it and see what might change for you from their input.

The ego will also be attempting to co-opt your affirmation for its own purposes. It will try to tell you that it is unrealistic, that you are not capable, that it must be managed by the ego. Wrong. The ego will try and pull you into the past or future. Remember, the affirmation is about the now.

After you say your affirmation just let it go. The unfolding of your affirmation will come from the Power of the Universe. Let It do Its work. You can make plans and take actions that will move you in the direction of your affirmation but understand that you are not doing this by yourself. You are co-creating with the Universe. The Universe is providing the energy and potential. You are affirming the vision.

Look for the synchronicities. Once your affirmation is in place the Universe will conspire to bring into your life people, places, things that are energetically aligned with your affirmation. This is part of co-creating the next step. If you aren't paying attention you can miss a promising and important opportunity. I have found that once the affirmation is in place that the Universe loads your present moments with synchronicities.

It is important to not get real specific in the final affirmation. At the same time it needs to have enough meat to give you a sense of where you are heading. This is a fine balance. If you are too specific you will shut life out and life will most likely barge in at some point necessitating that you adapt to change life has initiated without your conscious intervention. This can cause disappointment. If you leave your affirmation open it can easily adapt. I will try to give some examples.

When I completed my degree in counseling I went about setting an affirmation for my career. After some co-creative thought I came up with the following, "I work with people to improve their lives." Over a couple of years I found that my career moves were allowing me to work with people to improve their lives but not necessarily in a way that best used my talents. I wasn't comfortable in counseling as a generalist. While it offered more clients, I felt I needed to be more specific.

After much introspection and internal counseling with my Higher Self I found the works of William Bridges, related to change management. Having worked with change as a consultant in business I felt very comfortable in bringing this process into my counseling. At that time I re-visioned my affirmation to, "I provide counseling to individuals and groups, helping them to effectively manage change in their life." To date I am very comfortable and holding to this affirmation for my real work in life. It is the genesis of this book.

You can have many affirmations for different aspects of your life. Career can be one but you might also have an affirmation for relationships, health, prosperity, spiritual growth, etc. There are no limits for affirmations.

I had a client who was familiar with the affirmation process and was using an affirmation related to her current relationship. Her affirmation was, "Charlie and I have a happy and harmonious relationship." The problem was her affirmation was going nowhere after six months.

In my work with her I challenged her as to why she was specifically putting Charlie in her affirmation. I asked her if she was absolutely positive that Charlie was synonymous with a happy and harmonious relationship. She said she didn't know. I then asked her if she was willing to try the affirmation without Charlie. After some deep introspection she agreed to leave Charlie out and see if the relationship shifted to her vision. Within three months she had dropped Charlie from her affirmation and her life.

About six months later I ran into my former client and she told me that she had met her 'soul mate' and she was living happily and harmoniously in a new relationship. I asked her if she was still holding to her affirmation. She said, "Yes, I feel at this moment that I am living my affirmation but I am also open that it might change. Even if this relationship is not the final fulfillment of my affirmation I know I am getting much closer." I complimented her that she was leaving room for her and life to continue with the co-creation process.

Affirmations Verses Goals

I would like to make a distinction between affirmations and goals. Most of us are familiar with goal setting as part of the planning process. Goals are designed to be specific. The common acronym is SMART for Specific, Measureable, Achievable, Realistic, and Time bound. Goals are excellent ways to move your feet. They are also ways to test a specific direction to your affirmed outcome. Goals, however, are a function of the ego/mind and do not completely allow life into the equation. Goals are fine but don't confuse them with affirmations and don't expect that you will always achieve each and every goal you set.

This isn't being fatalistic; it is just a proven fact. We are often moving forward without all the facts. Bits of reality are missed and can cause the direction we are moving in to quickly change. Goals still play in the future and the future is an unknown. Goals are a story that can unfold as reality, but usually not exactly. Unmet goals held in the wrong framework can be demoralizing if not achieved and can cause a loss of connection with the Higher Self. Hold all goals in the proper perspective.

Affirmations help us to stay in the flow of our experiences and life as a whole. It keeps us from falling back into old patterns and provides greater resiliency. Resilience to move with your intuition but not resisting any variation that may enter into the unfolding. Pema Chondron expressed this in *Taking the Leap*,

> "But behind our views and opinions, our hopes and fears about what's happening, the dynamic energy of life is always here, unchanged by our reactions of like and dislike.

> How we relate to this dynamic flow of energy is important. We can learn to relax with it, recognizing it as our basic ground, as a natural part of life; or the feeling of uncertainty, of nothing to hold on to, can cause us to panic, and instantly a chain reaction begins. We panic, we get hooked, and then our habits take over and we think and speak and act in a very predictable way."

Affirmations inspire change and provide a point of reference to a new way of being. Affirmations provide a source of positive energy for change through the co-creative process with the Universe. Affirmations are the doors to who you are to become. Allow yourself to 'play' in the world of affirmation. Life is a lot more exciting and fun. Change then becomes a synchronistic link to your own path through life.

Mikayla was frustrated and depressed about her life. She is black, comes from a family living below the poverty level, and she has to work while she is finishing high school to help the family survive. Mikayla has met with her school counselor, who has encouraged her to focus on graduating and gaining some technical skills for 'blue collar' work. The vision painted for Mikayla based on her current conditions and the advice of experts is not what she wants for her life.

When I started to meet with Mikayla her focus was more on what she didn't want her life to be like, rather than what she would like her life to be like. It took several meetings for her to get it all out of her system. I just listened, waiting for the negative energy to dissipate. One day Mikayla said, "Well, what should I do?" At that moment I knew we were ready to move towards building her an affirmation that would bring new energy into living.

I began to move Mikayla through the process if formulating a core affirmation that she could get behind. We started with some free association related to experiences that would make her feel alive. A wide variety of topics and ideas came up. Within this vast array of ideas a central theme started to surface. Mikayla became excited whenever she could see herself free from the bonds that held her, allowing her to fly free of all restraints. In a visioning process Mikayla saw many birds flying overhead and she joined them in flight. The feeling of flight excited and energized Mikayla and the more she visioned on it the more energized she became. When I asked her to inquire deeply into what her visions meant she almost immediately said, "I want to fly." I encouraged her to set with this idea for a while and to come back with a general idea of how this would look like for her.

Within a month Mikayla knew she wanted to become a pilot and fly airplanes. I asked her to keep her vision to herself, and to start to research this concept so that it could become more *real* for her. Mikayla immediately started to come with reams of information about pilot training, career opportunities in flying, and various options she might pursue. For a brief time Mikayla considered entering the military, but she eventually ruled it out as being too constraining. She had had enough of constraints in her life. As we worked towards a final affirmation for her it became clear that her intent was to become a commercial pilot, working for an airline.

Mikayla became driven by her newfound love and her affirmation. I saw Mikayla occasionally over the next several years. She would come to me in an effort to refine her affirmation even further as she moved closer to flying. She aligned her final two years of high school around the sciences she knew were necessary to becoming a pilot. She brought her grade point up to the scholarship level for college. At the same time Mikayla found a local program, privately funded, that taught students the basics of aeronautics. It included flying lessons in small, private aircraft.

Mikayla was awarded a scholarship to attend a local college that had an aeronautics program that would lead her to the licensing required to become a commercial pilot. None of this was easy for Mikayla. She had to work hard to gain her education while finding sufficient financial support to keep going. It was her complete faith in her vision and affirmation that kept her going.

Mikayla graduated from college, acquired her commercial pilot license and has a job flying private jets for large corporations. Mikayla is truly free from the earthly bonds that made her feel confined and depressed. Mikayla was exceptional in her ability to stick with her affirmation, even in the face of the harshest, present moments along the way. Perhaps it was her deep desire to escape her childhood or just the strength of her vision in flying. I really don't want to know. I am just happy she is living her affirmation.

As a treat to me Mikayla took me for a flight one day in a small, private plane. As we twisted and turned through several aerobatic maneuvers I retained the contents of my stomach by focusing on Mikayla's uncontrolled laughter with each spin and dive. Mikayla was living her vision and affirmation. Mikayla was really flying!

CHAPTER SIX

OPENING INTO GRACE BY OVERCOMING RESISTANCE

Grace is all around us, if we only have the eyes to see it. The good moments are grace, the difficult moments are grace, the confusing moments are grace. When we can begin to open enough to realize that there is grace in every situation, in each person we meet, no matter how easy or difficult we perceive them to be, our hearts will flower and we'll be able to express the peace and the love that each of us has within us.

Adyashanti, *Falling into Grace*

I'm becoming more and more myself with time. I guess that's what grace is. The refinement of your soul through time.

Jewel, (contemporary American Singer/Songwriter)

Change begins with letting go, but we are usually resistant to letting go. Our instincts tell us to react in an effort to maintain where we are. Frequently we see change as unknown, threatening and aggressive; we feel like we are under attack.

When I was studying martial arts I was taught to relax when faced with aggression. Allow the energy from the aggressor to flow though you. Use that energy to your advantage. Adjust, adapt and deflect. Stay calm and clear headed. Do not take the act of aggression personally. The aggressor has only had a momentary lapse of reason. Reason and balance will prevail if you step aside and wait.

I discovered these teachings to be sound, as I found myself during my youth in a variety of uncomfortable situations. In later years, when I started to become more interested in change, I found that these same principles applied as a part of the change process. Change brings with it a tremendous amount of energy. If we resist it we are quickly drained. If we step aside and move with the energy we can use it to our advantage. We are responding to change and not reacting to it. We can redirect the energy of change to our advantage. Confidence replaces fear as we go with, rather than resist. It is just a matter of letting go.

So how can we get to the place of response rather than resistance? It all starts with trust. Trusting that we don't have all of the answers immediately at hand. Trusting that there is always a deeper meaning, a broader purpose to what is really happening, as compared to what we initially perceive when first encountering change. Trusting in the fact that this broader purpose is exactly what we need for growth and our higher good. Trusting that we are part of the Whole and we receive exactly what we need to move forward within the Whole. Trusting that the Whole is our true nature. As Adyashanti indicated in the quote above, grace comes in various forms. Our challenge is to discern the ultimate good that it brings and to trust in the Power of the Unknown.

STOP STRUGGLING WITH WHAT IS

Whether we are conscious of it or not we are constantly struggling with what is. All of our stories that we create are about the ego struggling with 'what is'. 'What is' can be external or internal and is always associated with change. 'What is' is always changing, becoming something else, something different. The more we resist and struggle the tighter the grip 'what is' seems to have on us. Even if we momentarily free ourselves from this grip, through fantasy and delusion, there is nowhere to hide. So struggling is a no win scenario.

I remember when I was a little boy my uncle gave me some Chinese Handcuffs. You know, that five-inch long tube made of woven bamboo. You stick your index fingers from each hand into the tube and then try to pull them out. The tube responds by tightening its grip and you can't get your fingers free. I would struggle and struggle, much to the delight of my uncle, until I just relaxed. Then I finally got it. I can't pull away but how about pushing in, going deeper into the tube. When I did the tube relaxed. If I then used my thumbs to hold the tube in this position I easily remove my index fingers.

This is a great example of how to stop struggling with change and to just *lean* into it. Get as close as you can and then hold in that position. Suddenly you are set free. Spontaneously the right course of action comes to you and there is a new level of confidence. You just know what to do, right now.

'Leaning in' is not an act of aggression. It is just stopping our resistance to and becoming inquisitive in 'What is happening'. Inquisitive to what we are to learn, what doorway is being shown, what path is being revealed. Trusting that this is the moment of our next step forward. What may seem like retreating is just selecting a new direction. 'Leaning in' is a learning experience.

Have you ever been in a situation that is so intense, so restrictive that you are at your mental and emotional whit's end? When you got to that point did you just give up, let go? If you did, how did it feel? For most people they are overcome by a calm and sense of peace. They have regained their balance by stopping the struggle. The original thought was to struggle until you could achieve a desired outcome. This requires a tremendous amount of effort. But by simply stopping to struggle we quickly reached the peace and calm we were trying to attain and gain a clearer vision of how to achieve our desired outcome, or whether we even really desire the outcome we have become attached to. As we step aside the intensity passes and we can inquire into a deeper meaning related to our struggle. We quickly move from our emotional limit to our emotional well-being. We gain the ability to accept what comes our way and to work with it not against it.

When I was working in healthcare management for a large corporation that was in bankruptcy I struggled to bring the billing and collections system into some sense of viability. The problem was that all of the systems that fed the billing and collections process were broken. As hard I tried to fix the processes the more resistance I got from other parts of the operation. I couldn't control what they wanted to do. I also couldn't control all of the billing centers that reported to me. Some were operating well and others were a mess.

My problem was a sense of personal responsibility to fix it all, and with that responsibility the need to control all the elements involved. The harder I worked at it the more messes I uncovered and the pressure mounted. After three years I hit the wall. I was mentally and emotionally broken and I just collapsed. I took a medical leave of absence and during that break I discovered a great sense of peace and calm. My health improved and my state of being came back into balance. It came to me that I was not the right person for this job. I took too much on myself and didn't hold others more accountable. I couldn't control everything and I needed to let go and find a different path. So I quit.

I felt an unbelievable sense of freedom. Here I was, without a job and no income, without any immediate prospects, but I felt great. What I came to discover was this job was as far from my soul purpose as I could get. I was financially set, but spiritually bereft. This was a major turning point in my life, just by letting go.

Since that time I have grown to look for the peace related to letting go during change. I no longer resist it but step into it. I am eager to see where change is going to take me. I am much more aware of when I start to struggle with something or someone and just stop. When you stop, everything, you can look for that place within you that is not struggling. The mind and ego aren't going to take you there because there is nowhere for them to take you. Their goal is to maintain control and separation. This is a dead end and a source of great pain.

When we let go we are not surrendering to someone else. We are surrendering to the Higher Being within. The way forward lies in the hand of our Higher Self. It is already within you, always was always will be. It is that part of you that is real, composed, at peace. You just need to give it your attention.

Why do we continue to struggle?

Even if you understand that struggling is senseless, it doesn't mean that you won't continue to struggle. Why? Because struggling is a key, energizing force for the ego and ego consciousness. The ego feeds off of the energy of struggle and, in turn, we momentarily feel more alive. There is a sense of security that comes from the power of struggle. We contract and separate, which can seem to give us more definition. When we struggle we hope that we are doing something that will cause a change for the better. We have been historically conditioned to take the next step because the next step will get us out of where we are right now.

The assumption is there is something wrong with right now. Stop for a moment and ask yourself, "What is wrong with right now?" Right now always has a lesson to show us. If we don't take the time to understand the lesson it will reappear at a later date, sometimes with a lot more intensity. We have to gird ourselves from the false sense of security that struggling can provide and learn to understand that letting go can be just as beneficial and much more productive. Letting go opens the door to many more possibilities and pathways moving forward. If we take the time to look deeply into all that is offered when we let go we can often find a more productive path from the one presented by struggling.

Finding a Greater Power by Letting Go

Struggling consumes a lot of energy to create this sense of power. So at some point we just run out of steam. When we let go of struggling we come to find a greater, unlimited source of power coming from the Whole. It is a different kind of power. It is a power not based on resistance but assimilation. This power is attractive in nature and draws more energy to it. All it takes for us to tap into this power is to stop struggling and just be. We must step beyond the veil of our perceived power in struggling and find the real Power that lies beyond.

How can we stop the struggling? By stopping the mind from its continued attempts to define what it thinks should come next. At the height of struggle the mind is usually in hyper drive. It literally has a mind of its own. We have all had a time when we just stand back, look at our mind in action and wonder what it is doing. It's like it is on autopilot. Rather than finding a way out of our struggle the mind usually is just making it worse, coming up with a plethora of linear thoughts that continue to reinforce a given position. This is fun for the mind. As the mind continues to contrast its position from another it creates greater definition, which is something the mind is seeking. It's insane but the mind thinks it is very rational.

Resetting the Mind by Stopping the Madness

This is the time to hit the reset button on the mind. Just stop and let go. Rest in the present. Smell a flower, feel the wind, hear a bird singing. Don't rush the reset process. Allow the reprogramming to take place. Just allow yourself to experience without thinking. You can do it!

Your mind is probably having a conversation with you right now about the words you have just read. You know, "That doesn't make sense. What about this or that? I don't get it!" Just stop reading for a moment and use your senses to lean into the present moment. Release the thoughts that are struggling with this concept and just be. Be in a place of peace and calm.

Was it easy or hard? Did your mind just reset or did it resist in a way that was beyond your control? If you struggled don't worry. You now have the awareness of what to do. Keep looking for the opportunities to stop and reset the mind. It becomes easier with time and will eventually be second nature.

In high school my friend, David, and I were leaving a football game when a car full of boys from the opposing high school drove by and peppered us with eggs. David's anger was immediate and he began to struggle with how to get even. After a moment, in which I had temporarily bought in, I just let go and thought, "Why do we have to get even?" I didn't really know why. I continued to think about this while David continued to plot some sort of revenge. The more I inquired into the value of revenge the less I thought of it. I began to feel that we really had nothing to gain.

I finally shared this with David and he became furious with me. How could we not plot some form of revenge? I asked David, "What do you think we will gain from getting revenge?" David came up with a variety of answers, but they all seemed hollow to me. Finally I told David that I didn't want any part of a plan to get even. He stomped off in a huff.

Days later, when David was ready to speak to me again, I asked him if he still felt as strongly as he had about getting revenge. He said no, he no longer felt the need to get even and he was willing to let it go. I asked David if he felt any less about me because I wouldn't bite on getting revenge. He said that, looking back on it now, it was probably a pretty stupid idea, but he was so angry at the time and he really struggled with his feelings. We shook hands and stepped back into life without the burden of revenge.

MAKING ROOM FOR INSIGHT

During the reset process you have a unique opportunity to experience a different way of thinking. Rather than allowing the mind to create the next thought just be open to what will come. Be patient and expect that what you need will be delivered from the Higher Self within. If you can hold the mind at bay long enough, *insight* will come. I love where Webster's goes with the definition of insight, "the act or result of apprehending the inner nature of things." Insight is an awakened act of knowing when we let go of the mind and allow thoughts to spontaneously arise. When we stop our egoistic chatter for a moment the doorway to insight opens to reveal 'the inner nature of things.'

The mind is so used to having its way that it is going to resist. Don't jump back into its game by resisting back. Just continue to hold the space you have created in silence. Gently allow yourself to drift into 'no thought'. If you slip back, don't resist but just note the slip and return your concentration to the openness of 'no thought'. If you just wait a second insight will step up. Insight will come quietly from nowhere. Observe it as it unfolds. What unfolds will start to form as thoughts. These thoughts are different from the ones the ego creates. They are spontaneous, present, clear, often carrying input from multiple senses with them. The mind is quick, so insight is usually co-opted by a thought the mind creates to take back control. Note the different feel between these two types of thought. This will help you discern between thoughts related to insight or the ego in its efforts to define a singular picture of the future. Don't struggle; just let go of the thought and return your attention to insight. There is probably more that the Higher Self wishes to share. Remember, the Higher Self is about the present moment and the ego is about the past and the future.

This process takes some practice. It is a new way of having thought. It is a process where mind becomes a tool rather than the boss. Once you get the hang of it, this new way of co-creating thought can become quite easy. In fact it has a much more natural feel to it. You feel you are just in a rhythm, in the flow, thinking without straining. Thoughts are not contradictory but synergistic. One feeds off of the other. There is no resistance as the mind processes each insight. All of your senses are involved and present to your thoughts. You feel awake, rather than in a dream.

The more you practice this way of using mind as a tool, rather than giving it unlimited authority over your thoughts, the more you make the shift from struggling to being. It doesn't mean that there are not times when the mind is useful in inquiring deeper or in putting a plan together. Insights provide a reorientation to our true nature and what is real. The mind builds on this information to help us take action on our insights. You need both to make real progress on your path, but you must always be diligent in remembering that the mind is just a tool.

The trick is to work insight and the mind together; always letting the mind know who is the real boss. We will run into times when the mind tries to reassert itself. Sometimes we will probably slip back into letting the mind take total charge. This is especially true if the ego is feeling threatened, which will be anytime that you are fully engaged in insight. When someone pushes hard against our egoistic sense of self the mind leaps to our defense, making arguments, assuming positions, creating its own form of truth. We step into reactive thinking, resisting. This is our clue that it's time to let go again. Allow grace to enter into the external situation. Become at ease with what is currently unfolding. Allow your curiosity to take you back to insight. In this way inquiry and insight replace resistance and aggression. Insight and the mind can work together in this way that creates clarity and peace from chaos and unrest.

For the last couple of years I have contemplated writing this book. Every time I would get inspired the mind would take charge. First would come the struggle with what is the perfect outline for this book. Next came the questions: "Do I have all of the right information needed? Do I know how to write this book the correct way? Am I worthy enough to create a book on this topic? Will I be successful in getting my message out or am I just wasting my time? Will the book be a flop?" It's a wonder with all of this resistance and contradictions that I ever even started.

My salvation came through this new way of thinking. I just let go. I opened into the Grace of the Whole, via my Higher Consciousness. I had been moving in this direction for a while but had not fully applied it as yet to the idea of this book. I just let go of my egoistic questions, doubts and needs related to this book. I had the insight that I just had to do it, even if no one ever reads it. I experienced the grace that comes with surrender. I gained energy from coming to the understanding that writing this book was just the right thing to do. I moved from seeing the book completed to knowing the book had started. No future, just now.

So I have continued to write daily from this process of insight thinking. I have no idea what the next word is coming from my fingers. When something comes I write it down. When there is nothing there I just stop and wait. Remarkably, the words have flown onto the pages. I am not worried about having writer's block, not having the correct structure, not concerned if the words are perfect or not. I just know this is what I am supposed to be doing at this time, and I am willing to get out of the way and let it happen. I can come back and use my mind as a tool for editing. What is important right now is to capture the insights related to change. I have had years of experiencing and contemplating change. It's all there. I just need to get out of the way and let the insights I have gained over the years surface.

This book could be a great success or a flop. I really don't care. That is something others may judge and opine upon, but I don't care. This book isn't about me or about them. This book is a Divine creation by a Power that I am a part of and an instrument for revealing. I am allowing it to change my life and in the process change who I am. All I know is I am not going to fight it. It just is.

EMBRACING THE UNKNOWN

Because the mind thrives on separation it is also naturally inclined to know. Very seldom do we question our thoughts. We just accept them as they are. Even when thoughts are proven to be wrong we often jump to justification of the misperception. We didn't have all of the facts, conditions have changed, we were given misinformation. So what is known shifts, but very seldom do we acknowledge that we were actually in a time of not knowing. The egoistic mind has such a need to be right that it will go to no ends to defend and protect.

When I was seven my parents would occasionally go next door to the neighbors in the evening, leaving me alone in the house after going to bed. During the winter our old furnace would start to creak when it fired up. The sound was just like someone walking up our staircase to the second floor. Creak, creak, creak, I knew it was a burglar who had broken in. I would lay frozen in fear in my bed, my heart racing a mile a minute. No one ever came, but my mind was convinced that there was someone there. Time and again this would happen when my parents left me alone.

It wasn't until I sat down with my father and explained my terror that he figured out it was the furnace. I still didn't believe him. One night he came into my room after turning up the thermostat on the furnace. He lay in bed next to me and said, "Hear that, the gas just came on. Hear the creaking sound, that is the pipes expanding from the heat." Then he jumped out of bed with me in tow and we bolted to the stairs. He pointed down the stairs and said, "See no one is there, but you can still hear the creaking." The world suddenly looked a lot different. Without the mind's concept of a burglar in the house, I was left with my raw feeling, which I then told my father, "I get afraid when I am left alone." This was real and something my father could understand.

While this is an example of a childhood fear it is a prime example of how we allow our mind early on to create reality. As we get older the process just becomes more complex and convoluted, making it harder to recognize fantasy from truth. Most of these fantasies of the mind are based in fear. The ego is fear based so creates its energy through fear. When our mind falls pray to this constant way of thinking then it becomes automatic and habitual. We become centered in fear-based thinking. We become continually fearful of our reality, believing we are separate, alone, vulnerable. It takes a concerted effort to replace this pattern of thinking. To break this pattern of thinking is the key to approaching the unknown with curiosity, rather than fear. It is our curiosity that will allow us to embrace the unknown.

Change is almost always draped in some level of unknown. We are moved from what is usual and customary to a different place, different experiences, and different interactions with new people. We get uncomfortable. Rather than accepting this period of unknown we leap to solidify our thoughts, opinions and beliefs. We resist, rather than accept change, foolishly thinking that resistance will keep us in control. Why? In part it is the fear-based pattern of thinking just described, but it is also a natural process for the ego in supporting the creation of its own being. The ego hates change because it naturally changes who and what the ego is. Like the Wizard of Oz behind the curtain, continually attempting to make everyone think he is something more than he really is, the ego attempts to exhibit its power by resisting the unknown, by resisting change, by attempting to control the uncontrollable.

In part two of the book that covers the change process, we will come to understand that uneasiness with the unknown frequently short-circuits the change process, leading to an incomplete or unsatisfactory outcome. We don't allow ourselves the opportunity to fully explore the unknown. We don't embrace the mystery of the unknown. As a wise friend of mine, Evan Hodkins, would say, "We go cheap instead of deep." The ego will constantly resist change to keep us from becoming the next person we are destined to become. In this way the ego is an inhibitor of our own evolutionary process.

By missing the opportunities presented by the unknown we are putting on blinders to all of the possibilities and potential that the unknown has to offer. As a result choices become limited and decisions are based on incomplete information. Our ego cowers behind the curtain, fearful of being discovered as weak and ineffectual. We give away our real power, centered in the Higher Self, to seek a false sense of security. We miss a lot when we don't embrace the unknown.

By allowing ourselves to embrace the unknown we open up to the wondrous mystery of life. It is the only way we can break out of the limits of our current paradigms. The unknown is the home of inspiration. It is a shift in consciousness from limited to limitless. I love the following passage from *Falling into Grace* by Adyashanti:

> "Once you get to the frontier of your mind, to the farthest outreach, you'll come to a place where you cant go any further, where the next thought would just take you back into the mind rather than beyond it. When most people get to this point, they either turn back into their mind, or they just start to move along this imaginary frontier, imagining what it would be like to move beyond it. This is the doorway to the place beyond suffering.
>
> When you find yourself at this boundary of your mind, when you've gone to that placed where you realize that you can't go any deeper within the mind, then you begin to stop. You begin to let go. You begin to embrace this unknowing. Embracing the unknown makes us wonderfully and beautifully humble – not humiliated, but truly humble. True humility is a very open state. It's a state of great availability, and it's from this state of great availability and openness, from this willingness to realize how little we really know, that our consciousness begins to shift. It begins to shift from the mind and ego into its natural state. By "natural" I mean something that is not conceived, something that's not staged or altered, something that doesn't take effort to maintain. In order to find the end of struggle, we have to find a state of consciousness that's totally natural, that doesn't fight against our inner or outer environment. That's what I call "aware spirit," or "awake spirit." It's an awake emptiness. That may sound abstract, but simply put it's the openness to a lived sense of not knowing."

Change is often our ticket through the doorway of not knowing. Change allows us to return to our natural way of thinking, a state of creativity emerging from formless infinity. We need to merely suspend our egoistic thoughts, release our fears and embrace what lies ahead in the unknown.

ATTRACTING OUR REALITY

Science and esoteric thought seem to be converging on a similar perspective related to energy; we attract what we put our energy towards. Scientists now know that we are not just matter but enormous energy fields and that all of the energy fields are connected, influencing each other. When energy is focused in a given direction it attracts the energy to which it is pointing. So where we focus our energy we attract that energy to us. This energy does not carry any labels, like good or bad. That is a perception of the mind.

Thoughts become focal points of energy; therefore, the type, frequency and intensity of thoughts will attract to us that type of energy that those thoughts attract. Simply put, thoughts collect energy that becomes things. Since this energy is neutral it can react to any thought, ones that we consider good and ones that we consider bad, creating through us the energetic charge of the thought. This energy becomes the power of the thought to manifest. If we are thinking positive thoughts we will create a positive charge to our energy and we will draw to us energy with a similar charge. The same holds true for negative thoughts. Energy then holds no intrinsic value but becomes directed by the context and texture of the thought.

The Power of Thought-Driven Energy Fields

When we become obsessed by a given thought, positive or negative, we are an energetic magnet to another's, similar energy. When we feel a deep sense of love for a person, if they have any level of sensitivity, they feel it. How they react to this energetic alignment may vary, but the connection is made through your own focus on that person. This principle is behind the mystery of why people with opposite personalities, interests and tastes are attracted to each other. The energy is not visible on the surface but is a deep undercurrent of attraction. The energy is not centered in external factors but comes from the depth of our internal feelings and very being. External trappings mean nothing to a heart emitting love.

This same principle holds true for fearful thoughts. In working with managers I have consistently found that employees who are afraid of being discovered for illicit activity at work invariably come under the scrutiny of their manager, no matter how careful and covert they are. Their fear attracts the attention of the manager. Then there are those employees who could care less whether they get caught by their manager for illicit activities. They frequently go undetected for years. Then one day they become obsessed with the illicit activity and their continued focus on the activity brings about attention to their actions. In some cases the increased focus is obvious and the attention comes from observation of their overt activity(behavioral psychology). There are other cases, however, where the manager just got a feeling and started to check the employee out. This is one reason why I have always coached managers to go with their gut.

Much of the time we have mixed feelings and emotions related to the area of our attention. What we get is the attraction of a mixed bag of positive and negative energy. This can be very confusing, concerning and disorienting. This is frequently what occurs when we enter the unknown of change. We ride the rollercoaster of experiences unaware of the role we are playing in the unfolding through attraction. We put forth both positive and negative energy, creating a mixed reaction and manifestation in our self and others. In this way change becomes more confusing and uncertain. Change is not the problem. The real problem is our mixed, energetic reaction to it.

The Influence of Our Energy on Finding Employment

This is easy to track with people who are looking for work. They search for a new job and put in lots of applications. Some jobs they have positive feelings about and others they have negative feelings for. Frequently they will get calls for a job they have negative feelings about. In questioning many of these job seekers it became apparent that they had stronger, negative feelings towards a job they really didn't want than they had positive feelings for another job they really desired. They end up taking the job they don't want because they never got the call on the job they wanted. Why? I will tell you that they sent out stronger, attractive energy for the job they didn't want and immediately released the attractive energy for the job they wanted once they were called for an interview for the negative job. In short, they settled for what they didn't want and released the energy soliciting the job they wanted.

In other situations I have worked with job seekers who are obsessed with getting a certain job. They put out immense amounts of attractive energy towards the desired position. In some situations they get the job but in others they are deeply disappointed when they are passed over. Again, why? Just like in personal relationships, the hiring manager senses the intense, attractive energy and becomes concerned. In interviewing hiring managers, who have passed over qualified candidates for hire, I frequently hear that their rational was, "just had a bad feeling about the candidate. He/she was just too intense!" So even intense, energetic attention to a desired outcome can end up in disappointment. Not because the energy wasn't there. It was just too strong for the situation and made the receiving individual uncomfortable.

When we operate from strong, egotistic needs and desires we frequently can go overboard. If we step back and allow ourselves to be open to what is now, and accepting of what is next, there is a tendency to be interested but not obsessed with any area of focus. The energy of attraction reaches a natural balance. That which holds a reciprocal attractive charge is drawn to us. This is a natural form of synergy. We may attract the focus of our attention or something totally different, but when we come from a position of interest then the synergy happens. As we reflect on what we have attracted we can see the fit, even when it is not evident at first. Replacing obsessive, egotistic thoughts with an open, inquiring posture allows us to move forward naturally, guided by the Higher Self within.

To continue with the employment example, I worked with a woman who had been unemployed for over two years. She had suffered many disappointments related to positions she was obsessed in getting. Nothing clicked. I counseled her to just let go, to stop focusing so intently on a single position. I asked her to vision in general terms the type of work she would most like to be doing, without focusing on any one potential position. I said, "Be open to positions of interest and do the work of applying, but also stay open to all opportunities without focusing on just one." She reluctantly followed my advice.

A week later an old friend, who she hadn't seen in over a year, contacted her and told her about a job she thought she would be perfect for in a neighboring city. My client wasn't particularly interested in moving but decided to apply, as the job seemed interesting. Two weeks later she was starting the new job. Five years later she remained thrilled with the company and had been promoted twice. She also loves the new city and home where she is living. I attribute her success to releasing all of her resistance and being open to any and all possibilities. She allowed the attractive energy to do the work; she fell into grace.

The other side of the coin is unwanted experiences. If we focus on unwanted experience, especially to the exclusion of a focus on wanted experience, then we attract more of the unwanted experience. Ester and Jerry Hicks summed this up in The Law of Attraction, referring to this concept: "Once you understand this law and begin to pay attention to what you are giving your attention to, you will regain control of your own life experience. And with that control you will again remember that there is nothing that you desire that you cannot achieve, and there is noting that you do not want that you cannot release from your experience."

When we allow our egotistic mind to storm in with fear, doubt and negative energy we are attracting disappointment. It is a hard pill to swallow, but I firmly believe we attract our unwanted experiences.

I would add that the term 'desire' in the above quote is of a general, rather than specific, nature. The important point is to become aware of where you are placing your attention, and to focus your attention on the direction you want to go in, rather than what you want to release.

The Law of Attraction in Relationships

I have counseled men and women who have gone from one relationship to another, with little satisfaction. As we looked at why they broke off the relationship they would present a litany of negative experiences. As we looked at each subsequent break up they would invariably list similar, negative experiences. Further inquiry uncovered that they had a tendency to get into subsequent relationships that were just like the prior. I asked them what was their focus of attention as they got into the new relationships. More often than not they would say that they were focusing on the negative aspects of the last relationship. The Law of Attraction has no idea of where you want to go; it just knows where you are putting your energy.

I have asked them to work with me to get through all of their fears related to the negative experiences they had in the prior relationships before moving on. At the same time we looked at what they really wanted in a relationship and turned their attention to these qualities. While there are no guarantees, almost all of these clients moved into much more healthy and long-lasting relationships.

Working with this law of attraction requires us to achieve a delicate balance of openness, acceptance, attention and intention. Feelings also play as important a role in the process as does our thoughts and desires. Our feelings will offer a doorway to our Higher Self. It is much easier to communicate with our Higher Self through feelings than through a thought process. This is why most of our intuitional hits come first as feelings. We need to be aware of the source of our feelings. If the source is a product of our thinking then it is coming from the mind. When the feeling has not been solicited by the mind then it is coming from our connection to the Higher Self. Be suspect of the feelings generated by thought and accepting of 'spontaneous' feelings.

In the relationship example, feelings coming from negative, unresolved thoughts were a strong attractive force in new relationships. Part of the attraction to the new partner was a desire to understand the prior negative experience. We have a tendency to draw ourselves toward and relive experiences until we understand them.

ALLOWING GRACE INTO CHANGE

In summary, successful management of change requires an openness and acceptance of grace. Grace requires us to let go of control. We have to become more open and accepting, knowing that all of our experiences are increasing our awareness, if we just allow ourselves to relax and understand. Through our understanding we can release the unwanted and focus on what is now. From the now we are open to whatever life has to offer; we are free to accept our good. We are free from the mind's incessant need to label, free to connect with the Universal Force behind all that is. Grace is not something bestowed upon us by God; it is what is always there if we just are willing to accept it. Change is the perfect opportunity to accept grace in our life. Don't allow fear and resistance to block the way into grace.

PART TWO

EMBRACING THE PROCESS OF CHANGE

Part One was designed to create a paradigm shift for you with respect to change. This paradigm shift is based in the acceptance of change as inherently good, rather than bad. More significant is a full understanding of the fact that change is the doorway to who and what we are to become.

Also covered was a wide variety of tools to assist you in moving through change. Most of these tools seem contrary to our old habits of managing change. It will take some concerted thought and effort to break through old, unproductive patterns of reaction and resistance to change to successfully utilize these new tools.

Part Two is dedicated to the process of change. The three chapters in this section outline the three phases of the change process; saying goodbye, exploring the present, and moving on. These three phases of change apply to all aspects of your life, work, relationships, health, soul direction, prosperity and more. No matter what the event or situation you will navigate change more easily and with greater success by having a heightened awareness of these three phases. This comes from a better understanding of how to respond in each phase of change

While these three phases are sequential they also have significant overlap. As an example you may be finishing up the process of saying goodbye while being fully engaged in exploring the present and beginning to consider moving on. It is important to remember that you must be complete with each phase at some point to be successful with the entire change process. If at any point in the process you try to move on to the next phase without having made significant progress in the prior one or two phases you will short-circuit the entire change process. Change unfolds based on our willingness to be open and accepting; it is nothing that we can force into a successful outcome. We can definitely influence the process but we are not its master. Change is life in action and life has no master.

I provide this warning, as we have a natural tendency to rush forward, particularly if we are experiencing some level of pain or perceived suffering during the process. Rushing forward may allow us to ignore the pain or suffering but it doesn't alleviate it. You have to be courageous and face each phase of change with a deep desire to understand and gain closure to all that each phase has to offer. Part Two will give you a broad understanding of each phase and what you should be looking for to assure you have completed each phase.

Of course the change process is as individual as you are and will not exactly fit the descriptions in this book. As you work with change you will adapt the change process to best fit your personality and style for engaging life. While the three phases are universal in their application you will need to tweak them to fit your needs and situation.

As you read through this section of the book I would suggest that you apply it to one aspect of change currently going on in your life. Attempting to use it in multiple areas of your life at once will invoke some confusion and make the learning process more difficult.

CHAPTER SEVEN

SAYING GOODBYE: LEARNING TO LET GO

We must be willing to let go of the life we have planned, so as to accept the life that is waiting for us.

Joseph Campbell

When I let go of what I am, I become what I might be.

Lao Tzu

There are a lot of well-traveled phrases that you frequently hear to describe the first phase of change:

"Unload your old baggage."

"Just let that ship sail."

"Lighten up before you leap."

My personal favorite, "When I was a child, I talked like a child, I thought like a child, I reasoned like a child. When I became a man, I put childish ways behind me." I Corinthians 13:11

All of these phrases are pointing to the same requirement for initiating change, releasing what no longer serves you. Frequently we jump to the conclusion that this releasing process is associated with external people, places and things. While these are a part of the 'saying goodbye' process it really begins within. We release and let go from the inside out.

This inside-out process begins with self-reflection. We have to take stock in what mental, emotional and physical changes we need to make, and identify what no longer serves us internally before we turn outward to release what is no longer needed in our life. If we don't go inside out we may carelessly discard someone, something and even some idea or belief that is still of benefit to us in our growth process. We may also needlessly hold onto things that no longer serve us because of habitual, old ways of living out our experience. Self-reflection is critical to make sure we sort out what to keep and what to let go.

Frequently some of the most painful things in our life are very beneficial. We feel like running from them, but they are actually just what we need. If a friend challenges us in a way that makes us feel uncomfortable we don't just dump that person. We take a long look at what they are trying to tell us and see if we are in denial about anything related to what they are sharing. Our best friends are those who are honest, open and willing to challenge us. They uncover our blind spots, where we are stuck, and reveal to us what we fear. This is the real gift of friendship, which many people just discard. Suffering helps us to build our emotional muscles and increases our capacity to move forward without fear. This can only occur, however, when we take the time to see what we have gained from a painful experience. What has it taught us? How are we different? What will we do differently in the future? These answers and more are the benefits of painful experiences.

Several years ago I joined a men's group that meets each Monday, all year long. We took a pledge to be authentic, open, sincere with our feelings and willing to challenge each other on our beliefs and stories. There is no wrong or right. We just share openly without judgment. Sometimes we just need to be heard and nothing else is said. I cannot express how far this men's group has brought me in managing change. Without their courage to challenge me and get me out of my story I would have not as easily managed many of the growth opportunities that have come over the last few years.

So saying goodbye is a thoughtful process of exploration starting from self-inquiry and expanding outward. It is an acknowledging and releasing of the past physically, mentally and emotionally, so that we are free to explore the present without the blinders of past regrets and can start to vision the future without the limitations of past beliefs and feelings. In 'saying goodbye' we become an empty vessel ready to receive what is next. We release our ego-facades and look towards who we are becoming. These old masks are the greatest resistance to change. In fact, they represent a bundle of old beliefs, expectations and programmed responses, all based in creating resistance to change. Saying goodbye to our old persona is critical to allowing in what is next for us. Stop for a moment to reflect on this truth and allow it to show you your internal resistance.

EXPLORING THE INNER CANYONS

We are constantly evolving, outgrowing old ideas, thoughts and beliefs. Releasing these constrictive, mental fixations makes room for our awareness to expand our understanding of life and how we fit into this unfolding reality. These mental fixations have defined how we connected with our outside world. Even if the connection was broken with an external person, place or thing that caused us pain and suffering we will most likely connect with a similar replacement unless we change the mental fixation. We repeat the old patterns of the past because we look at life through the same mental and emotional fixations, no matter whether we consider them good or bad. We must face these fixations and deal with them before there can be meaningful change.

Harriet was a 23-year-old client, who had lost her mother a year before coming to see me. She was deeply attached to her mother and consulted her for every major decision in her life. When her mother died Harriet turned to a close friend and started to seek advice from her on major decisions. After a year Harriet was distraught over her relationship with her close friend. She felt her friend was giving her bad advice and attempting to replace her mother. She didn't want to loose the friendship and sought help regarding how she could change and improve their relationship.

Rather than diving into the relationship I began to discuss with Harriet her own, internal thoughts, ideas and beliefs related to making life decisions. What surfaced was Harriet's belief that she was incapable of making her own decisions regarding almost every aspect of her life. As far back as Harriet could remember she had always relied on her mother for making major decisions.

We then explored how well that worked for Harriet. She admitted that the advice her mother had given her did not always help. The deeper we looked into a variety of decisions based on her mother's advice it became apparent that some of the advice given was actually detrimental to Harriet's growth. In several situations Harriet could now see that her mother's advice had the affect of keeping Harriet as her mother's little girl, dependent on her. Harriet came to the awareness that her belief that her mother always provided the best advice for her was false. I asked her to let this belief go.

We next explored her belief that she was incapable of making her own decisions, independent of others. Was that true? We first explored small, financial decisions she had made and whether they were successful in assisting her to move forward with her life. Saving money by changing her cell phone provider. Finding bargains while shopping. Refinancing her car. As we moved to larger and larger decisions she had made it became apparent to Harriet that she was capable of successfully making her own decisions.

We then explored further decisions her mother had help her make. What were Harriet's preferences going into the discussion with her mother? Harriet came to realize that frequently her mother was just confirming her own preferences and ideas. Harriet was actually making her own major life decisions, but was just looking for confirmation from her mother. We also explored situations where her mother disagreed with Harriet, leading to Harriet changing her decision. Did it always work out as her mother advised? No. Would Harriet have been better off following her own instincts? Well, yes.

In short order Harriet discarded her old belief of inadequacy and became confident in her own decision-making capabilities. With a new belief in place we turned to Harriet's relationship with her friend. I asked her to what degree her friendship was based on her dependence for advice. Harriet's response surprised her. It was significant. I asked her, if she no longer needed her friend to help her make decisions, how that would change their relationship? Harriet admitted that it would not be as close. I asked her how she felt about that? She felt guilty, like she had been using her friendship for selfish needs. I further explored with Harriet if her friend was also getting a need met and what she thought that might be. Harriet answered, "To be my mother." I asked her if her friends need was really benefiting Harriet's personal growth. She just shook her head no.

We were then ready to move to the next phase in changing Harriet's relationship with her friend. Over the next few weeks we looked at what she really wanted in this relationship and if she was willing to initiate the changes needed. Harriet initially backed off on her friendship as a cooling off period. She then approached her friend with an honest appraisal of her wishes for their relationship. Her friend was surprised and relieved that Harriet was no longer seeking advice on major life decisions. She admitted that she liked being helpful but, at times, it made her uncomfortable.

Over the next two months Harriet and her friend redefined their relationship based on mutual desires and trust. I continued to work with Harriet on co-dependency to assist in releasing old needs for support, based on a sense of inadequacy, and developing an inter-dependent friendship. Years have passed and Harriet and her friend continue to share an intimate and fulfilling friendship, centered in trust and respect rather than need.

Sifting Through the Past

How do we know if a thought, idea or belief is no longer useful? First, thoughts, ideas and beliefs are just as impermanent as everything else in our lives. Even in the hallowed halls of science few theories, and laws stand the test of time. Our physical world is not constant, so we must adapt what we think. This is even more true to thoughts, ideas and beliefs about less tangible things, like people's intentions and feelings. Creating judgments from our thoughts, ideas and beliefs take us even further into unreality and create fixations that are the root of suffering. Thinking, not grounded in the present experience, is a recipe for disaster.

So how can we break free in our thinking? We can start by looking at the validity of long-held thoughts, ideas and beliefs. It is especially important to look at those mental and emotional fixations that are holding you in an uncomfortable state of being. Mental fixations that are nebulous in nature, but significant to being stuck in a certain physical, emotional, mental state. These mental and emotional fixations represent significant, subversive barriers to change. On closer examination we find that these mental and emotional fixations are usually fear based. If fear is holding us back, then this is a good indication that we need to take a close look at what we need to let go. If it hasn't helped us to move forward in the past, what makes us think it will help us now?

Lying beneath and supporting our mental state are emotional fixations that also restrict how we engage in life. Even when the mind has moved on there can be a feeling that creates a sense of hesitation. We just feel that we can't move forward, that we need to retreat. Limiting emotions are just as powerful, if not more so, than limiting thoughts. Limiting emotions are subtler and are frequently unconsciously experienced. They are also entirely based in past experience. It is critical to do an emotional review when we are performing self-inquiry during the 'saying goodbye' part of the change process. We will spend more time on this topic later in the chapter.

Philip was a 52-year-old business executive, who was extremely distressed over his state of health. He held a high-pressure management position, which was sedentary by nature. During a recent doctors visit Philip was informed that he had high cholesterol and blood pressure. He was 80 pounds overweight and borderline morbidly obese. He had made several attempts over the prior two years to 'get on a program' but was not successful. We first worked to identify Philips core belief regarding his health. What Philip discovered was a strong belief that he was past his prime and unable to garner good health, no matter what he tried.

Rather than taking this deeply held, core belief head on we started by breaking it down. What had happened in the past that leads Philip to this belief? Philip and I spent several hours detailing each of his efforts to get healthy and why they had failed. It was obvious that Philip had several beliefs that were creating artificial barriers to his road to a consistent, health improvement program. Work didn't afford him time for a regular exercise program; he felt he was at risk in starting any exercise at all; he couldn't manage his diet due to travel and eating out. The list was extensive.

We started by deeply inquiring into the validity of each long-held belief. After an initial discussion of each belief I asked Philip to go out and research the validity of that belief over the Internet and report back. In the majority of cases Philip would return each week, enthusiastic about what he had found. There were reasonable ways for him to overcome each belief barrier and to get on the road to health. I asked Philip in each case if he was willing to release these long-held beliefs and experiment with what he had learned. He agreed and we took it slow. I gave Philip time away from therapy to work on each belief. He was to come back when he was stuck or if he felt he had achieved success in creating a part of his plan for health.

Over a years time we tackled diet, exercise, work, stress and relationships. Yes relationships! Philip found through inquiry that his current girlfriend actually liked Philip 'full bodied' and was supporting his negative beliefs about his health. Eventually Philip had to decide between the two and he chose health, ending the relationship. One by one the belief barriers fell.

When I stopped seeing Philip he had a well-rounded, sound and stable health program in place. He had committed to and made several significant changes to a variety of aspects of his life, to include work, exercise, habits, hobbies, eating and relationships. Philip had already lost 45 pounds, had a goal to be at or below his ideal weight and to run the Bolder-Boulder 10K race by May of next year. In May I joined Philip for the race and he beat the pants off of me at the finish line.

Too often we try to tackle a broad, core, fixated belief when, if we just go after its parts, it will eventually evaporate on its own. Just by saying goodbye several, small, long-held negative beliefs, that no longer served him, Philip radically changed his life. This was not a quick and easy process for Philip to see and feel differently about himself. Some old beliefs are so strongly entrenched that they have to be broken apart to be dispelled.

In addition, we had to deal with hidden emotions that were reinforcing Philip's beliefs. Philip had been overweight as a child. His father frequently called him a 'fat little boy', which lead to feelings of helplessness and melancholy. These feelings of helplessness and melancholy were now attached to his belief that he as 'over the hill'. This reinforced his new belief on a subconscious level.

With a concerted effort at in depth inquiry we can uncover the truth about any strongly held belief and emotion. This was the case with Philip as he is proof that no mountain is too hard to climb.

The Impermanence of the Strongest Held Beliefs

It makes sense that if life is impermanent then beliefs are as well. This has been proven time and again as we move forward with the physical sciences. The world was flat and now it is round. The universe was disjointed and chaotic and now it is connected and interactive. The most enlightened scientists not longer completely accept any law of science. Unfortunately we don't normally inquire into and challenge our personal belief systems in the same way that science has adopted. We just blindly accept them as fact. Sometimes life just comes up and demands we take a deeper look. Other times we just get that sinking feeling that something is wrong. Whether external or internal we must respond and adapt our beliefs to the now. The more willing we are to inquire, challenge and say goodbye to negative, restrictive thoughts, ideas, feelings and beliefs the more resilient and responsive we become to change.

WHEN CHANGE AND LIFE COMES A KNOCKIN'

Change always seems to come at the most inopportune time. Just when we feel like life is under our control we hit that bump in the road. The unexpected arrives. What is known becomes cloudy. What is fixed starts to break apart before our eyes. What is comfortable is now uncomfortable. Why?

The Soul (Higher Self) seems to know when we are getting stuck; when the ego-self has gained an unreasonable upper hand. When the Soul knows that we can soon be totally lost in the dream that the ego has created

It steps in to shake us awake. The Soul is like an internal emergency alarm. "Watch out! You are asleep at the wheel!" Change calls us to awake from our dream, yet we are so lost in the dream that we fight to stay there. This is the main reason why we struggle so with change; but the Soul is relentless. If we ignore the early invitations to change our Soul, in the disguise of life, just seems to ramp up the circumstances of our experience until the need for change is undeniable.

It is at this point where the battle of wills begins. Of course the reality is that the ego can never win against the Soul, but the ego will create the illusion that it can stop our experience and keep life from effecting change. This is the seed energy for resistance. We have a choice at this early stage in the change process. We can either allow change to have its way with our reality or we can resist it. Giving way to change may seem like an act of weakness, but, in fact, it is an act of strength. Accepting and moving into change is an active process that takes courage and forbearance. We acknowledge the unknown and greet it with a sense of discovery, rather than dread. So when change comes a knockin' we can stand with the ego in resistance or stand with the Soul in acceptance of what is to unfold. If we decide to stand with the ego we can hold off the tide of life (under the direction of the Soul) for a time, but change always wins in the end. Embracing change early on is a far easier battle because change always wins out.

The Two Doorways of Change

Change will manifest through two doorways. We access these doors either externally or internally. When it comes internally it is the Soul pushing its way beyond the ego. When it comes externally it is the Soul attracting to us the circumstances and situations that will initiate the change process from without. Either way it is the same source. Our Higher Self is ready to move on, whether we consciously like it or not.

There are many ways that an internally initiated change will begin to manifest. Our first clue usually comes to us through our emotions. Feelings like emptiness, boredom, depression, disorientation, fear, doubt, loneliness, sorrow or lack of energy can frequently indicate the precursor of internal change. In general we loose interest and enthusiasm for what is going on around us. We disengage from work, relationships, play and routine daily activities. There is a generalized discontent that seems to be building. We can't seem to define it but it is there and it is affecting and effecting how we are interacting with life. This sense of discontent seems to gain energy over time, robbing us of our energy, motivation and desire.

We normally have little recognition initially as to what is going on as the ego tries to distract us from any internal discomfort or distress that is not focused on it alone. The ego will pick up the dialog in the mind to distract and divert our attention from our feelings. Frequently it is not until the emotions are overwhelming that we mentally take notice of what is going on. The ego knows change is coming, but it is going to resist for fear that it will loose control. It may take an external event, like being fired from a job, to shake us awake. Many people I have counseled after loosing their job have failed to realize their general discontent with the work they were doing and how it negatively impacted their work performance. They were on autopilot, not realizing their feelings were taking them in for a rough landing. Internal change takes our full attention to feelings in an effort to realize early on that change is starting from within. We must listen intently to the song of the heart.

Jayne came to see me because she was having real problems with her employer. She was in a senior management position and was deeply troubled by where the leadership wanted to take the business. She was angry and upset with her boss and felt little support for the direction she wanted to go with the business.

I asked Jayne to detail for me the different duties that she performed in her position. As we looked at each one I asked Jayne how much personal satisfaction she got from performing each of her duties. Jayne came to discover that she had lost interest in many of the functions she was performing in her position. I asked her if she was performing at the same level that she did when she originally took the position. She had to admit that she was not. When I asked her why this is Jayne suddenly got in touch with her feelings. She didn't really like the work she was doing. She didn't see it as her life's calling, but she made great money and had excellent benefits.

We explored some of the reasons that she originally took the job. She focused on financial security and increased job responsibility and authority. Jayne also stated that she had had some misconceptions as to what her duties were going to be and that she was disappointed to find out what her job actually entailed. We then explored how this had emotionally affected her over the last two years. She responded by detailing many of the feelings I had listed above. I then asked Jayne what she really wanted at this time. Jayne said she wanted out.

From that point forward I worked with Jayne in developing a solid exit strategy and to explore what she really wanted to do. Early on Jayne identified that she wanted to run her own small business. We explored many possibilities and Jayne finally notice that she was drawn to small, unique boutiques, offering specialty clothes and products for women. We began to put together a plan to move her in that direction.

During this time I asked Jayne to focus her attention on doing her current job to the best of her ability. I asked her to look at the skills that she would transfer to her own business and to hone them in her current job. I also asked Jayne to let go of her discontent on the direction that leadership was moving the company and to focus on giving her best effort. Jayne agreed and her performance improved, along with her relationship with her boss. More important, Jayne no longer dreaded going to work each day.

When the day came that Jayne was ready to move on she had no problems or regrets in giving her notice. Her boss was sorry to see her go but understood her desire to have her own business. With business plan in hand Jayne had already secured the financing needed for her own boutique and her new business was successfully launched within 120 days.

I am in no way inferring that Jayne was wrong about the direction her company was going. What was important for our work together was for Jayne to take ownership of her feelings for the work she was doing and to let go of what no longer served her. Being an employee for someone else, despite the financial security it provided, was not the life that Jayne envisioned for herself. By owning her own deep desires and needs Jayne was able to make a decision that benefited both her and her former employer.

Change can also come from the outside. Frequently it smacks us on the side of the head and we are deeply shaken, disoriented. In many ways we unconsciously draw to us the instigators of change. Sometimes what we draw leads to positive change, like an unexpected invitation to join an expedition to a long dreamed of land we have wanted to visit or maybe a job opportunity that will take us in a totally new direction. Whatever the case, we easily accept this new opportunity because it usually is not threatening to the ego-self. Change can also appear unexpectedly and painfully, deeply challenging who we think we are. We are often thrown into a state of shock and we look to retreat, regroup, and defend our position. Adyashanti calls this "fierce grace". Unfortunately we don't normally see it that way. When fierce grace arrives we are already internally conflicted, but unaware of it. This unconscious state of uneasiness makes external events even more seismic in their effect upon us. Externally initiated change is the mirror of our internal conflict, drawn to us in an effort to create awareness. Either way, internally or externally, we are attracting the elements necessary to allow us to evolve to the next level. The storm is upon us and yet the alternative is mental and emotional stagnation.

Guy came to see me in deep distress. Guy had been married for 15 years and had three children he loved dearly. During the last year Guy had become involved in an affair with a woman at work. Guy's wife found out about the affair, demanded Guy move out and filed for a divorce. Guy immediately ended the affair and pleaded for forgiveness. His wife was having no part of it. Guy wanted me to help him fix his marriage. I said I could help him sort things out and he could decide what was next, but I was not in the business of 'fixing marriages'. He agreed to move forward, primarily because he was so distressed and wanted help.

We started with his reasons for getting into a relationship with another woman. Guy's first response was that she had come on to him. This is a common male defense, "I was wrongly lured into an affair and I couldn't help myself." I confronted Guy with the fact that we always have a choice and I didn't believe it was due to any weakness on his part. After some discussion Guy accepted responsibility for entering into the affair. We had made it to first base.

Next I explored with Guy his motivations for getting into the affair. At first, Guy didn't want to go there (typical ego defense). With much effort Guy began to reveal his thoughts, beliefs and feelings. Guy had felt himself drifting away from his wife over the last several years. They had different interests, beliefs and he just didn't feel emotionally close to her anymore. I asked Guy if he found a greater alignment with the woman he was having an affair with. Guy admitted that he didn't really know. Guy realized that the woman he was having an affair with was not that different from his wife. Now Guy was even more confused.

We next started to define what Guy really wanted in life. We also took a hard look at who he was and how he felt about that. Guy did not like who he was. He stated he felt like an actor, playing a part in life but totally board with it. I inquired as to what aspects of life he felt most like an actor. Guy admitted that he had been very ambitious at work for years, looking for the next opportunity for promotion, but he didn't feel like the work he was doing was meaningful. He felt that he was just going through the motions. I asked Guy what would happen if they found out at work that he was having an affair with one of his employees. He said he would be fired. I asked Guy if that was what he really wanted. He was shocked into a long silence.

We then returned to Guy's marriage. Had he and his wife drifted so far apart that he no longer felt that he loved her? After much soul searching Guy discovered that he still loved his wife, but he didn't love himself. I told Guy that he would not have any hope in 'saving his marriage' until he figured out who he was and approached his wife as that person.

Over the next few months we worked on who the unfolding Guy was and what brought meaning into his life. Guy explained to his wife that he was seeing me and what we were doing. He asked her to allow him some time for her to get to know who he really was. Guy's wife recognized how unhappy Guy had been with himself and she admitted that she was not very happy with who he had become either. She was willing to give it some time.

Guy was able to redefine what 'moved his soul'. He quit his job and took on a new position in an industry that interested him. Guy took his wife out on dates and on day trips with the children. He worked hard at being honest and authentic with few expectations. Guy's wife liked the new him and they grew closer. As the family grew closer and Guy became a better father. This had been an unspoken issue between Guy and his wife. She felt that Guy had become disengaged from the children prior to their separation and this had made her feel more distant. Guy cried at this revelation and was sincerely sorry to his wife and the kids. He took the ninth step and made amends to all of them.

A month after I stopped seeing Guy he reported that the divorce had been cancelled and he was returning home. Guy's wife welcomed home her new husband. I doubt seriously if she would have ever accepted the Guy from whom she separated.

For Guy life had sent him the most direct message as possible as to what needed to change. He came to see that his affair had more to do with his own self-discontent than the growing differences with his wife. Guy saw his affair as an attempt at self-sabotage in a effort to exact a change in who he was. Guy saved his marriage by making a change in himself. In his book, *The Shift*, Dr. Wayne Dyer writes, "I have now made almost 70 trips around our sun, and the one thing that stands out very clearly is that all of us want our lives to have purpose and meaning." Guy was willing to destroy his marriage and himself to make the move to meaning. To his good fortune, Guy woke up and realized the shift he needed to make did not require that he destroy what he really loved.

Whether it comes from outside or within, once the change process begins it requires our full attention. We need to become cognizant of what no longer serves us, starting with a full assessment of who we think we are and extending outward to all that we have been connecting with in life. Unless we release what no longer serves us then we cannot become the receptacle for what is next to come.

What is next will most likely not be evident as the change process gets underway. In fact it might be weeks, months and even years before what is next is fully revealed and manifest. This makes the 'saying goodbye' process even more difficult. It is like the trapeze artist that must let go of one bar, in hopes that the other bar will be there when she arrives. We must trust the process, trust our self, and trust life to work on our behalf.

Indicators for Saying Goodbye

In his original book, <u>Transitions</u> William Bridges talks about four indicators/feelings that can be signs that change is underway and it is time to start letting go. To quote from his book, *The Way of Transition*, he describes these four indicators, which he calls cardinal aspects of the experience of loss:

1. *Disengagement*, which is the separation from whatever it is that you have lost.
2. *Disidentification*, or the way that the loss destroys the old identity you had.
3. *Disenchantment*, which referred to the way that the loss tears you out of the old reality you previously accepted unthinkingly.
4. *Disorientation*, was how, as a result of losing the object of your feeling and the identity you had together with that shared reality, you feel bewildered and lost.

Bridges speaks of these four feelings in the association with loss, but that is not necessarily true. As in the prior case study with Guy, he experienced all of these feelings related to his work without loosing his job. His loss was internal, a loss of purpose, of moral and ethical orientation, and of self. His feelings towards work were not fully understood until we discussed them during the course of therapy.

Each of these feelings not only helps us to understand that change is underway, but also provide clues as to what is changing and the direction it is going. The area of our life that is starting to change will be the focus for these feelings. If we take the time to ask ourselves why these feelings are present and what do they mean then we have the opportunity to get a 'jump start' on the process of 'saying goodbye'. Each of these feelings also helps us with different aspects of the change process.

Disengagement helps us to create distance from what we are releasing in our life. We are stepping back from our attachment and creating space for clarity. As we disengage we can use inquiry to understand why we feel this initial disconnection and what is the source of these feelings. In deeper inquiry with Guy it became clear that he had been disengaging from his current position for years prior to the affair. He frequently would find his mind wondering at work from the assignments and tasks before him. Guy lost interest in his performance and, more importantly, the outcome of his work. Violating company policy with regards to fellow employees was an unconscious act on Guy's behalf to further disengage by putting his position in jeopardy.

Disidentification starts to break down the ego identity that is holding us to whatever we are starting to release. We frequently establish an ego persona related to a given attachment. This persona does not represent our true self, but we feel the need to project this persona in defense of our attachment. As we start to release there is no need to continue with this persona and we start to let it go of this external identity. For Guy he no longer liked who he had become at work. His self-image had deteriorated dramatically and he had outgrown the his specific ego persona at work that he had spent years developing and defending. Guy was feeling the need to be more authentic, more real, but couldn't summon the energy to move into change in a conscious and deliberate manner. In part, Guy's attraction to the female employee was her willingness to openly share her disenchantment with their employer and the work she was performing.

Disenchantment is an often, negative manner in which we overtly destroy our current reality. Our unconscious will begin to overtly attack what our ego has spent years rationalizing and defending. This battle starts internally but quickly escalates into our outer world. The ego is attached to 'the way things are' and will divert much thought and energy to maintain the status quo. Our disenchantment is the active expression of our internal discontent and rebellion to the ego. This will often manifest as instability and inconsistency in our outward persona. While Guy's affair had many aspects involved, a big part of it that was revealed in our discussions was his need to move away from his current work, even if that meant initiating self-destructive behaviors as part of the process. Guy's ego was continuously preaching security, power, prestige, and persona validation as part of the pattern for resisting change. At the subconscious level Guy was forced to extremes in overcoming the pull of the ego. If Guy had been more conscious of his disengagement, disidentification and disenchantment he might have been more constructive in how he moved forward with change.

Sooner or later, when we are not inquiring and acting consciously with regards to change, we will become disoriented; we become aware that we have lost our internal compass. Our actions become random and not focused in the present. Often friends and family begin to question our state of being. Feelings of anxiety and depression are common. If the disorientation is strong enough, we succumb to their assessments and seek help. In Guy's disorientation he became incapable of disguising his affair any longer. His wife's awareness, acknowledgement of the affair, and move to file for divorce, caused further disorientation, leading Guy to seek my help.

While these feelings are all a part of the 'saying goodbye' process they do not have to be as dramatic and damaging as they were for Guy. If we inquire into each of the feelings, with an effort to make conscious what is unconscious, then we can discover and react appropriately to the releasing process. I have worked with many individuals who have come to me early in the disengagement phase and we have developed conscious, constructive ways to release what no longer serves them. Using the tools described in Part I of the book can go a long way to moving the 'saying goodbye' process forward.

The Dis's and Their Impact on Personal Will

We resist change during the 'saying goodbye' phase because of two gut reactions, fear and personal will. Personal will is a function of our ego that defends and supports its position, giving power to resistance. Personal will offers a compelling argument that it protects the self from harm, where harm births from our fear of separateness. Personal will gives us a sense of control over the circumstances of our life. Personal will is also a mechanism to discount and ignore reality. The resistance it offers frequently creates a ramping up of change, making it more traumatic when change wins the day.

The four dis's are significant in their impact on personal will during difficult change. They progressively break down our personal will and resistance, allowing us to surrender to change. They are the grease that allows the personal will to slip away. Disengagement, disidentification and disenchantment create external separation to the object of our attachment.

We loose the will to possess as the separation grows. Disorientation is an internal process where we distract the personal will, breaking its certainty, neutralizing fear, and allowing surrender to change. Simply put, we can't move into who we are to become until we are able to surrender who we currently are. The four dis's help us to achieve this transition.

Bonnie had made the decision to not engage into any intimate relationships after a string of failed encounters with friends and boyfriends. She had withdrawn into the security of 'self' and identified it as her way of avoiding further hurts and disappointments. While initially content with her position Bonnie was steadily becoming more lonely and depressed.

Our first few meetings required a significant amount of listening and clarifying on my part. As Bonnie gained trust in the therapeutic relationship she gradually became more comfortable. Bonnie felt comfortable in sharing with me since there was no chance of intimacy in our 'working relationship'. During this period I did not challenge Bonnie's personal will to not enter into intimate relationships; I just let her share her pain and need to resist.

Slowly we began to discuss her adamant attachment to being alone. In our conversations I treated her desire to be alone as an independent entity. In this way I was indirectly asking Bonnie to look at the desire to be alone as something separate from herself. During this period she disengaged, disidentified and became disenchanted with the idea of being independent and safe by being alone. As the separation grew her personal will lessened and she began to surrender to the need for intimacy in her life and the uncertainty it would create.

We turned our conversations to the developing of a realistic view of intimacy and relationship. Bonnie slowly inquired into the positives of intimacy, as well as taking a realistic look at the uncertainties that will arise in relationships. She surrendered to the idea that there are no certainties in intimate relationships but they offered something she needed that was worth the risk, love. We then began to identify and affirm for Bonnie those qualities she desired in a relationship. Her desires for intimacy, community and love became the budding elements of a new personal will. Bonnie was now ready to leave her personal island of isolation.

Slowly and carefully Bonnie allowed herself to be open to new relationships. She re-engaged with some former friends, who she had 'dumped' in a reaction to her failed relationships with men. What came to light was that she had turned away from these friends because they were willing to openly share their concerns for her as she jumped from one boyfriend to another. Bonnie came to understand that their comments were coming from a position of concern, but her personal will to make the current relationship work caused her to turn away from her friend's insights and concerns. Bonnie found that these friends were willing to forgive, forget and move forward. She was greatly relieved and appreciative.

Eventually Bonnie began to date again. This time she took things slowly and listened to the input from her friends. During our talks we continued to discuss Bonnie's needs in a relationship and whether she was expressing those needs and getting them met. Bonnie found that by being honest and authentic with her needs she could easily discern if the relationship was moving forward, on the right track. At the end of our work together Bonnie was feeling comfortable in the relationships she had created and was realistically seeking to increase the intimacy of these relationships. In looking back Bonnie could only laugh at her steadfast position of being alone. Her parting comment to me was, "I guess I am not a rock or an island."

Sincere self-inquiry is an excellent way to look at the validity of our personal will and to use the four dis's to create separation and clarity to our internal resistance that is holding us back from making progress on our personal path. For Bonnie she was able to 'say goodbye' to isolation by careful inquiry into her deeper needs that lie beneath her fears and the value of friends as sources of insight. This allowed her to overcome her fear of being hurt and rejected.

SAYING GOODBYE AND WHAT IS NEXT

One of the reasons that 'saying goodbye' is so difficult is the fact that there frequently is not a 'something else' awaiting on the other side. Saying goodbye is recognition of an ending, but it does not guarantee a new beginning right away. There may be a substantial gap between what we release and what we move towards. We will explore this more in the next chapter, called 'Exploring the Present'. It requires a leap of faith on our behalf to move forward into the unknown. I liken this to jumping from an airplane without any certainty that the chute will open after the free-fall. It takes great courage and faith to take that step from the security of the airplane and the free-fall is both exhilarating and terrifying at the same time. What gets us to jump is the belief that the chute will open when we pull the ripcord. In a similar manner, we have to have faith in our Higher Self to guide us through our free-fall to what is next in life.

William Bridges shares this view in The Way of Transition when he writes,

> "But the transition process does not depend on there being a replacement reality waiting in the wings. You are in transition automatically when some part of our life ends. Predetermined outcomes certainly make things easier, but we're in transition with or without them. If they are not there, we have to create the outcomes ourselves."

So there are no guarantees, but we cannot stop change because of uncertainty.

When we withdraw back into our old thoughts, beliefs and patterns, we may think that we are retreating to a secure position, but the reality is we are even more vulnerable. Our old way of being has died and, like a discarnate spirit, we try to return to what is gone forever.

Our natural laws teach us that resistance is always met by an increased, opposing force. So when we resist change it naturally becomes more intense. When we enter into change we are better off looking into what needs to be released and begin the process of saying goodbye. Looking at what needs to be released makes the process easier because, once inquired into, what needs to be released is not as big or bad as we first may have first thought. This inquiry also helps us to realize what we are carrying forward, and the resulting realization can be very reassuring. We are never asked to give up what we really need. It takes wisdom, however, to understand what we *really* need. Change helps us to understand what we really need from what we *think* we need. So the quicker we release into change the sooner we find out what we really need. Right now your Higher Self is saying, "That makes sense." and your ego is saying, "You have got to be kidding!" Learn to trust the small, quiet voice of the Higher Self.

Saying Goodbye to Self-Confidence

One of the reasons we resist letting go is the effect it has on our self-confidence. The ego is deeply invested in self-confidence. Self-confidence creates a sense of stability and well-being; both reinforcing the ego's self image. When we enter into change our self-confidence is naturally challenged. In the first phase of saying goodbye our self-confidence is challenged as our old persona begins to break apart. The ego immediately defends itself by invoking our sense of loss in self-confidence. As a result, we almost always have a knee-jerk reaction in an effort to retain our level of self-confidence. It is important to note that this knee-jerk reaction is emotionally based and not consistent with reality.

What is critical to discern at this point is the difference between self-confidence and awareness of our Higher Self. Self-confidence is an ego façade, a mask we wear to project an image of personal power and assurance out into the world. We come to believe that projecting self-confidence will help us get what we want and protect us from potential threats. Change easily strips away this mask, leaving us with a sense of vulnerability, as we struggle with feelings of uncertainty. This uncertainty may be real or perceived but its effect is the same. Time and again self-confidence fails us during change but the ego always seems to trick us into reconnecting with our self-confidence to support the ego's self-image. What the ego is looking for is an alley in resisting change.

During our most troubling situations the ego may use negative self-confidence to remain in charge. By negative self-confidence I mean where we take on the responsibility for bad things that happen to others. We take responsibility for negative outcome to others, as well as ourselves. We take on full responsibility for change, thinking if we just did some things differently everything would have turned out for the better. This negative self-confidence comes from the ego's view that it is better to assume full responsibility and remain in total control than to admit that there are some things we cannot control and just are. This negative self-confidence lays the groundwork for co-dependent behaviors. Our negative self-confidence provides support and resistance for another's loss of self-confidence when both are going through change.

In some cases we are so devastated by this loss of self-confidence that we cannot recover, becoming a perpetual, powerless victim. This is a fallback position for the ego. Our new persona is one of a helpless, clinging vine, always dependent on others for security and safety. The ego would rather perpetuate feelings of hopelessness than loose it's hold over who we think we are. This becomes an indirect control over our experience.

When our awareness of the Higher Self increases the need for self-confidence decreases. Our strength comes from our connection to Spirit, rather than being isolated within our ego-centric self. Our confidence comes from a Power flowing though us, offering infinite strength and ability. This Power is without limits and cannot be contained. Our sense of connection to everything leaves us without an enemy. Resistance is replaced with adaption. We adapt with, rather than resist, change and life. From a place of Higher Awareness we see our being as evolving, rather than being destroyed. Who we are is fluid, constantly in motion. We accept the fluctuation of motion, understanding that the long view sees progress.

We see that a perceived negative change is just a part of a natural cycle that evolves into a positive. We have confidence that a Higher Good is evolving in our life and that patience may be required to fully experience the outcome. Our confidence expands to a higher level, replacing our dependence on the self. Our confidence is no longer based in an ego-centric self thus eliminating any resistance. This higher level of confidence is rooted in the Infinite, without limits, and cannot be threatened.

The ego will continue to contest our awareness of the Higher Self as it is a direct threat to its authority and existence. It will call upon self-confidence to resist uncertainty and change. We can halt this process by letting go of the ego's need for self-confidence and just trust in our Higher Self. We replace self-confidence with faith and trust in our connection to the Infinite through our Higher Self. We trust in what we really are.

Over the years I have worked with clients who are in the midst of a career change, sometimes self-induced and other times forced. In all cases the biggest stumbling block is their ability to let go of their perceived, work persona. After years of working with their ego to design value, worth and self-confidence around what they do it is terrifying to think about a change. I always start with the question, "Is what you do the ultimate definition of who you are?" Sometimes the answer comes easily, other times it is quite difficult, but the eventual realization is 'no'. Once a client has come to this realization we can begin the process of saying goodbye to their old ego-persona that was based on what they did and move to a greater understanding of who they really are now, which will support what they are doing now.

In looking at who they are clients come to realize that they are constantly changing, always in a state of flux. By inquiring into a deeper need for stability clients inevitably find it in their Higher Self. As we work to define where they are in their evolutionary process and what is next self –confidence is transformed into *Self Awareness*.

Saying Goodbye to Perfection

Religion and society have joined forces to convince us that perfection is our ultimate goal. We bow to a prefect God and try to emulate It. The desire for perfection then becomes our deepest, internal stumbling block to moving forward and letting go. The desire for perfection leads us into a fear of moving forward with our choices, thinking they may not be 'perfect' and, therefore, lead us to disaster (even greater imperfection). There is also a fear of letting go as we perceive that whatever gains we have made towards perfection will be lost if we let go of who we think we are, what we do, what we have believed to be true. We become trapped in a self-conceived labyrinth that defines our quest for perfection. So our quest for perfection provides resistance to change and the initial phase of 'saying goodbye'. Simply stated, we resist saying goodbye as it reveals our imperfections.

The quest for perfection is, in reality, an attempt by the ego to achieve divine status. Its siren song is, "I must strive for my perfection and then I will be happy." Unfortunately this is not how life or God work. Life is evolutionary and is backed by an evolutionary God within each of us. This means that our goal is to grow and expand, rather than become perfect. When we let go of our egotistic need for perfection and accept our own imperfections as part of the growth process we remove the self-imposed obstacles of perfection. We understand that choices are often imperfect but are part of the growth process. The need to have a specific outcome to our choices (perfection) is replaced by a desire to move forward (growth). From this orientation change is natural and saying goodbye is not a loss but the beginning of moving on. We are just taking the next step on our path to who we are to become; and who we are to become represents growth.

It's not easy to let go of this ego-centric need for perfection. Over the centuries it has become the standard perception of the Divine for many religions, especially Christianity. God is perfect and man is the fallen son of God, fraught with imperfection but striving to return to perfection. From this initial perception comes the genesis of original sin and judgment. Our only salvation is to strive for and achieve perfection or to pray for redemption. This perception is inherently resistant to choice and change, yet we have so ingrained this perception into our psyche that it is often a reflex reaction to change.

I would like to paraphrase from a recent lecture by Sister Joan Chittister, a world-renowned contemplative, mystic and Benedictine Nun. 'God is the God of Creation, where God humbly shares the power of creation with all life. God is also the God of evolution, the God of becoming. It is God's inherent urge within us to grow. That is the Divine Seed within each of us. The purpose of life, then, is growth not perfection. Life from this perspective takes on promise, possibility and invites us to change.'

From this perspective God, in Its infiniteness, is dynamic, rather than static. Perfection is a static state, so if God is dynamic then God is actually evolving instead of being perfect. This allows us the opportunity to be co-creative in that evolution with God; partners in change, rather than separate from a God who is an observer of change and who dishes out judgment. Change then is an aspect of God and not a separate event. Change is inherently Divine and worthy of our attention and involvement. Quite simply, all change is Divinely inspired and a good thing.

My first marriage covered a span of thirty-six years. During the last ten years we had both stagnated into polite interactions that, for the most part, were without love or meaningful interaction. Our individual interests and lives were drifting further and further apart. A question I was later to take into deep inquiry was, "Why did it take ten years to decide to make a change?"

After years of reflection and therapy I became increasingly aware of how perfection handcuffed my ability to say goodbye. My sense of self for the first twenty-five years was based on a desire to be perfect. I constantly strived to be the perfect husband, perfect father and perfect provider. This need for perfection trumped any desire for growth and discovery. My unrealistic desire for perfection restricted my thinking and behavior, limiting in my options and willingness to change.

To be blunt with myself, the desire for perfection became a major stumbling block to facing my internal desire to actively attempt to repair or leave the marriage. I was afraid to loose the level of perfection I had gained with my children, friends and employer. I had invested years in creating an inflated, false persona and it took tremendous energy and effort to just keep it up. I secretly pursued my passions for psychological and spiritual growth but, at the same time, could not see how my desire for perfection was actually inhibiting my own internal growth. I was intellectually knowledgeable but emotionally underdeveloped. In short, my need for perfection left me emotionally dead.

Fortunately I was subject to fierce Grace. All aspects of my life began to unravel and my false persona was fully exposed. Forced change became my salvation, allowing me to give up perfection for evolution. As painful as the process was at the time, I look back and realize it was the only way I was going to awake from my emotional hibernation. I would not become authentic and whole unless I successfully navigated the changes before me. Saying goodbye was difficult at first, but as time went on it became easier and easier as the need for perfection dissipated.

Today I recognize and honor my imperfections and allow them to guide me towards whom I am to become. My imperfections offer the doorway to greater clarity and help to initiate the next phase of change. Change is now an integral part of my evolutionary cycle and I am much more alive for it. I honor who I am without any need for perfection.

THE EMOTIONS OF SAYING GOODBYE

Emotions have been shown to be the seat of our memories, and in the process of 'saying goodbye' memories are frequently a major stumbling block. Memories can hold us to 'what was', even if 'what was' is no longer serving us or has simply disappeared into the past. While our minds may have accepted change our emotions will pull us back to our memories. These memories often support a desire to resist and deny that life has moved on. We become deluded into thinking that if we just somehow reconstruct the past that all will be well. In our minds we may know that this is not realistic, but our feelings, as we well know, aren't always coherent with thought. We can become delusional to the past, painting a false picture of 'what was', which, in turn, leads to confusion in the present and freezes our inner need to move on.

The fourth wave of psychology is based in Emotionally Focused Therapy, where it is recognized that our feelings and emotions are the 'first responders' to all external events and will often not be coherent to thought. Simply, we feel before we think and these feelings can influence and even override any thoughts we have about a situation. Change will commonly bring up feeling of uncomfortableness, which may be attached to old, integrated feelings of fear. The fear may be based in a past event that is totally unrelated, but its integration with feelings of being uncomfortable will combine to cause resistance to change. The emotional construct of being uncomfortable and fearful will override the reality of change. We find ourselves resisting without actually knowing why.

This is where the tool of inquiry once again becomes critical. If we stop to look at the genesis of our resistance by diving into the related emotions we can test the legitimacy of what we are feeling. If we can separate the origins of 'feeling uncomfortable' from the origins of 'fear' then we can see what is behind the emotion of resistance to saying goodbye. It is natural to experience some level of feeling uncomfortable as we let go of something long held dear to us. Yet the fear of loss is often unfounded, based on a past event that may be totally unrelated.

Christy was having difficulties in saying goodbye to a relationship that she understood neither her partner nor she was invested in any longer. As we investigated her feelings about saying goodbye she expressed a deep fear of ending the relationship, but was not able to immediately articulate why.

As we took the inquiry process deep into her fear what surfaced was repeated incidents as a child where her attempts at independence were harshly responded to by her parents. Christy was emotionally expectant that ending her current relationship would end in harsh retributions from her partner.

As we look at her fear in the light of the present Christy became convinced that her partner would not react like her parents. We discussed the difficulties of saying goodbye and it was clear that the situation would be uncomfortable but was not anything she should fear.

Christy was able to then end the relationship without drama or incident.

Our emotional responses play a critical role in the entire change process so we will discuss them at the end of each chapter in this section. Emotions seem to be the most intense during the first phase of 'saying goodbye' as this phase is where we have frequently stumbled in the past. It is important to look carefully at the genesis of our emotions as we start the change process and make sure we are not dragging unrelated experiences from the past into the current change process. Change is difficult enough to initiate without dragging in old feelings and emotions.

SAYING GOODBYE, THE END OR THE BEGINNING

Make no mistake about it, saying goodbye does herald an end to some aspect of our life. What has been will not be as we move forward; at least not exactly as it has been in the past. It is difficult to start change when we realize that we may be letting go of a significant personal investment in time, energy and self to allow change to move us forward. If we honor these contributions as part of our evolution to get us to the current change then the loss is not as great. We invested to get us to this point. It is like a booster rocket, which is essential to get us to orbit but would only drag us back into the atmosphere if we didn't jettison it. In this way nothing is wasted or lost. In this way 'saying goodbye' becomes a right of passage to who we are to become.

So 'saying goodbye' is an ending and a beginning. The beginning cannot successfully occur without the ending. While people, places and things may be physically lost we carry forward the meaning they have provided within us. We would not be able to move forward without letting go. It is with gratitude then that we say goodbye and fall into the mysterious arms of change.

CHAPTER EIGHT

EXPLORING THE PRESENT: WILDERNESS TRAINING

It seems terrifying not to know what's coming next. But there is another time, a better time, when we see our lives as a series of choices, and What Now represents our excitement and our future, the very vitality of life. It's up to you to choose a life that will keep expanding. It takes discipline to remain curious; it takes work to be open to the world - but oh my friends, what noble and glorious work it is. Maybe this is the moment that you shift from seeing What Now as one more thing to check off the list and start to see it as two words worth living by.

Ann Patchett, <u>What Now?</u>

Life will give you whatever experience is most helpful for the evolution of your consciousness. How do you know this is the experience you need? Because this is the experience you are having at the moment.

Eckhart Tolle

At some point in the change process we have let go of the past enough that our attention now turns to the present. It is the present where we actually live and breathe, no matter where our ego and mind try to take us. It is the present moment that will give us the clues we need to set our new direction and new way of being during the change process. If we ignore or deny the clues given us as we navigate the present, then we will not maximize our potential evolution to the next level of being that we are destined to achieve. We become weighed down or stuck in old ways of being. The outward appearances may change but the way we respond to life will remain the same. The present offers us the opportunity to understand and create *real* change.

It is for these reasons that we need to give our full attention and time to the present moment during the change process. The present moment brings us a clear understanding of the shifting internal and external changes that will influence our ongoing development and growth.

Internally we are responding differently to life; but we are frequently unaware of these differences unless we take the time to be fully conscious of all that is taking place within us. Thoughts, beliefs, feelings, emotions and desires are all taking new forms. How we view and react to life has shifted. These responses are instinctual in our evolving orientation to life. They represent a shift from our old methods of responding. They are adaptations to what we have experienced and learned. If we ignore them we will fall back into old, familiar patterns of responding and we will quickly lose our new, more effective, ways of navigating life. So change facilitates the recognition and acceptance of new ways of responding to life, but change cannot force meaningful adaption and incorporation of these new ways of response. We must consciously decide to embrace our new ways of responding to life.

Change also subtlety or overtly altars our external world. Our present moment becomes less predictable, old patterns are broken and we are left with uncertainty as to what comes next. It is this uncertainty that often causes us to attempt to ignore the external happenings of the present moment and to drift back into the past in search of our lost sense of security. It is important to note that this doesn't change what is happening in the present, and it leaves us less capable of responding effectively to our external environment. This is where many people start to become dysfunctional and maladaptive. So it is essential that we hold our awareness in the present and look carefully for the meaning that change is creating in our life. To quote again Eckhart Tolle, "Some changes look negative on the surface but you will soon realize that space is being created in your life for something new to emerge."

The present moment is creating that space for something new to emerge. This is a birthing process and requires time and patience. Like a mother in labor we cannot force the natural process of change. Each contraction may be painful but the mother has to keep a larger view of what is happening; something new and wonderful is being birthed. We must have this same, larger view when we are set adrift in the present moment.

Oscar had received an offer for a new sales management position with a competitor that brought a significant increase in pay. Oscar quickly accepted the offer and was in his new position two weeks later. Not having been in management before Oscar became concerned when he discovered he was not going to get any, significant management training and was just expected to lead and perform. He quickly became uncomfortable and was wondering if he had made the right decision. He was great at sales but had no idea on how to lead a sales force. Oscar was considering asking his old company to take him back. He sought my help in making a decision to stay or leave his new opportunity.

We started with a deep inquiry into his current position. As we reviewed his first month in the new position it became apparent that Oscar was fearful of his management ability but he also admitted that he was not overtly failing. His sales staff were receptive and accepting of what direction he was providing. The floor had not fallen out of sales, in fact, sales were actually up slightly. By observing what was really going on in the present Oscar's fear of failure abated to a point where he was thinking more clearly and not frozen the fear of failure.

We then turned our attention to what was different inside Oscar. First, Oscar could no longer just take direction; he had to provide it. We started to look into the basic skills that Oscar had related to the sales process and how he could apply them to directing his sales staff. Oscar was able to provide a list of sales techniques and methods, which he had learned over the years that might be valuable to his new sales staff. We also uncovered that Oscar had been successful in leading various groups at his church resulting in positive outcomes. We agreed that several of the skills Oscar had tested with his church would be applicable to leading the sales team. In short, Oscar had something to offer as a manager.

Next we explored where Oscar felt he needed help. We reviewed a variety of management skills necessary for success and where Oscar would rate himself for competency. First, to Oscar's surprise, we found that there were several areas that he already had some general competency. We then outlined the areas where Oscar felt he had little competency and developed a plan. Oscar would ask his boss to mentor him in these areas. He also was committed to researching and attending some specific business courses, like finance, where Oscar felt weak. On approaching his boss with his perceived short-comings and desire for help Oscar found his boss quite receptive and willing to pitch in with mentoring. In the weeks to come this strengthened the relationship between Oscar and his boss as he was open and honest about where he needed help. Oscar attended a finance course at a local college and was better able to read the company financial statements as they related to sales and revenue performance. His personal commitment to growth was also well received by his boss.

As we looked back Oscar was now happy that he had decided to stick with his new, management position and he now trusted that he had made the right choice. Slowly, as we dealt with each fear and need Oscar became a manager and grew in internal confidence. Oscar finally came to the conclusion that, whether he succeeded or not in this position, he is capable of leading a sales team and is an effective manager.

Oscar's instincts told him he was ready to make the change into management; however, he had not taken the time to explore what that meant in the present moment. Through our work together we were able to take an honest look at the skills Oscar already had for management and how he could quickly improve. Oscar was internally ready for change but just didn't fully understand how that would translate into his new job. Inquiry in the present moment helped Oscar to get over his fears and arrested his desire to retreat. Another Tolle quote fits here,

"You find peace not by rearranging the circumstances of your life, but by realizing who you are at the deepest level."

WHY THE PRESENT MOMENT IS SO DIFFICULT

When we get to this point in the change process it is like stepping out into the wilderness. The wilderness is exciting and intriguing, but uncertain and scary at the same time. There is great beauty and great, perceived danger. The wilderness is wild! We have a general idea as to where we are going but nothing is certain. The fear of getting lost is always, to some degree, in the back of our mind. We cannot tame the wilderness, just survive in it. All of this is a real threat to the ego, who desires complete control.

The present moment is just like the wilderness. We can't control it, no matter how hard we try. There is always some aspect that we cannot fully influence or manipulate towards our desires. The present moment requires that we adapt and it is this adaption that threatens the ego the most.

While the present moment is not controllable it does offer unlimited opportunities. Anything goes in the present moment. This is why it is so unnerving and so exciting. We just need to understand how to work with it.

When we are surprised by change we are like a camper going into the wilderness without adequate camping equipment. We have no idea if we are carrying enough water, if we have enough food and if we have enough clothing to keep us warm. This is exactly why we need to take our time in exploring the present. We need not rush into any situation that will put us at odds with the present. At the same time we need to be hyper observant and fully take in our surroundings. The more we take in, the more clues come to us as to how we are to proceed and in what direction. Change requires our full attention and patience.

While change frequently offers subtle clues as to who we are becoming and what direction we should lean towards, the present moment doesn't offer the comfort of certainty. The future is often muddled by what is going on in the present moment, so it is natural to have feelings of discomfort. It is paralyzing, however, when the ego co-opts discomfort and ramps it into deep-seeded fear of change. The affect and effect is resistance to the present moment specifically and change in general. Our response is fright or flight, freeze or retreat. When we freeze our behaviors become dysfunctional and we do not respond properly to our current situation. When we retreat, we go back to the past and the old ways, even if they no longer serve us.

The ego uses the mind to pull our attention away from the present moment, either retreating into the past or visioning a future that is not congruent with the present moment. The past offers the comfort of more of the same. A fantasized future offers the comfort of the return of a false sense of certainty by crafting a vision of stability that is congruent with the needs of the ego but not our current situation. Neither is real, we just wish they were.

Unfortunately society is not much help during change (transition). William Bridges summarizes this point quite eloquently in The Way of Transition,

> "If a transition goes satisfactorily, of course, it finishes with a new pattern of meaning emerging from the chaos left by the destruction of the old one. But since we lack the societal acknowledgement of (and any social support during) most of these disenchantments, the experience easily degenerates into simply one of personal loss. In that case, it is stripped of its significance. The person in such a transition is no longer someone shedding an outlived shell of reality, but simply a victim of an unfortunate (and essentially meaningless) personal experience."

I have found that most people come to see me because they are unable to fully connect with and respond to life in the present moment. Emotional dysfunction is commonly a result of the ego in control and the person turning their back on what is going on now. Most of the initial work I do with people is focused on a greater awareness of the present moment. Many are lost in the ego's story of the past. They resist the circumstances of the present by creating a story that often represents the 'tragic hero', who has been unfairly treated by the present. The story is filled with explanations why they are not responsible for what is happening to them. It is critical to put a halt to the story and ground consciousness in what is really happening in the present. By halting the story it helps us to move towards more appropriate actions and responses to current circumstances. Our only reality is in the now. Eckhart Tolle from <u>The Power of Now</u>, "Realize deeply that the present moment is all you have. Make the NOW the primary focus of your life."

ALIGNING WITH THE WISDOM OF THE PRESENT

Before we can fully explore the present we have to allow ourselves to step outside our perceived realities, strip bare our ego-persona, and become acutely aware of our connection to everything in the now. We can only find the wisdom of the present and that wisdom can only come when we are no longer separate from it. The key to the present comes with being fully immersed in the now. Through this deep connection with the present we align our experience with life as it unfolds. It is like floating in a river and allowing the current to carry you forward. This unfolding is evolutionary, so it is always, eventually, to our benefit. Whatever comes, good or bad, if we just stay with it and don't turn away the result will be metamorphic to our soul. Your soul understands this and encourages you on, even in difficult times. The ego, however, wants to cut and run.

Belief in the evolutionary power of the present is the only real way to break down the resistance of our ego. Quoting again Eckhart Tolle, "Life will give you whatever experience is most helpful for the evolution of your consciousness. How do you know this is the experience you need? Because this is the experience you are having at the moment."

There are several steps we can take to align with the wisdom of the present. They require an open mind and a courageous heart.

Taking Responsibility for the Present Moment

While we may take some comfort in telling our story about how we got to this present moment, our story holds no relevance in the present moment and does not help us accept and deal with the here and now. When we don't take responsibility for how we got to the present we become disconnected and respond in an inappropriate manner to our present condition. It is not uncommon to engage in magical thinking, where if we ignore the present imagining that it will just go away. We devalue life's circumstances, thinking we can assume control, by denying, what is happening right now. All of this magical thinking may make us feel better in the short-term, but the present moment and life keeps moving forward. The longer we stay in our story/fantasy the further we drift away from the reality of our condition and the harder it is to regain connection with the now. In our distraction from reality we get into deeper difficulties and suffering returns with a vengeance.

It is important then that we fully accept our role in how we have arrived to where we are. It is just not possible to be where we are now without our active acceptance and participation in past, present moments. We may not be totally responsible for where we are now, but we did play a significant role in how we got to the now. Our thoughts, beliefs, feelings, decisions, expressions and actions all played a part in shaping the present. Fully realizing our part in our evolution is a critical alignment with the present. By taking the time to become fully aware and accepting of our influence in getting to the now we become open to discovering and aligning with the direction our life is taking. In this way, taking responsibility is key to discovering our path through the wilderness.

Nathan was applying for college and had become extremely distressed because he was not getting accepted to the schools he most wanted to attend. He felt their criteria were too strict and that his score on his SAT exam was not a true reflection of his capabilities. Nathan was angry and frustrated with his current situation and his parents had not been able to set down and discuss his troubles with him to his satisfaction. Nathan sought my help in getting out of his current situation.

My initial meeting with Nathan was spent tracing backwards through his educational history, looking to find how it had brought him to his current position. Nathan told many stories of classes he didn't like and teachers he thought did a poor job in teaching. Nathan was angry with his parents for not pushing him harder and angry with his school guidance counselor for attempting to direct him towards a career in the trades or possibly accepting going to a local, community college. I asked Nathan what responsibility he had accepted to his current level of education and preparation for college.

At first Nathan was unwilling to accept any responsibility, but I continued to press him. I refused to move forward with his decisions until he accepted responsibility for his role in getting to the now. Slowly, reluctantly Nathan began to accept that he had chosen to not seriously study for his classes in high school and that he was more interested in socializing and dating than in getting good grades. When I asked Nathan what vocation he was moving towards he didn't have a clue. His immediate response was, "Isn't that what college is for?" I inquired as to how he knew which college was the best fit for him if he didn't even have any general areas of interest he wanted to pursue. I asked Nathan to take some time to consider what he liked to do, what inspired him, what brought meaning to his life. I also asked Nathan to consider what responsibility he had in his poor grades and weak selection of electives during his high school year. I told Nathan to not schedule another appointment until he was ready to honestly discuss all of these topics.

Six weeks passed before Nathan rescheduled. To his credit Nathan had done some deep soul searching and was starting to accept some responsibility for his current condition. Nathan admitted that he did not take his high school education seriously and had very poor study habits. He just wanted to get buy; doing only what was necessary to get average grades. I asked Nathan if he had earned the right to attend the colleges he wanted to attend. Reluctantly Nathan admitted he had not. I praise Nathan for accepting his role in arriving at his current situation.

We then began to explore what interested Nathan. Nathan, like many youth of today, was obsessed by computers, the Internet and video games. As we inquired deeper into why he liked all of these areas of technology, he said he was fascinated how it drew people in and influenced their decisions. He was especially interested in Social Media and how Facebook and Twitter influenced his friends. I asked Nathan to meet with a career counselor I knew to dive deeper into these areas.

Two weeks later Nathan returned all excited about his discussion with the counselor. They had discussed the area of Internet marketing and it struck a chord with Nathan. They had discussed good schools that provided majors related to Internet marketing. The counselor also suggested that he might want to get a minor in computer sciences. The problem was, Nathan did not have the grades to get into these schools right away. The counselor had discussed community colleges that offered great, preparatory courses to get into the schools he wanted to attend. Still confused, Nathan returned to work through his newfound knowledge about himself and his college career.

I returned to the topic of Nathan's acceptance of responsibility in being where his is now. Through our conversations Nathan accepted that he was not prepared to go to a four-year college and was willing to accept attending a community college for one or two years. I asked him how he was going to change his behaviors going forward, based on where he was now. Nathan understood that he could not expect anyone else to improve his study habits. He had to focus on completing the work necessary to get good grades. He also came to accept that he could not blame others for poor performance. Nathan was excited about the classes he was planning to take at the community college and saw it as a way to motivate him to better study habits. Nathan was finally grounded in the present moment.

Two years later I got a note from Nathan telling me he had graduated from the community college with a 3.7 grade point average and had been accepted to the four-year college he most wanted to attend for Internet marketing. Nathan was confident in his ability to succeed at the next level of his education. Nathan's willingness to accept responsibility for his present situation freed him to explore and make wise choices in his present moments. He aligned himself with life and used that energy to forge a path towards his newfound dream. A dream based in the reality of the present.

Nathan's story is not just a story about the hubris of youth. Falling into our story and fantasizing away from the reality of the present can and does occur at all ages. This is really a story of all human nature. What is important is when we sooner than later take responsibility for our getting to our present condition and to move forward fully aware of our connection to what is now.

Becoming Patient with the Present

There are no set timelines as to how long we spend exploring the present before we experience the insights and gain the confidence that will define how we move on. This period of exploration could range from minutes to years. The key to exploring the present is to suspend any expectation of a defined timeframe for definitive action. This doesn't mean that we don't start taking baby-steps in the exploration process. When we are lost in the wilderness the best action is to explore several paths in an effort to gain clarity in choosing one path forward. This process can be slow and tedious, with initial feelings we are going nowhere. Trust and patience is required to allow us to get reoriented.

For the western mind this need to be patient flies in the face of all that we have learned. We have been raised to set a vision, establish goals, monitor closely our progress, and take immediate and decisive action. Yet we are also advised in the Bible, Ecclesiastes 3:1, *"To every thing there is a season, and a time to every purpose under the heaven."* So who and what are right? Yes, it is important to establish a rhythm to our lives. We often call this rhythm our routine. Our routine helps us to survive, act efficiently and be productive. Routine is necessary for our daily existence. Yet change breaks, in some part or whole, our routine; and it is in this break that we must allow the old to be released and the new to be defined.

Routine is managed by the mind, but when it is broken we require the insight of the Soul to help us determine what the new path and new routines will be. It is the wisdom of the Soul, through its connection with the Infinite, that takes the higher view, the long view of our evolution. The Soul will provide the insights needed but it operates in the infinite, without specific timeframes. We cannot force insight. In fact, the more we try to force it, the longer it will take to find it. Insight appears in the quiet spaces when the mind is at rest. This rest may be a second, a minute or longer. Resting the mind is the fertile ground by which we allow insight to sprout into the light of thought.

So our job in exploring the present is not to try and think our way to what is next and who we are becoming. Our job is to be patient, aware of the present moment, attentive to events as they unfold, and willing to look for the patterns that develop in the present, which will lead us to the keys for insight. In the present moment we are provided with small pointers, which help us to position our whole being for insight. By being patient we are being open, and it is in this openness that the way is revealed.

I am not intimating that exploring the present is a totally passive experience. Being open and aware does not equate to being passive and not taking action. Exploring is an action verb and it is in thoughtful actions we gain further insights and truth. There are several tools we can call upon to help us in exploring.

TOOLS OF THE PRESENT MOMENT

There are some principles and techniques that can assist us in exploring the present. Each has a quality that promotes insight. I will outline a few that I have found to be most helpful.

Using Meditation to Create the Space for Insight

The use of meditation during our exploration of the present is a sound way to allow for this fertile ground to flourish with insights. Whatever meditation practice you learn it will serve two purposes.

First, meditation slows the mind and allows for us to see the 'space between'. It is in these gaps that insight is born. It is in this silence that we can hear the quiet voice of our Soul. The longer you can allow the 'space between' to be present the greater the potential for insight. At first it might be only a second or two. The critical point is to give this space your full attention and rest in this space as long as you can. The ego/mind will be resistant at first, wanting to regain control and to take you in its direction. With some practice even the ego/mind becomes intrigued and wants to observe what is going on. Once you have the ego/mind hooked it is easier to get to the 'space between' and to stay there for some time.

This special place offers more than insights. It is also a place for gaining great clarity around the present. It also provides almost instant emotional rebalancing. When you are upset with your current situation going to the 'space between' takes the edge off of the situation and allows you to expand into a new perspective. It is a place to find some relief from your story about what is happening and to find a greater reality in the present. This special place also provides an opening into the second benefit of meditation.

Meditation also helps to ground us in the present. We simply are open and observant during meditative practice. When we see our mind start to wonder into the past or future, we simply note this movement of the mind and gently allow our thoughts to return to the present. Meditation helps us to sustain our observation of the present moment by being aware when our mind desires to go elsewhere. The ego hates meditation because the ego lives in the past and future. That is why so many of us struggle with a consistent meditative practice. Over time, if we are persistent in regular practice, the ego learns to live with the present moment. It realizes that the present moment will create changes but it is not a direct threat to the existence of the ego. The ego learns to play with the Soul in the present moment.

The Buddhists commonly use a technique of just observing the breath as a pathway into deeper meditative practice. They observe the inhalation, the slight pause and the gentle exhalation with each cycle of breathing. This focus on the breath provides a landmark that makes it easy to see when the mind begins to wonder from the present moment. We see the shift and gently return thought to the breath. This is initially torture to the busy ego/mind. The observation of the breath is very mundane and the ego/mind quickly becomes bored. With practice, however, we become able to see the many dimensions of the breath. No two are alike. Each breath seems to hold its own special purpose. Some breaths clear the mind; others release an emotion; and some sustain our actions. We live because of the breath. And finally, when we begin to see that pause between exhalation and inhalation, we discover a place of deep peace. In this peace are further seeds of insight.

After practicing the breath meditation for some time you will become aware of the role that the breath can take in making you more aware of all that is occurring as you react to the present moment. It is particularly helpful in sorting out emotional reactions to the present. If you notice the breath quickening you will be able to stop momentarily and see what is the emotion behind it. There might be excitement or fear. Being aware of your emotional state in present moment will lead to clearer evaluations of what is taking place and in making positive and effective decisions.

These are only two aspects of how meditation helps us in navigating the present. There are many more to discover the longer you practice. Meditation has much to teach us about our connection with all things and our interdependency with the simplest elements of life. Meditation leaves the mind open, responsive and flexible; a perfect vessel for change and exploration of the present. With sustained effort meditation moves from being a practice to a way of being. Start with the simple breath meditation and see where it takes you with even moderate effort.

Exploring the Present Is a Time to Slow Down

When we become grounded in the present we come to understand that there is so much to take in. We realize that the present moment is jam-packed with information, events, activity, people, animals, nature and more. We can become overwhelmed by how much there is to take in when we are first fully awake in the present. It is incumbent on us to slow down if we are going to take in all that is essential to understand all that is taking place and how to respond in a positive and productive manner as we move through the change process.

As change breaks our patterns for living we enter into new territory. When we feel lost in the wilderness we have an instinctual tendency to want to slow down, reorienting our self to our surroundings. Change beckons us to realize where we are now. Change, however, will also trigger a level of anxiety that urges us to move faster to escape what we find uncomfortable or unpleasant. It is critical to realize that we have opposing emotional and mental responses during change. The advantage to slowing down is the opportunity we gain to not miss what is important. During change we are surrounded by a plethora of important signs and information. Don't speed by it in fear. Take a deep breath and slow down .

As we slow down and become more aware of where change is taking us we also gain clues as to our Soul's involvement in creating and supporting the change we are experiencing. Our Soul knows that change is coming long before the mind is conscious of change and it is the Soul that understands the purpose and importance of current changes to our evolution. It is the Soul that conspires with life to bring forth events and interactions, which facilitate the change process. When we slow down it is easier to discern the meaning of change and to allow ourselves to go with the flow. Slowing down will decrease our resistance and increase our Soul awareness, as we learn a new way of being.

As mentioned when we have that uncomfortable feeling that comes with change, we have a tendency to want to speed up rather than slow down. To push on, hoping that things will return to how they were. By speeding up we will most likely miss the real purpose of change and not be aware of its importance to our growth. Like a stone hurtled into a pond, we can skip across the surface of change and loose the opportunity to become immersed in its wisdom. When this happens change will return with greater force, and it is this greater force that will require us to eventually slow down. It is wiser to recognize the importance of stepping back and slowing down with the initial changes that come our way. It is a lot less painful.

The Importance of Slowing Down with Addiction

I frequently encounter this reluctance to slow down and seek the meaning of change in interacting with people who have addiction issues. Their addictions will start to create small changes in their life; trouble in a relationship, difficulties at work, the withdrawal of family members. They move quickly past these changes and discount them in a manner that deflects attention away from their addictions. It normally takes a much more significant change, like getting divorced or being fired from a job, to get the person to stop and be fully present with the issue at hand. I believe that the person's Soul is crying out for conscious recognition of the addictive behavior and conspires to ramp up change until the person is willing to slow down or stop and honestly assess his or her current state of being.

The Soul desires freedom from addiction and a return to mental and physical health, and it will assist in bringing about events to shake the self from its dream and into full awareness. But the mind and body must slow down long enough to become fully aware of the impact that their addiction is having in order that they can gain the insight needed to accept a change in behavior. In the world of addiction this is called 'hitting the bottom'. In my way of thinking it is just the Soul getting the ego to step aside so that the individual can slow down and become aware of who and what they are in the present. In addiction we run from who we are in the present. The Soul knows we cannot make a change for the better without stopping and taking stock of where we really are and, more importantly, who we really are in the present moment.

This section is meant for all of us. We all have addictive behavior that supports the shadow side of our being. Big or small our addictions point to the shadow. It is up to us to slow down, stop and to inquire with an open mind into the shadow of who we are. We must shine a light into the darkness to find the path forward.

Slowing down is a tool to greater awareness. Slowing down allows us to see our connection and interplay with the world around us; it is the opportunity to understand that how we have been is no longer effective and that we need to change, we need to evolve. Slowing down allows us to align with and reconnect with life on a mental, emotional and energetic level.

Slowing Down to Recognize Our Connection to All of Life

When we slow down and become more aware of the present, we naturally become more aware of our connection with life. We come to experience that we are a part of and not separate from all that is around us. As we begin to see our connections we also fall into the rhythm and flow of life, which releases our fears and reveals all potentials and possibilities. Through this connection we can begin to explore what could be, without restrictions and limitations. We can also connect with our Soul and listen to Its *yearning* for our next step forward.

In the light of our connection to life change becomes a process, a continuum, not an ending without any sense of a new beginning. If change is an end to who we have been and a transformation to who we are to become, then change in this sense is death leading to rebirth. In a way change becomes a mini-death of self. Without a sense of the continuum, through our connection with life, change can be quite foreboding. By finding our connection in the present moment endings no longer exist. We become aware of the experiences that were before and the lessons they bring to the present. These lessons are the groundwork for the future. These lessons define what no longer works so that, through inquiry, we can gain insight into other ways of being.

Harriet and I met when she was discharged from a 48-hour suicide watch. She was classified as not in immediate danger of harming herself, properly medicated and now alone. Harriet had been in a long-term relationship that ended abruptly and badly. She had been totally committed to her partner, to the point that she had isolated herself from former friends and family. Even her work relationships did not extend outside of the office. Harriet had slowly, surely narrowed her interactions with others and was without substantive connections to life.

Like many suicidal patients, Harriet had seen the dark, confining tunnel after her break up. The tunnel was her pain and sense of isolation. She saw no way out and the tunnel was unbearable. Death seemed to be the only potential relief from her suffering. I knew that we needed to shine a light on this tunnel to allow Harriet to break free before she once again came to the conclusion that suicide was the only relief she could find.

We began our work inside the tunnel by challenging the rigidity of its structure. Harriet was in a self-imposed isolation and she needed to realize that she was capable of reconnecting with the world. We spent several hours together exploring her perceptions and feelings about the tunnel. The longer we spent in our inquiry the more porous the tunnel became. Harriet came to realize that she had created the tunnel through her single focused desire to please her partner. She also came to realize that her contraction was fueled by a fear of more broadly connecting with life. We explored the impact of allowing herself to become more and more isolated from her world. This put Harriet back in the drivers seat.

I started to work with Harriet on reconnecting, first with family and then with friends. Fortunately Harriet had caring parents, who her partner had convinced her to turn her back on. It took work and courage to get Harriet willing to make contact again with her parents. Overcoming her guilt and shame she summoned the courage to make the call. Like the prodigal son, or daughter in this case, Harriet was welcomed with open arms by her parents, who tearfully opened their home to her. Harriet found that this first, major hurdle was founded in unrealistic fear. Breaking this bond with fear was a critical, first step in gaining the courage to face other fears in connecting.

Now, with a loving and supporting home base, we started to work on other connections. I pursued with Harriet her relationships at work. She actually felt close to two female co-workers, but had never thought about getting together with them outside of work. I came to find out that her former partner had actually discouraged friendships at work, telling Harriet that she needed to be more committed to their relationship (a classic, co-dependent ploy). Harriet was worried about having to talk about her past. I assured her that there was enough to talk about in the present to fill any conversation. Harriet made the connection with an invitation for dinner after work, her treat. To her relief the two women focused on discussing the ins and outs of their lives, allowing Harriet to slowly open up about her self. She found that these two women shared many of the same hopes and fears that she had. They also offered vary different perspectives of how to deal with these hopes and fears. All of this helped break down the tunnel and offer new ways of change for Harriet.

Finally, I turned to Harriet's religious connections. Harriet had been raised in a Unitarian church but had not attended since she entered into her long-term relationship. She seemed comfortable with the open nature of the Unitarian church but held the belief that she would not be accepted back, since she had abandoned the church. Harriet's parents were instrumental in being her emissaries back into the congregation. She came to our next session tearful about the warm reception she had received on her return. Harriet reconnected with some old friend she had grown up with in the church. Another significant fear, long held, fell in the face of love and understanding.

At this point we had reconnected Harriet back to life and this gave us the opportunity to focus on the lessons learned. As we entered into an objective inquiry regarding her self-imposed isolation, created by her total surrender to the wishes of her partner, Harriet began to see the unhealthy nature of such a commitment. We discussed co-dependency and looked deeply into her own wounds that were fostering her behavior. Harriet's sense of self was changing dramatically. She now saw herself as a vibrant, independent woman, who was capable of developing deep connections with life. At last the tunnel completely collapsed upon itself. The new Harriet emerged with courage and few limitations.

Suicidal ideation is very common with individuals who have become isolated and disconnected from the life around them. Harriet came to realize the blessing bestowed upon her with the ending of her relationship, and she became mystified by her ever considering suicide. By bringing Harriet into the present and helping her to reconnect with a life she had abandoned Harriet's suffering had come to an end. More importantly, Harriet was now firmly committed to never giving herself totally to any relationship where her sense of connection with life would be sacrificed. She had come to realize that ignorance and fear had built her tunnel to suicide and it took her willingness to stop and seek the love around her to bust her free.

Connecting with life goes against the ego's need for separation. The ego uses separation to establish a sense of lack in our being. The sense of lack empowers the ego to drive us in the direction of seeking something more and different. This leads us to aggression or surrender. Harriet's ego had led her to surrender. By connecting with life we see that what is available to us is unlimited. We don't have to fight or give up to get what we need. Lack is replaced by choice. All that we have perceived to be missing in our life is now available to us when we allow ourselves to be present in the moment.

Many of the great masters have stated that we become enlightened when the seeker no longer seeks, when we stop and see it is all right here, right now.

Falling into Freedom

Change can be positive in nature and that makes it easy. However, change frequently will have a negative side that makes us resistant. In this case change is falling from the precipice that the ego has carried us to. A fall, however, that is really the beginning of our next evolution.

Before a fall our ego has lead us down an ever-confining path, creating and supporting a persona that is separate and unique. The ego defines who we are as 'special' and with this 'special' we are entitled to certain rights and privileges. In truth Life is based in equality and offers no privilege. This is where the fall comes. The fall is our wake up call to reality of equality with no privilege. It breaks the fantasy that the ego has created, leaving us bare and exposed. Yet is in the loss of privilege and a sense of separation that we find connection. Connection to all that is and the unlimited power and possibility that it provides.

Countless stories by survivors of plane crashes, who have been stranded in the wilderness, have recounted the sudden need to forget who they have been and to focus on the present situation. There is great energy in the desire to survive. Suddenly they were back to basics; food, water, shelter and calling for help became their central focus. Stories often recall these life-changing events as a discovery of a greater sense of being and the need to connect and support fellow survivors. Those who have gone through such ordeals come out a changed person.

In my own life I can look back and see that every great leap forward seems to be proceeded by a fall. Mine came in a successive flurry of events. It seemed to never have an ending. Loss of my corporate position (money and power), the end of my marriage and bankruptcy created a succession of falls for my over-inflated ego. As I look back now, without these events and the energy and insights they have brought me, I would have never awakened from the fantasy perpetrated by my ego over the years and I would have never became grounded in a more authentic way of being. It took the *good fortune* of all these falls to allow me to move into the present where I could find my purpose for this life. What a gift. What fierce Grace to the door of my next evolution.

Using Synchronicity to Help Guide Us Through Change

We are not left without guidance in the present. As noted, in the present moment we find our connections to all of life, and in those connections are the threads to what is possible. The word synchronicity was first coined by Carl Jung, as an aspect of the collective conscious and has become popular through the works of James Redfield. Synchronicity is defined in Wikipedia as, "the experience of two or more events that are apparently causally unrelated or unlikely to occur together by chance, yet are experienced as occurring together in a meaningful manner."

Jung saw that the interconnectedness of our minds draws us together in inexplicable ways that defy causal explanation. To Jung synchronicity is continually occurring in our lives but we normally just ignore it. Why? When we are unavailable to the present moment then we are often incapable of recognizing any synchronicitous events as they occur. They're there; we just choose to ignore them. Why? As I have discussed, the ego is working overtime to keep us locked into the past and the future. In the absence of present awareness we are blind to what is now, and synchronicities are only available in the present.

Suspending egoistic rule and turning our awareness into the present open our eyes to life's connections and the possibilities they bring. Change is often the catalyst needed to suspend egoistic rule, but we need to understand the opportunity that change is offering us.

Many people I have connected with over the years have shared countless stories of where they have been wondering about a long-lost friend only to have them almost simultaneously call on the phone. What transpires is a deep, evolutionary conversation that creates a shift for both individuals. I have also heard numerous stories of people thinking about a change in careers only to pick up a magazine or newspaper that has a story about the career they are thinking about. I have long experienced and become convinced that synchronicities abound in our life. The more focused I am in the present moment the more they appear for me. Finding these synchronicities does not require us to gain some special skill. All we need to do is tap into our awareness in the present. Often this is preceded by a decision to take the road less traveled. Synchronicities are most often found on unfamiliar grounds.

Finding the synchronicities, when we are exploring the present is a key tool to discovering where our Soul desires to take us. It is the language of the Soul through Its connection with the Infinite. Learning the language of synchronicity can help to accelerate the process of exploring the present. Following these thread of the Infinite can exponentially reduce our time in the wilderness.

WORKING TOWARDS MEANING IN THE PRESENT

By now I hope it is evident that the present moment is full of hope and opportunity. Allowing ourselves to get comfortable with the uncertainty of the present and to dive deeply into its lessons is the only sure way to discover what is next. Our lives are full of mini-deaths and rebirths. We evolve, we become and our Soul, through Its connection with life and the Infinite is our guide. Exploring the present is necessary to connect with the Soul and life, to gain clarity related to the reality of the now, and to reorient away from a selfish, egotistic self to a Self filled with purpose.

It is only fitting to end this chapter with another quote from Eckhart Tolle, "The primary cause of unhappiness is never the situation but thought about it. Be aware of the thoughts you are thinking. Separate them from the situation, which is always neutral. It is as it is."

CHAPTER NINE

MOVING ON: CREATING THE NEW SELF

"If you do follow your bliss you put yourself on a kind of track that has been there all the while, waiting for you, and the life that you ought to be living is the one you are living. Follow your bliss and don't be afraid, and doors will open where you didn't know they were going to be."

Joseph Campbell

"Making decisions about all the little things we will do with our lives out of all the possible things that life has to offer is one thing. Deciding what we want to become as a person as we do them is entirely another. What we will spend our lives doing is often a far less important question than what we want to end up being while we do whatever it is we do with however much time we have."

Joan Chittister, *Welcome to the Wisdom of the World*

Moving on is an awakening, followed by actions that move us forward. By awakening, I mean a mental and emotional trigger that says, "I'm ready for what is next!" It doesn't have to be a well-thought-out plan with a vision, mission and key objectives. An awakening is more of a gut sense of certainty that provides the energy to get moving. We may well have a fully developed plan, but it is not necessary. We may only need to be certain of the next step we are taking.

Moving on is overcoming our fear of failure, accepting that we could make some wrong decisions in the future, and also being willing to take the next step. There is no set process for moving on. We just are driven to the call for action by the energy generated from our 'ah, ha' moment of awakening.

A true awakening for moving on comes after we have been exploring the present, and not before. Many people are eager to get to what is next in change and short-circuit the process by jumping from saying goodbye to moving on. Usually the sense of certainty at these times is fragile at best, and can easily evaporate with a slight bump in the road. We often refer to this as making a 'snap decision'. What we gather by exploring the present becomes a key component to the awakening, which triggers moving on. We can't fall pray to a sense of urgency and must rely on our inner Self to let us know when the moment has arrived to move on.

I had been working on change with Dorothy for a couple months, making steady progress moving through a significant change process for her. Dorothy had been a program designer for a major software company in Silicon Valley. She had made a comfortable fortune on options when her company went public. Dorothy had been totally committed to her company and job. Unfortunately, her work-a-holic style of living had cost her a relationship she held dear. Dorothy had begun to question her life and was looking for change.

Dorothy and I had worked through much of 'saying goodbye' and had extensively been 'exploring the present'. She came into my office one day and started off with the question, "When am I ready to move on?" I just smiled and said, "You'll know when you tell me." I knew she was close. On her next visit, two weeks later, Dorothy walked in and sat down with a big smile on her face and simply said, "YEAH!!!" Dorothy had begun to move on.

Pervading thought pushes the idea that you need to have a solid plan in place to move on. I disagree. Moving on is initiated within each person when we get that feeling, that sense of freedom and excitement, that confidence, which speaks from our Soul to say, "I'm ready!" There may be a plan in place, underway or nonexistent, but a plan is not where moving on starts. What matters is that internal Gestalt feeling of a shift. This is a feeling, a sense, that who we have been has undergone enough, significant change so that who we are to become has initiated the birthing process.

For Dorothy she had not totally decided on the direction she wanted to take with career, relationships, family life and many other important areas for her. What Dorothy knew when she walked in that day was she was not going back. She had released her old way of being, had gained a much better understanding of who she is now, and she had a core confidence in making life decisions moving forward. I had only been her sounding board as she stepped forward into the future. Dorothy was no longer defining herself by what she had, what she did and what others thought of her. Dorothy did not totally see her purpose in life yet, but she had made the shift to wanting to define her self and her life as one of purpose.

There are no trumpets to herald the start to moving on. The internal feeling may be imperceptible in the beginning. Slowly, as the feeling and energy builds, we become aware that something new within us has come to be. This something new will become our guide, it is the loadstone that provides the magnetic pull to show us the path forward. Uncertainty suddenly becomes replaced with a level of confidence and a deep-down desire to move on.

This doesn't mean that all doubts are suddenly gone and that we won't have some level of hesitancy in moving forward. We may stick with baby-steps for days, weeks or months until we get our footing. But the pull forward will always be stronger than the desire to freeze or retreat. Uncertainty will be challenged by a desire to experiment and to seek the wisdom of the outcome. Mistakes will be made, but our Spirit will have an elasticity that allows us to discover the wisdom of our errors and to bounce back with greater insight for our next step.

We have entered into the final, metamorphic phase of the change process and it is filled with excitement and hope for the future. Possibilities abound and there is a thirst to explore them all. Our minds hit hyper-drive and old patterns of thinking are being quickly replaced by new paradigms for life. Life now has new meaning. We may not be able to clearly describe that meaning yet, but we have a sense for it. We are *inspired*!

These are just a few of the qualities I have come to recognize from over the years, while watching many people shift into moving on. These qualities may vary greatly with regard to the strength and clarity they exhibit in each person. Yet I find that when some combination of these qualities is present I know that we are moving on.

Terry had been exploring the present for several months. Initially he was anxious to move on but came to realize the value of not rushing forward. Terry was motivated to move away from his career in finance but was still unsure of what career would add meaning to his life.

We had worked to tease out many of the qualities he was seeking in a career to add meaning to his life. It was clear that Terry wanted his new career to have a positive impact for others and also provide more enjoyment in his work life. Terry liked working with numbers but found his life in banking as very routine and boring. He liked his role as a loan officer, helping individuals finance new homes and cars, but there was little creativity in the process and he hated it when he had to say no to a customer that didn't meet the requirements of the bank. Terry was ready to let go of his banking career, but just hadn't found that spark as that would indicate to him what direction he would like to go in. He didn't have that inspiration to motivate moving on.

I continued to encourage Terry to actively explore his world and look at all possibilities. One day Terry came in and told me that he had coffee with a friend from the Chamber of Commerce, who was a financial planner. He was intrigued by the different aspects and focus of the work his friend was doing, but was unsure if this was the 'fit' for him. We outlined how Terry could find out more information about financial planners and what he would need to move into this field. The more research Terry did the more excited he became about the prospect of moving into financial planning as his next career.

Terry looked into the additional training he would need to be certified as a financial planner and he was frightened by the prospect of returning to school after so many years since getting his undergraduate degree in finance. I encouraged Terry to see if he could set in on a couple of classes on financial planning at a local college. Terry made the arrangements and attended three different classes for one lecture each. When Terry and I met next he had become *inspired*. He discovered that he could comprehend the material presented and found it very interesting. He could see the benefit financial planning could provide for securing financial futures for clients. Terry really liked the idea of being a consultant, rather than the decider in people's financial future.

Over the next month I helped Terry work through a plan to move on. In the end he was confident and ready to initiate his change of careers. Terry found that he could attend classes by cutting back on his hours with the bank. He successfully negotiated this physical and financial change in his life. Terry was moving on with excitement and enthusiasm. It is important to note that Terry didn't have a fully baked plan or all of the answers as he moved forward. What he had was the energy within to stick with an emerging transition in careers.

Terry was surprised that he found his next career so closely aligned with his former career in banking. What made the difference for Terry was the shift from decision maker to consultant. He felt that he had moved into a more meaningful career in helping others make sound financial decisions instead of having to make financial decisions for them. Terry didn't throw that baby out with the bath water. He took the time to explore what was meaningful for him and how he wanted to serve in the world. Financial planning was the perfect fit.

MEANING MAY TAKE MANY DIFFERENT SHAPES IN MOVING ON

The feeling that a meaningful change is underway fuels moving on. What form this new meaning will have for us is unlimited scope within a limitless nature. There are two major directions that meaning may take, one is egocentric and the other is purpose focused. It is easy to make these definitional distinctions to the meaning behind change, but in the real world it is normally some combination of the two. Like Terry we have a tendency to blend personal needs with altruistic desires as we move on.

There is no good or bad to either approach to meaning. During any one of the many changes we navigate during our lifetime we may find greater meaning in one approach over the other. Often we can find ourselves flipping between egocentric and purpose driven meaning and motivation as significant change unfolds. This provides a complexity to moving on that may lengthen the time before we become stabilized into our new way of being. For most of us we find the greatest meaning where we can make an impact on our world but also find some personal gain or growth.

The circumstances of change can influence whether our primary meaning will come from a self-centered perspective or a world view. Losing a job can put sudden, financial burdens on us and will naturally have a more self-centered focus. Deciding to cut back on personal spending and giving a greater amount of time and money to a specific not-for-profit organization reflects a deep desire to have an impact on your world. In either case if you can find meaning in your decisions moving forward. It doesn't really matter what your orientation is as long as you have the internal motivation to move forward.

Self-Centered Meaning to Moving On

Sometimes change can move our focus to our own wellbeing. Employment changes, health issues, changes in relationships will have a natural tendency to move us into a more self-centered perspective and decision process. We are forced into making changes that support our most basic of needs. We gain greater meaning if these changes can serve others as well as ourselves, but meeting our primary needs is paramount. The old adage holds truth, "You must help yourself first before you can help others." There are some purists who believe that making changes for self-centered reasons is coping out. I think it is more reasonable to consider that we can help others more when we come from a strong, internal base.

There are also times in our life, especially early on, where our focus is to please ourselves. Acquiring provides motivation to work harder and acquisitions provide some perceived level of meaning. Serving self seems to be part of the evolutionary process. While there may be some sense of accomplishment and gain related to self-centered goals and objectives, these gains are often short-lived. These gains have some satisfaction when attained, but we quickly turn to 'what is next'. This is because these gains hold minimal meaning to our Soul and Its evolutionary process.

Self-centered meaning holds little staying power in our lives. After attaining what we believe to be meaningful, the transient nature of our acquisition becomes apparent. What we acquire, things, positions, power, all have no staying power. At some point in our life we seem to come to the point where self-centered meaning no longer has a point. Like clouds in the presence of the intense light of the sun, self-centered meaning evaporates into the eternal sky. Some call this a mid-life crisis, mainly because it seems to occur around that point in our life, but age is not the real determinant. What seems to cause this shift is an increased awareness and identification with our Higher, authentic Self. There is a point where the ego needs lose meaning to our sense of Self and we desire a deeper purpose.

In his book, The Shift, Dr. Wayne Dyer lists six key indications that we are moving away from self-centered meaning in search for a broader, more encompassing purpose to our existence. Here are his six indicators:

Signs of Readiness to make the Turn to Meaning (purpose)

1. Ego's repetitious insistence to do and have more becomes less attractive.
2. We begin to shift from doing more to doing less.
3. We begin to shun the spotlight and function more from the shadows.
4. A belief in unity replaces our belief in separation.
5. We begin realizing that we're connected in Spirit to everything we perceive to be missing from our life.
6. We begin trusting the wisdom that created us.

In working with people I do not discourage self-centered intent in the process of moving on. It is not productive to shut down what is motivating someone forward. I do ask them to clarify what meaning these perceived goals have for them and what they think it will mean to there greater vision of life when the goal is achieved. In attempting to take the 'long view' I look to have my clients find the enduring value in their and the world's evolution that will come from achieving their goal. Whether I agree or not doesn't matter. I simply ask the questions to help gain some sense of continuity in meaning and purpose. In the end, it is what's important to the individual in motivating the desire to move on.

Often, immediate ego-centric needs seem to demand that we rush forward. Usually the decisions to be made seem black and white at the time. It is at this point that it is important to remember the lessons covered in exploring the present. If we step back and allow some time to take a broader view, what seems like the obvious choice at the time takes on a different appearance. We may still choose the same path, but it will now have greater significance, centered in a broader understanding of the present.

I had worked with Frank on and off over a ten year period as he started and built his own homecare company. All this time Frank had one, central goal; build a successful company that he could sell to a national buyer and become financially set for the rest of his life. Frank was successful in achieving his over-arching goal, but scheduled an appointment to see me four months after he had sold his business.

Frank was feeling lost in his success. While able to not work, he could not find any activity that satisfied him. He was lost in change. We started back at the beginning, saying goodbye. Frank had been so dedicated to his goal of selling the business and becoming rich that he had blocked out almost every other aspect of his own evolution. Frank lacked any sense of connection with his family, his community and his world. I asked Frank what he had gained besides wealth from his goal of selling his company. Frank listed the many skills as a manager and business owner, which he had honed over the years.

I challenged Frank to take some time and explore what he could do with his skills that might bring him more connection. Frank's wife had been involved for many years in an organization that assisted homeless children. The organization was currently struggling and was thinking of closing its doors. I inquired if Frank might consider volunteering some of his time and talent to help his wife's charity get back on its feet. This seemed like an area that Frank might be interested in exploring. He felt it might bring him closer to his wife and his community.

After several months Frank was totally committed to helping this homeless children's charity succeed. He came back to see me with another decision at hand. Frank had been asked to step in as acting executive director for the charity and had looking for advice if this was the right decision in moving on. What we discovered together that Frank had a deep need to find connection. He was not afraid of the fundraising requirements for the position and was unconcerned about being paid. When I asked him, "Why would you want to take this position?" Frank replied, "It's the kids. I know we can make a difference. I have seen it, and that is what is giving me meaning at this time in my life."

Frank took the position and was so successful that they offered him a salary after his first year. Frank took the salary but donated it back to the charity. I asked him why and Frank said, "I am done with having money be my motivation in life. I just want to see these kids get off the street." Frank had made the shift.

Was Frank's first goal of growing and selling his own business for wealth meaningless? The answer for Frank was absolutely not. It put Frank in a position where he could seek a deeper meaning for his life in helping homeless children, without concerns for making money. Frank's homecare company was valuable for sale because it effectively served in meeting the homecare needs of its patients. Frank had already been in the business of helping others; he just didn't see it as a driving purpose in his life at that time. He was able to use his same skills at a later point in his life to serve a higher purpose for others and his Soul.

Finding Purpose in Moving On

What does it mean to find purposeful meaning in our life? Purpose driven meaning is always bigger than we are. It is based on connection and a sense of unity with others and all things. It is often challenged by the ego as being not as important as ego-satisfying meaning.

Choosing purpose does not depend on having all of your needs met. Unlike, Frank I have worked with many people who have not achieved financial security before finding purpose as more motivating than self. In fact, there have been many who have chosen a purpose driven change for moving on when they have been in dire straights. What seems to give purpose more strength is this sense of Oneness, connection and a desire for everyone and everything to move on together. It is making a choice that keeps you in the flow of the life that encompasses you.

Moving on with purpose becomes an integrated effort and requires cooperation and collaboration with our immediate world. Our meaning is found from a greater source that lies within and without. It is a powerful force because it is based in unification, rather than separation. This powerful force is often ignored when we are totally focused in self-centered needs and desires. Yet once we recognize meaning in purpose we are powerfully drawn to it. This is why clients who are seeking meaning in purpose seem to make the move more quickly and in a more decisive manner. When they lock on to their purpose there is no turning back.

Kelly had become a local political figure and her star seemed to be on the rise. Conservative by nature she seemed to fit well into her conservative community. Kelly had desires to move forward with her political life and had decided to run for a state senate seat that had been vacated.

Kelly came to see me to sort out a difficult platform issue that could potentially derail her campaign. The state had same sex union legislation being proposed for the next state assembly session. Kelly is conservative by nature, but she is also a strong feminist that believes in the rights of same sex partners. She knew it was going to be a campaign topic and was concerned about how to respond.

Kelly and I took the time to fully explore the present moment of her internal debate. What was at stake was her own political aspirations that seemed in opposition to her internal, personal values. I stayed neutral in our discussion, just assisting with the inquiry process. The deeper we went it became apparent to Kelly that her personal values held more value and meaning than any political position.

We then turned our attention as to how she would move on. Kelly decided to be up front on the subject, rather than waiting for it to surface on during the campaign. Kelly held a press conference and made her position clear. Her male opponent jumped on the issue and took a strong, opposing position. The issue remained prominent all through the campaign. On Election Day Kelly narrowly lost the race. The level of support she had received from all women in her district had heartened Kelly. She also felt that she had faced the demon of her political aspirations and had stood for what she believed in. For Kelly standing by her principles and being up front on her views made her a stronger candidate, which would serve her if she decided to run again for the state legislature. She went on to serve on the boards of two non-profits, one dealing with women's rights, supporting lesbian interests. Kelly ran in the next election for a representative position in the state legislature and won with strong support from the women in her community. This time it was a narrow victory, where the deciding factor seemed to be Kelly's honesty and transparency.

At times it seems that our personal goals and our principles, based in purpose, can be at odds. For Kelly sticking to her commitment to equality was more important than an election outcome. Kelly's increased connection and recognition with her community, based on her principles, garnered the support needed to seek office again and to win. Kelly took the long view and was able to 'have her cake and eat it too'.

Idealism and Purposeful Meaning

The roots for purposeful meaning in our life come from a desire to attain specific ideals. Idealism is seeded in our Soul, and as such is a function of our Higher Self. These seeds of idealism spark the desire for a better world, positive change, greater connection and a belief in universal, evolutionary growth. When we hold to our ideals all things move forward with a sense of purpose. Well, not always. Idealism is very fragile and can be easily fall pray to failures, rationalization and doubt. Our idealistic principles need continued reinforcement from our mental and emotional bodies to keep the connection to Spirit. With reinforcement during times of doubt we are able to sustain purpose as a meaningful aspect of who we are and what we want to accomplish. So to retain our ideals as an integral part of who we are we must keep a mental and emotional focus on our ideals, no matter what is going on around us.

In our youth we often spawn many ideals and see them as creating meaning in our lives. Frequently, when these ideals are crushed by a seemingly uncaring world we have a tendency to retreat back into the self. This return to self-centered meaning has a term with the younger generation, 'coping out'. This was very apparent during the 60's through the 80's when the idealism of the 'hippies' became the ego gratification of the 'yuppies'. Today, however, many of the yuppies are seeking to return to the ideals they held during their hippie years. Their idealism was suppressed, but not crushed. The Spirit within held watch over these ideals, allowing them to resurface when the environment was ripe for their continued growth.

The need for power and possessions that derive from self-centered meaning loose their shine over time as their temporal nature becomes evident. Something deeper, more lasting, with meaning that aligns with our Soul is yearned for again. Feelings become more important than things and we yearn for the intangibles like love, connection and understanding. This shift is a sign of the need for change and the desire to move on. As we age we gain the desire for more purpose and meaning in our lives and the ideals are resurrected from the Spirit within. This time, we take the long view. We take meaning in the journey forward and not necessarily the end result. We are more willing to put energy towards a specific purpose without the need for an absolute victory or personal gratification. The effort has as much, if not more, meaning than the outcome.

We all have ideals that set the ethical and moral fiber of our being. Frequently life will deliver them a harsh blow and our energy to support these ideals shifts to sustaining the self. These ideals are also part of the collective consciousness and it is from this wellspring that we find the energy and commitment to return to our ideals as we seek a higher purpose in our life. We discover that some ideals will not come to fruition just because we think and believe in them. When we return to these ideals we come to realize that they are held and connected to others, and this newly discovered connection provides the energy to revive the purpose of these ideals. In her book, *Welcome to the Wisdom of the World,* Joan Chittister states the following about ideals, *"Where did we loose our idealism? In our hunger for approval. How can we revive it? By refusing to ignore the cries of the people for the sake of the system, by refusing always, to be silent."*

Change can be triggered by a conscious or unconscious desire to find a higher purpose in our life and to revive our ideals from our youth. It brings back a vitality that has been missed. Changes to return to purpose and ideals will be more dramatic and more difficult. The ego will resist creating an internal, as well as an external, struggle. To a certain degree we often meet resistance from society at all levels. Depending on where the collective unconscious is with the purpose and ideals we hold dear will dictate the level of external resistance we face. Yet the energy to revive this level of meaning in our life is stronger, reinforced by our now perceived connection to the whole. We are sustained by the new knowledge that the participation in the process is as important in its contribution, making the end result less critical. As Malcolm Gladwell has noted in his book, *Tipping Point*, this is why a few can create a wave of change within society. Wherever our position is on the wave of change we can make the contribution that can tip the tide to a change for the better.

MAKING A PLAN FOR MOVING ON

As I already stated the decision to move on may or may not be associated with a plan. Plans are not necessary for moving on but they are helpful in many ways.

A plan adds structure to making progress and gives us a greater sense that what we are looking to accomplish is achievable and realistic. This increased confidence provides greater energy and focus to the process. Planning has been an axiom in business for decades and has produced mixed results. The main reason for its failure in business has been the fact that some plans, while well conceived, are not fully aligned with the group that is charge with implementing the plan. Without energy and commitment the best-designed plans will fail. When putting a personal plan in place it is important to look for and understand if you have any conscious or emotional resistance to your plan. It is not uncommon to find people self-sabotaging their own well-designed plans for moving on.

Frequently resistance to a plan is based in not having completed the saying goodbye portion of the change process. As we will discuss in more detail later, each phase of the change process will most likely overlap with the others. It is not uncommon to be at the point of moving on and then discover the last remnants of some goodbyes not completed. We need not get discouraged, but we do need to return to and complete the process of saying goodbye.

Plans also help to provide a vision that others can recognize and identify with. This can solicit much needed support for moving on and can also provide critical input and additional ideas to enhance the plan. Moving forward in change occurs more readily when we have a strong support system in place. Plans are a great way to find the support we need to get through the rough spots that eventually surface with moving on. This support will frequently save the day and prevent us from retreating in the face of perceived obstacles.

Plans and planning can have some negative aspects as well. The planning process can become protracted and complicated. This will cause us to expend an unnecessarily high level of energy before we get into moving on. Excessive planning may be associated with fear of moving on. We need to be cognizant of any fears that seem to arise, while putting a plan together. Planning can also get to a level of complexity where it is more confusing than constructive. It is important to remember that plans are helpful in achieving what we vision but are not a guarantee. Sometimes we keep looking for the perfect plan that will guarantee success, but in the process we fail to get started.

Plans can help us find gaps that need exploration. This usually occurs when we want to move on before fully exploring the present. When a plan starts revealing gaps we may need to return to exploring the present to gather more information. There is a happy medium that can be achieved in having sufficient information to move on and not having enough information to avoid getting lost. No textbook on planning can define this happy medium for us. It is as individual as every cell in our bodies. In the end, this is a personal call and it often will not be perfect. Change is a process and is never perfect. The important part of planning is to be aware of the energy it is creating. If planning is energizing you to move on great, if it is draining your energy then rap it up and take your first steps. You can always return to a plan later on. Knowing when enough is enough is more of a Gestalt feeling, rather than a process reached in the mind. Finally, plans were made to be living documents that evolve as our vision for the future evolves. If you have a tendency to be a perfectionist, get over it if you really want to effectively manage change.

Roger had spent the last year developing a strategic plan for launching his own business. He looked to build upon his prior employment experience working on software for large corporations to enter into the field of website design and support. Roger had developed an extensive plan but was having difficulty pulling the trigger.

When we first met I asked Roger to review for me the plan he had put together and to let me know where he felt the plan lacked sufficient detail to move forward. All areas of Roger's strategic business plan were very detailed and thoughtfully developed. One area where Roger seemed hesitant was his marketing plan. While he had loads of data regarding the market and demand for his specific market segment, it was obvious that Roger had doubts.

I began to explore with Roger the origins of his doubts. What first surfaced was Roger's experience with his father, who had attempted his own business start up and failed. The impact that this had on his family was significant. They went from a level of financial security to just barely getting by. It became obvious that Roger feared he was going to travel down this same road. I explored with Roger the reasons why his father's business failed and if he saw similar risks in his plan. After much discussion Roger came to realize that he did not have to carry his father's business failure forward with him. Yes his plan had risks, but his plan was much more thoughtful and realistic than that of his father. In fact, his father didn't have a business plan at all and just jumped in using the family savings to advance his start up. Roger didn't need to touch his current savings due to the low capitalization required. Roger came to see that he just needed to say goodbye to his dad's business failure.

Roger's second level of hesitancy had to do with concerns about marketing his business. Roger had never had to seek customers and felt very inadequate as a salesman for his new enterprise. While Roger had done his research on how to market Internet services he had not achieved a personal level of experience to give him the confidence needed. I suggested that Roger needed to spend some more time exploring this area to get more comfortable. Roger did and in the process found a small Internet marketing firm that would work on a commission basis for helping Roger acquire customers. Roger had a good feel about this group and decided to put a limited contract in place with them. He also felt he could learn from them how they marketed his business services and eventually take over.

The next month Roger quit his corporate job, set up a small office and, working with his contracted marketing firm, had his first customers in three weeks. His business has grown steadily since then to a point where he has hired another person and he is spending some of his time marketing on his own.

Roger's story is a common one. The entrepreneurial spirit is strong and many people have great visions, plans and desires to be their own boss. In Roger's case he needed to revisit saying goodbye and exploring the present to come to the point where he had the energy to move on. The best-laid plans still need the *heart* to succeed.

Designing A Plan for Moving On

There have been thousands of books written on the planning process for business or personal use. I have no desire to wade into this conundrum of information. What I would like to share is some ideas about how to decide upon and put together a plan for moving on that would work for you.

First, I would like to dispel the idea that there is a perfect way to plan. With over 30 years of assisting business and individuals in setting plans into place I know of no, one plan that fits all. So planning is what you make of it. Planning can be a simple as no plan at all, "I'll make it up as I go." Or it can be an inspired treatise, hundreds of pages in detail.

What is important in a plan is that it energizes us, it gives us the confidence we need to move on, and it helps us to take the first step forward. A plan should reflect our internal guidance, as well as the wisdom provided through the thoughts of others, which strikes a chord with our hearts. A plan can be a thought that guides us through today or a detailed outline to map our path for the next five years.

Plans are not fixed, but fluid. A fixed plan is a dead plan. Things change as we move forward. We are tinkering with the future and it will impact what comes next. We are not omnipotent so we cannot see all the variables as they come into play. In working with businesses I have seen many good plans fail because of an unwillingness to refresh a plan based on current information. If a plan is not viewed in the present moment then it only reflects the past, and the past is over! Plans are evolutionary entities that must be tended if they are to stay alive. Like a good gardener, plans must be tended on a regular basis if they are to bare fruit.

I am not advocating that we should ignore all of the wisdom that has been written over the years on planning. I am just saying there is no one-way to plan successfully. What makes a plan successful is our own personal commitment to it and a willingness to let the plan grow as we grow, learn.

Working Without a Plan

When does it make sense to move on without a plan? Often this is a good approach when we are somewhere in between 'exploring the present' and 'moving on'. When we are at a point where we know we need to get going, but we still feel that we don't have a clear vision of the road ahead. So how best to proceed?

I have frequently told people I work with to take 'baby steps' in these situations. What I mean is ultra-short-term planning. This encompasses a combination of outlining the next reasonable step forward with a need to continue to search the present for more information. If we continue to look for the synchronicities, intuitive moments and the wisdom of our friends and mentors, then the road forward can become more and more clear. Continued personal visioning and affirmations will encourage more insights. Trusting that the Universe is conspiring to help us move forward leaves us open to connecting with new information. If we start with small steps forward and stay alert the perfect plan will come together. I have never seen it not when a person is patient, awake and willing.

Lucinda was a budding, high school tennis star, heading to the state championships. Her road to champion was abruptly interrupted by an ankle injury during a late season match. While she had physically recovered to a level where she could return to competition, Lucinda remained hesitant in practice with her coach. Her parents, who saw a potential college scholarship going down the drain, were pushing Lucinda to 'get back into the game'. I was asked to see her by her parents to help her in overcoming her fear of re-injury and to motivate her to get back into competition. Normally I will not work with a set goal prescribed for one individual by another, but I was interested in where Lucinda might be coming from and where she really wanted to go.

In my first meeting with Lucinda she was very hesitant and withdrawn. She was fully aware of her parents' motives and thought I was just a salesman. After we got over that impression, Lucinda began to open up. We explored together Lucinda's hesitancy in returning to competition. Lucinda shared how the injury had deeply affected her and how difficult and painful the recovery process had been. Having had a similar injury like Lucinda's in the past, I could empathize. Lucinda also expressed how tiring the practice schedule was and how fearful she had become of losing to opponents. She felt her parents and coach did not understand her feelings and she was being pushed over the edge of an imaginary cliff.

I asked Lucinda if she liked playing tennis. She told me that when she started she loved tennis, but over the years it started to become work as she became better and the competition became more intense. Once again, I asked Lucinda if she liked to play tennis, *now*. Lucinda told me she still liked the game but was fearful of failing once she returned to serious competition.

I asked Lucinda if she might be interested in playing tennis again, just for fun. No competition, just a game of tennis to see how much she still liked the game itself. This was a 'baby step' that Lucinda seemed eager to pursue. I arranged for Lucinda to play a couple rounds of tennis the next week with her high school friends, but without any coaches or parents. Lucinda returned the next week to share how good it felt to just play tennis. Her ankle felt fine throughout the games and she had a great time connecting with her friends. She felt like they weren't competing with each other, but just enjoying each other's company. Lucinda definitely still liked tennis.

I asked her what she would like to do next. She told me that she did like competition and a part of her missed it, but she was still afraid of the pressure. Together we worked on a plan to get Lucinda back into competition without the pressure of having to win. This took some negotiating with both Lucinda's parents and her personal coach. Luckily they were all most interested in Lucinda's mental, as well as physical, health and were willing to back off on the need to win.

Lucinda returned to competition with mixed results. As we met it became apparent that her desire to do her best was growing stronger, along with her confidence in her ankle. She stepped up her work on technique with her coach and her parents kept to their pledge to not push to win. In fact they became Lucinda's best cheerleaders, win or loose. They let Lucinda take the lead in discussing how each match unfolded. Lucinda described the mistakes she made in the match and how she could do better. Her parents just listened and smiled.

Lucinda went on to take third place her senior year in state tennis competition. She was offered a tennis scholarship, but her parents did not push her to take it. Lucinda made the decision by herself and accepted the scholarship. We will never know if Lucinda's ankle injury was an accident or subconsciously induced to get her off the competitive merry-go-round. Lucinda and I stepped back and explored how she felt about tennis in the present moment. She rediscovered her love of the game and competition. With the help of loving parents and a coach that really had Lucinda's best interest at heart Lucinda was able to make small steps forward to reengage in the game she loved to play.

Planning to Move On and Moving Your Plan

Putting a plan in place can increase our confidence and facilitate moving on. By fleshing out our inspirations it adds substance and energy to stepping forward, even if there is not a clear outcome in sight. Since there are no magic plans that will guarantee success what seems to work best is to put together enough of a plan so you can get started. This allows you to remain flexible as you move forward, while still seeing if the start you have planned out makes sense.

Over-planning is usually a sign that you still have some fear and hesitancy related to the direction you are planning to move in. Extremely detailed plans create rigidity, and we become resistant to altering or abandoning a plan that is not working. It is hard to give up all of the effort put into an extensive plan. This has been a critical weakness that I have run into time and again in business. Negative outcomes can be often overlooked as the decision makers focus only on the next steps in the plan. The ability to see what is happening in the present moment is lost as the focus moves to the past, where the plan was originally conceived. I have also seen this happen in personal planning, especially if finances are involved.

It is critical to look at what is causing you to continue going deeper and deeper into putting a plan in place. It is also critical to do a 'fear check' at this time to determine the causes for requiring more detail. Crucial questions at this time could be, "Does additional planning help build my understanding and confidence in moving on?" and "Is the additional detail helping me to move forward or holding me back?" and finally, "What am I afraid of in moving on?"

Roberto was an accomplished businessman with years of successful experience in consulting related to company strategy and operational planning. Roberto had been is a relationship for five years. Neither he nor his partner had a desire to get married but were interested in moving into a single home together. As they began looking for the 'right home' Roberto went into high gear in putting a decision plan in place. It covered an extensive list of their requirements, a detailed financial plan and even had a geographic, target area map, which both found acceptable.

Roberto came to see me as the execution of the plan was taking a toll on their relationship. Roberto's partner wanted to be more flexible in making a decision, while Roberto wanted to stick to the plan. She had challenged Roberto as to whether or not he was getting cold feet about moving in together.

Roberto did most of the talking in our early meetings, detailing and justifying why they needed to stick with the plan. I simply continued to listen and ask Roberto to look at how important each aspect of the plan was to the outcome they desired, finding a suitable home together. The more Roberto presented his case the weaker his arguments became. After the third meeting Roberto had run out of steam. I then asked Roberto to focus in on his feelings, and I asked him to consider his partners question and face any fears he held related to moving in together.

Roberto initially went into denial, detailing how happy he was with their relationship and explaining why his plan was a good plan. I asked him why he was so rigid in sticking to the plan when it seemed to be getting them nowhere. Roberto's initial response was, "I want this to be perfect." We discussed for some time the merits of seeking a perfect relationship and whether that was realistic. As we continued our inquiry Roberto's uncertainties began to surface.

Roberto shared how his parents had divorced after 19 years together and the subsequent fight had taken a financial and emotional toll on the family. Roberto had just entered his senior year of high school and was forced to make a change in schools, as the decision was made for him to move in with his father. Roberto didn't understand why he couldn't stay in their house, where he had grown up, and live with his mother. It became apparent to him that his mother wanted the house but not Roberto. He was devastated by the decision and the changes he went through.

It only took a brief reflection on my part, pointing out some of the similarities related to his parent's divorce and his commitment to finding a common home with his partner, for Roberto to discover his hidden fears. As the realization sunk in all Roberto could say was, "Oh my God!" It was the first time that Roberto had been able to cry over this loss from the past. On further inquiry what was uncovered was a deep fear that once in the house his relationship would deteriorate and end in a bitter dispute over the house and Roberto needing to suddenly move out. Roberto realized that his rigidity to the plan was really fear based from his past.

We dove deep into the reality of his fears. It took some effort for Roberto to separate the two situations in his life. He had to face the fact that there were no guarantees in his current relationship, but that it was also not a replay of his parent's divorce. We spent time helping Roberto deal with his perceived rejection by his mother. It also took some work to separate the women he now loved from the mother he loved and missed in the past.

As we worked though Roberto saying goodbye to his trauma from the past he became more flexible in seeking a new home with his partner. Within a month they had agreed upon a home and were moving forward with closing. Roberto's plan was not going to guarantee that his relationship with his partner would never fail. Roberto found the courage and commitment to move on without having to meet all of the specifications of his original plan. Roberto was also able to confront his mother about his feelings and they came to a better understanding of each other through a frank and open dialogue.

Keeping Inspiration Alive

Moving to planning can sometimes, inadvertently cut off the inspirational process. We can't help it. Planning calls on a different part of the brain and our centers for inspiration take a back seat or just shut down. That is why it is important to continue to take the time to stop, reflect, meditate and look into the infinite gap once more for continued insights and inspiration.

In the creation of this book I started with a basic outline of what I wanted to share. I have been writing now for over eight months, taking time each day to read, reflect, meditate and pray for guidance. Each day inspiration has contributed in ways I would have never foreseen. Whole sections of chapters have been added or rewritten from the insights I have received. What I have learned is that I am growing, evolving along with the book, and that insight and inspiration play an important role in making this work more meaningful.

My timeline for completing the book has continued to be extended, but it doesn't bother me. I am willing to invest the time and effort to seek more insight and inspiration from the Universe, receive it in gratitude and translate it into each chapter. Sometimes it is humbling to even write sections based on insights received. I know I have not fully mastered the insights, but I don't think that detracts from their value. I hope you feel the same way.

REVEALING THE NEW YOU

The process of moving on includes revealing our new self to the world. Through the process of change we have said goodbye to who you were, sought to define who we are to become, and now we are birthing a 'new being' into the world. Like a newborn, the 'new you' has had a period of gestation within each of us. As it has taken form, while we have held our 'new being' close. Many who know us will have no idea that a 'new being' is about to be revealed. When we reveal the 'new being' we have become it will be a shock to many.

We will often face resistance from friends, family and co-workers to our new way of being. This occurs for many reasons. First and foremost, we have evolved while others may have not taken their own next step in change. Without an understanding of what has brought us to our 'new being' others may see this a folly. Like a newborn baby our new way of being will be vulnerable. Others may challenge or even threaten our 'new being', demanding a return of the 'old self'.

Others may resist our 'new being' for very personal, and sometimes quite selfish, reasons. Some may feel threatened by the our new being. Some may feel that they are being abandoned. Still others may resist a broader worldview held by our 'new being', which they have not come to understand or accept. This list of personal issues could go on indefinitely, but the point is that these issues are not the responsibility of our 'new being'. Things have changed, and it is their, not our, responsibility to adjust, adapt and accept.

The birth of a 'new being' during the change process has ended marriages, friendships and business relationships. This is not a condemnation of the development of our 'new self'; it is a reality of the random evolution of all beings. We just all don't become aware, reflect and evolve at the same pace. Often relationships are challenged when one of us changes. We can often adjust and adapt, but sometimes the new void is so big that the relationship ends. No one is at fault. In an age of rapid change and evolution the ending of relationships and the forming of new relationships is happening at an accelerated pace. We can't ignore the loss this creates, but we can accept that this is sometimes a necessary part of the process of change and evolution. We must honor what has been as we 'say goodbye', but we must then have the courage to move on.

By far the greater loss is when this 'new being' is dismembered by the pressure from others to return to the old way of being. This is a far greater loss, but one that often occurs in the moving on process. Dismember may seem like a harsh word, but there is no other description to fit. The vulnerability of our 'new being' is threatened by what has been and there may be some willing to do whatever to make this 'new being' to go away; even intellectual dismemberment. This is done by using old thoughts, paradigms, and feelings to tear appart this 'new being', our new self. We must have the confidence, energy and determination to not allow our 'new being' to be assaulted and extinguished.

In moving on we have to be perfectly clear as to who and what this 'new being' represents, we need to have the confidence and commitment in support of our 'new being', and we must resist the temptation to fall back, negating all of the work accomplished in the change process. What we can create by falling back is an existential suffering with our Soul. This is a profound level of suffering that can color all of our other experiences. Countless books, movies and plays have portrayed this process of falling back and entering into profound, existential suffering. Seen in the light of an evolutionary God, even the fall of Adam and Eve in Genesis can be seen as a reflection of falling back from our new being, becoming trapped in the 'old self'. This is why it is so important to not rush into moving on until we are clear and confident as to who and what we are becoming.

Christie was a college student, who was exploring, like most college students, her beliefs. Christie had been raised in the Jewish religion by orthodox parents. During her study Christie had taken comparative religions and had come to realize many of the restrictions that she felt were evident in Jewish doctrine. Christie had come to see common themes in all religions that made them all valuable. She felt that holding a view of being 'chosen' was not right. She felt that the God she recognized was inclusive, not exclusive. Christie was considering leaving the faith.

On her next trip home from college Christie shared her views with her parents. The reaction was abrupt, intense and negative. The Rabbi for her parent's synagogue was called and the three moved to an 'intervention'. Christie attempted to share and defend her new way of viewing religion, but crumbled to the pressure. While Christie's views had not changed she capitulated to a false persona of a good Jewish girl.

Christie came to see me because she was miserable in presenting this false image. She was relieved to return to college, where she could openly share and debate her new views of religion, but dreaded returning home. She loves her parents, but she did not like the person she became when she returned home.

Christie and I spent the first couple meetings allowing her to share her knowledge and convictions related to her new view of religion. Christie needed to be heard without judgment or interpretation. This helped Christie to solidify her knowledge, feelings and newfound beliefs. I then helped Christie uncover a more open view of religion within Jewish faith. I suggested a few, more progressive Hebraic theologians that I was aware of and encouraged her to do more research into her faith of origin.

Christie came back a month later with a high level of newfound knowledge and enthusiasm. There were authors in Hebraic theology that were much more inclusive and shared some of her views on commonality. These authors did not discount other religions but showed the deeper, more mystical aspects of the Jewish faith. In particular, Christie became intrigued with the teachings of the Kabbalah. She now felt there was some common ground between the Jewish faith and her broader view of religion in general.

I worked for a few weeks with Christie on fully integrating her newfound beliefs into her core being. Through inquiry I challenged but did not threaten. In this way Christie was able to dive deeper into her feelings, changing some and reinforcing others. I saw and heard her confidence and conviction rise as we shared. We finally got to the point where Christie felt she had the strength to open the discussion of her faith once again with her parents.

Christie's next conversation with her parents met with similar resistance. Christie was in a different position this time. She was not totally rejecting her Jewish faith, but she made it clear that there were other interpretations of Jewish teachings that held a broader view and that she agreed with these teachings. The Rabbi was called in again and he attempted to discount the theology of her new authors. Christie listened but went on to explain that the Jewish faith had several divisions, some more liberal and some very orthodox. She firmly stated that she was in the liberal camp.

Christie held her ground and in the end her parents and Rabbi resigned themselves to the 'New Christie'. She birthed her 'new being' and withstood the threats to survival. Many are moving away from traditional religion in this new age of knowledge. In many cases the old faith is summarily rejected, without much inquiry. This is what happened with Christie. By helping her to dig deeper into her traditional faith Christie found that it was also evolving. Christie was able to bridge the gap between her old and new faiths, letting go of what no longer served her and embracing the new.

We had traveled back through the change process. I helped Christie to review what she was 'saying goodbye' to. She discovered that she didn't have to say goodbye to the entire Jewish faith. Next we spent some time in 'exploring the present'. Her willingness to dive back into Hebraic theology helped her to expand and strengthen her new belief structure. By going back and clarifying the first two phases of the change process Christie gained the clarity and conviction to birth and defend her new faith.

GOING BOLDLY . . .

While we can be supported in the process of moving on, in the end, we complete the journey on our own. This is a unique experience that is specifically designed by and for each of us. It is intimate and personal in many ways. The personal stakes are extremely high. Failure to successfully navigate moving on can be crippling for years, if not a lifetime. I am not trying to be dramatic. It is just that I have seen so many people in therapy due to the scars created by not successfully moving on. Most call it personal failure. I just see it as a setback in a person's evolution.

Not being able to become who you are meant to be is not an end. We need to look with an inquiring mind as to what happened. Usually, like Christie, we have not completed all of the work necessary in the first two phases of the change process in a way that allows us to succeed at moving on. If we take the time after a setback to look for what is incomplete with regards to 'saying goodbye' and 'exploring the present', then we can find the missing pieces to successfully 'moving on'. We need to overcome the melancholia of a setback and find our determination to become who we are meant to be.

Setbacks to moving on can also be attributed to our underestimating the level of resistance we will face. Christie was not anticipating her parents bringing in their Rabbi for support. Such a foreboding figure from Christie's religious past resurfaced deep seeded doctrinal angst from her established, childhood faith. Christie was unprepared for this external and internal pincer attack on her new belief structure. Our resulting work together helped Christie to clarify and strengthen her beliefs, allowing her to withstand the winds of her religious past. It is often impossible to foresee all of the resistance we will face in becoming who we are meant to become. Sometimes we will be overwhelmed and suffer a setback. It is death to just give up. Inquiry is the tool to greater insights and depth, needed to move on. To quote Sister Joan Chittister from *Welcome to the Wisdom of the World*, "Life is a process made up of many experiments, many mistakes, many learnings, many possibilities. Sometimes it is only error that can possibly teach us the value of goodness or show us the path to our own growth."

There Are No Wrong Paths, So Just Take One

The biggest resistance to moving on is an egoistic need for perfection. Our ego/self believes that the ultimate goal is to achieve some mythical level of perfection. Therefore, when we decide on a path forward in our life there is a great hesitance as we obsess as to whether the path chosen is the 'right one'. This is, by far, the greatest failing of the ego/self as we navigate change. The reality of life is there is *no perfect path forward.*

If this gave you cause to pause then it is time to look at the truth of life. No single path forward is free of obstacles and potential conflicts. There is an old Buddhist saying, "The road to Nirvana is paved with Samsara." This means, that the path to being fully awake to and fully knowing of truth is filled with illusions. By illusion we are talking about an inability to experience reality due to the need of the ego/self to create a perfect world that we find by traveling the perfect path. If this was true, why do histories enlightened beings, Jesus, Mohammad, Buddha, as well as all the saints, continue to run into difficulties even after they have achieved 'enlightenment'? The answer is, 'There are no perfect paths forward, even for the fully enlightened.' What is different for these beings is they see the illusions lining the path forward and choose that path anyway. Then they travel that path with calm and equanimity, knowing that what is encountered will expand their understanding of the truth of life, or what really is.

This may seem counter-intuitive to all that I have presented so far on the process for change, but it really isn't. We need to go through the entire process of change, being as fully awake as possible, but also knowing that the path we choose in moving on will not be perfect and free of obstacles and potential conflicts. By following the process of change, however, we will navigate these obstacles and conflicts with greater ease and grace.

As I mentioned earlier in this chapter, you will come to a Gestalt point when you know it is time to move on. At this point you will still have reservations. This is the ego/self attempting to keep you in the current state of being. It will call for you to find the perfect path. Know that there is no perfect path and resolve to just move on.

It's Just the Beginning

It is important to remember that moving on is not the end to who you are becoming. This is an endless process, facilitated by change, throughout our life. Sometimes life will provide a rapid sequence of events that trigger a successive group of 'growth spurts'. Like an adolescent during their growth spurts, we may find ourselves off-balance, a bit disoriented, and feeling like we are struggling to catch up with ourselves. We can only decide for ourselves what pace is acceptable, how much we can tolerate, when we need to slow down. We must remain engaged in the flow of life in our own way and allow us to stay afloat by not resisting and conserving our energy. Lao Tzu would call this 'the wisdom of the Tao'.

PART THREE

GETTING INTO THE FLOW

In part one of the book I have discussed some key precepts that will help to make working with change easier. In part two I reviewed the change process with details relating to what can be expected in each phase of the process, and how we can recognize our progress as we move through each phase. It is important to remember that rarely do we complete one phase before starting another. There is a point where we naturally begin to explore the next phase of change, and this will frequently occur before we have finished our work in the prior phase. In fact, it is not unusual that, midway through the process, we might find ourselves in all three phases of change. What is critical is to stay diligent in completing each phase of the change process before declaring that we have successfully navigated a change in our life.

In part three of the book we will look at the transformative aspects of change, as we live life to the fullest. Change plays a critical role in our physical, mental, emotional, and spiritual growth. It is the lever to get us unstuck from the routines in life that are holding us back. It is the alchemical element that brings forth new ideas, beliefs and actions. It is the teacher for a new way of being. Change expands our awareness, keeps us fluid, and allows us to engage in life, without resistance and fear. All we have to do is accept change as it presents, and not fight it.

In this section, I will speak to the role change has played in my life. It has definitely been a learning process for me. I was not as accepting of change in the beginning, even as I was facilitating change with others, and I had to personally learn all of the lessons presented in this book. While there are some general patterns to change, it is unique in each of our experiences and it is our responsibility to understand how and why it is presenting in our life. How change has operated in my life is not how it will present and operate in your life.

While change is intimate and unique to each one of us, there are similarities. It helps to know that others have had similar experiences with change, and have been successful in navigating through change. To that end

I hope that my experiences with change will provide a light for others.

This section will also look at change as the teacher for the end of our life. The more we understand change the better prepared we are for the ultimate change, death. Understanding change lessens the sense of finality that the thought of death often creates in our mind. When we come to understand that in change we are uncertain of what is coming next we can then come to accept the uncertainty in death. Yes, there is uncertainty in death, but we come to realize that death will help us to understand what is next. We realize that change in our life is a series of mini-deaths, and this helps us to be prepared for the actual experience.

In closing we will look at how change awakens us from the dream we have created in this life. The past and the future are not what they seem, they are illusions that we place too much importance on. It is the present moment that is our reality and change is one of the best ways to stay present. We are not fixed beings, but changing expressions of the Infinite. So change helps us to awaken to our Infinite Nature. This is the miracle that change brings.

Change also broadens our perspective to include the intangible. As our lives have become more and more dominated by things, our vision has narrowed to exclude the intangibles. We have lost interest in what we cannot see, touch and feel. Change exposes the impermanence of 'things' and fills the void with Infinite potential. We become aware of the intangible, which then opens our ability to create from the intangible a new reality and new way of being.

The most significant elements of the intangibles are our feelings. Change increases our awareness of our feelings, allows us to inquire into their origins, and to see if they are real in the present moment. Change creates a fluidity in our feelings that enriches our life experience. It provides a continuity, which counters the impermanence of 'things'. Change helps us to take the road less traveled and, in so doing, we find what the Buddhists call 'the middle way'.

CHAPTER TEN

PERSONAL REFLECTIONS ON MASTERING CHANGE

"There is a space between what we are now and what we become in the future. This space is filled with the winds of change. Let us step forward with open eyes, an open mind and an open heart, knowing that the winds of change will always carry us to a better place."

Merl Will-Wallace

"So seeking God is a personal adventure that we can only take on our own. Our spiritual path cannot be defined by others and is as unique and individual as we are, is as unique and individual as God is within each of us. God has no desire to listen to the repetition of God's own revelations spoken through the words of another. God wants the fresh perspective that each of us holds within us. This is an evolutionary God that grows with all of us. It is in the accepting of responsibility for our own spiritual path that we accept the promise of 'free will'. God encourages us to choose, knowing that there are no wrong answers, wrong paths, wrong ways to becoming more awake and aware. Mistakes, then, become part of our evolutionary journey. In their own way our mistakes show the way."

Merl Will-Wallace, *Religion and an Evolutionary God*

As an author of a non-fiction book it is always easy to pontificate about what you know, or what you think you know. It is easy to paint a picture of yourself as having it all together. That is not my message when it comes to change. Over my years of contemplating change I have stumbled more than I have run. For all that I have learned change is still my teacher, each and every day. There is no perfect way for dealing with change. We just do the best we can with the knowledge and skills we have.

No one has all of the answers, and that includes me. Most people I meet with have faced change in their own, unique way, and will face their current changes in their own, unique way going forward. In working with others I learned to honor the uniqueness of each person and their situation. There is no set playbook for moving through the process, but I have found the general processes from this book as a great template in assisting others, especially when they feel stuck. Yet the crafting of how each person successfully moves through each of the phases of change is his or her own creation. As I have mentioned in this book many times, change is rooted in our own, unique interplay between our ego/self and our Higher Self. I can facilitate that interplay with my own creativity, but I am always aware that what I say is not the ultimate answer to making change. The person I am speaking to must personalize what I have shared to their current orientation and infuse it with his/her own inquiry and insights. No one can define our change process for us.

On many occasions, as I have worked through the change process with an individual, it has triggered within me my own insights as to how I could manage change more constructively as it was currently unfolding in my life. In the struggle of others I have uncovered my own struggles, my own resistance. I have a great sense of gratitude for all that others have taught me about change as we have worked through their issues together. Managing change in a collaborative manner can benefit all involved.

It is for these and many more reasons that there can be no dogma where change is concerned. Each change is unique and expands upon itself. Even the process and tools outlined in this book will not work in all situations. Change is clever and has a unique way of helping us to evolve, helping us to move on. I can only share the following thoughts based on my own experience with change.

Make Change Your Own

When we enter change we immediately start to undermine our own foundations to life. By this I mean, in starting to define who we are to become, we have to start to break away from who we think we are right now. How else can we embrace the change to come that will guide our evolution? A result to the loosening of our foundations is a feeling of insecurity. Insecure to the world we are changing in and insecure about who we think we are. After all, we are changing.

In our uncertainty and insecurity it is easy to look to others for answers. 'Help me fix this.' is the common mantra of insecurity. While seeking assistance and advice is helpful, it is a mistake to think that anyone has experienced and successfully navigated a change exactly like the one we are now going through. In addition, it is easy for their needs related to their own changes to get mixed into our changes. By accepting unconditionally their suggestions for managing our change we are merging our change process with theirs. These co-mingled changes may seem to be mutually beneficial, but will not serve either person in the end.

Over an eight-year period I had experienced a successive level of promotions in management with a national homecare company. All of my work to that point had been in field management, working with teams directly related to patient care. I was excited, motivated and successful in my work.

After a merger with another large homecare company several problems surfaced in the post-merger period. Some of my specific operational skills were known to executive management, especially an expertise in information technology, and I was offered a promotion into an executive vice president position within the corporate office. My instincts told me to stay in the field, but under significant pressure to take the position and the lure of a big increase in compensation I took the position.

I quickly found that corporate life was far different from the field. There was a significant amount of politics that came into play. This was not an area that I was skilled at. I fiercely stuck to my ability to analyze and recommend change. Unfortunately, I did not realize that any recommendations at this level had political implications. I sat between two camps, one that cheered me on and another that criticized and looked for me to fail. I continued to follow the advice of my mentor, who had brought me into the corporate life, as I navigated a set of successive changes at the corporate office. With each change that I proposed I found my self at the center of the battlefield for control of the company.

What ensued was the longest, most professionally difficult, two years of my managerial career. I gained significant weight, developed high blood pressure, and, for the first time in my managerial career, was unsure of who I was and my ability to manage change. Mercifully, at the end of two years I was offered a golden parachute, which I took. This was not the end to my personal changes, but just the beginning.

Unfortunately, my last position as a corporate executive made me most eligible for similar positions in other healthcare companies. These positions had nothing to do with direct patient care, which I loved, and everything to do with collecting aged accounts receivables, a job I hated. I held three positions over the next nine years in managing distressed accounts receivables. While these decisions were safe, logical and financially sustaining, I was also miserable. I experienced two severe periods of anxiety attacks, with the second resulting in a nervous breakdown and a medical leave.

I had already received my masters degree in mental health counseling several years before and decided to return to this work. There was nothing secure in this decision, but it was my decision. During this same period my marriage of thirty-five plus years ended and I was forced to file for bankruptcy. Still, I stuck to my decision to return to counseling. Once again, I was working directly with patients in healthcare and it felt great.

This period was very painful. Change seemed to ramp up to unbearable levels and was overwhelming at times. Yet the more change I faced the more comfortable I became in working my way through who I was becoming. More and more I looked to my own insights and inspiration as my guide through each successive change. During this period I came to find the principles and practices for change developed by William Bridges. I embraced Bridges work and made it my own. As time went by my insights into change expanded with each person I worked with and each personal change I continued to navigate. As a result I was inspired to pen this book.

As I look back over the decades it is apparent that not listening to my instincts, and following the advice of well-meaning mentors sent me down the rabbit hole. Like Alice, I entered Wonderland only to find it not to my liking. And like Alice, the path out of Wonderland was long and circuitous. Yet all of the changes and mistakes made was a learning that moved me to find my Soul purpose, helping others to successfully manage change. There was nothing particularly pretty or perfect about my succession of changes that has brought me to who I am now, but I wouldn't change them for where they brought me.

To those I work with I share, "I don't have all of the answers to the changes you are going through, but I have been there, and it gives me a sense of compassion for what you are going through and a desire to help."

Believe in the Good

Due to the uncertainty and insecurity it creates change frequently doesn't have a good feel to it. Externally initiated change is unsettling and unwanted. Internally initiated changes often are started by the unconscious and we tend to initially resist. Usually our long-established routines are disrupted and we are suddenly filled with uncertainty. We feel clumsy and out of sync. It is no wonder that change is commonly and unwanted event in our lives.

As I look back I see that I frequently resisted change, and, at times still today, resistance is my initial reaction. I will say, however, that more often than not, I now welcome change. I have learned to take a long-view of change and understand that it always, ultimately is good for my personal evolution. It may take several years and a compounding sequence of changes to birth the good. I have had to learn to be patient, continue to inquire into the nature of change, and accept the lessons it is teaching me. I share my thoughts with the understanding that I will always, perpetually be a student of change. I am only a practitioner of change, accepting the knowledge it brings as I become more awake to what is real, what is true, what is life. We are all practitioners of change, whether we want to be or not.

My transition succession of careers went through many changes and personal transitions. My careers progressively changed from corporate executive to business consultant to a professional and personal coach before becoming a personal counselor focusing on change. Why so many interim careers? I simply had trouble in saying goodbye. Saying goodbye to power and prestige, saying goodbye to managing and making decisions that others followed, and, most of all, saying goodbye to money.

As a corporate executive I was earning a strong, six-figure income, with plenty of perks and incentives. I had moved into a lifestyle to match. To change to a counselor was going to dramatically alter my income and lifestyle. I must say, I did not go easily into this change. As my income progressively dropped with each career change I fell back on my savings to prop up my continuing six-figure lifestyle. With the ending of my long-term marriage the divorce stripped me of my assets and my retirement. I was finally in a position that change was forcing me to take a hard look at how I was living my life. Through this new lens I have been able to see that simpler is better and the need for things has been replaced with a need for knowledge, understanding and purpose.

As I learned, with the help of current spouse Barbara, to Zen my life I came to understand the greatest lesson that all of the changes were trying to show me. I am not defined by what I have. This was a hard gift of fierce grace, which I was slow to assimilate. It took the foreclosure on my home and filing for bankruptcy to finally drive the point home. My lesson, I am just like everyone else. I am human, I am not perfect, I am vulnerable, and my life will always be in change.

As time went on I found that the less I depended on possessing things the simpler and more enjoyable my life became. I found a greater meaning in life, beyond possessions. I came to realize that acquiring was a form of addiction, and I had been an addict. I made the shift that Wayne Dyer talks about from ambition to meaning.

I now use coupons at the grocery store, delay purchasing decision, prioritize my needs from my wants, and have learned to create a saving the hard way, one small deposit at a time. I live a much simpler, but more enjoyable life. I get great satisfaction and a feeling of connections from the people I work with. Serving is more important than acquiring. Co-creating a smile on the face of another person has greater value than a BMW.

It would be an understatement to say I was a slow learner in change. I resisted and struggled with each change and frequently felt sorry

197

for myself. Today, in hindsight, I see what a blessing this all was. My Soul purpose has always been to help others. I knew this when my first professional career was as a respiratory therapist, working in hospitals. Ambition pulled me from my Soul purpose, but my internal yearning, manifesting through change, drew me back.

Today, I look at each change unfolding in my life as an opportunity, a positive lesson, a part of my evolution to who I am becoming. I no longer take a fixed view of who I am. I accept that I will constantly be changing throughout the remainder of my life. Most importantly, I see *all* change as good.

Don't Create a Tsunami

We can, for some period of time, resist change. There are ways around an impending change in our lives, and this circumnavigation can be quite effective, for now. There are two problems, however, with rejecting a change in our life.

We miss the new knowledge change is attempting to deliver when we resist. I have found that change always has a message, steeped in meaning. It provides guidance, clarity and insight. It is a wisdom that holds only the best for us in the future. Like a nurturing mother, change is sometimes comforting and sometimes stern, but always interested in our well-being. If we resist change, and the knowledge it brings, we fall behind in the learning curve. The next change will often repeat the lesson, with more intensity, in an effort to get our attention. It is always better to learn as we go, rather than cram for the final exam. We need to welcome the lessons that each change brings into our lives, knowing that change can bring joy or pain and accepting of whatever comes our way.

We will also miss becoming that interim, new being on the path of our evolution. This interim being may be much more accepting and more capable of adapting to what presents next. Adapting in small, incremental steps is often much easier than making a single, dramatic change later in life. What is critical is to see that we are constantly changing and accepting these changes as part of our continual evolution. Like a newborn, learning to walk, we will stumble and get up, stumble and get up until we master walking. Each stumble creates change as we learn how to stand and keep our balance. Frequently during significant changes in our life we are just like the toddler, stumbling, falling and getting up to try again.

It is easy to see from my explanation of my personal evolution that my unwillingness to accept my changing lifestyle continued to ramp up, creating a financial, physical and emotional tidal wave. The crash was hard and took a long time to recover. If I had learned the lessons of change and let go of my pride and persona of being wealthy I could have avoided the tsunami that eventually struck.

Have Faith in the Evolutionary Process

Thanks to the insights from Sister Joan Chittister I have come to see God as not perfection, but an evolutionary God, experiencing and expressing as we do. To quote Sister Joan, "God is a mystery that nobody wants." This means that we are not bound by a predetermined destiny that only God knows. God and we are explorers of our destiny, and the active ingredient is change. Change is the alchemy that brings together our ever-changing mortal being with the Divine in an evolution of consciousness.

This view brings faith into alignment with science through the process of change. Science is no longer static but fluid. Even laws in physics are only temporary directional indicators, which can change with each new discovery. Our only constant is the impermanence of everything and the resulting evolution as consciousness continues to expand. So change is the catalyst in our discovery of what is next. We must have faith in the fact that change, in all ways and forms, is critical to the unfolding of our lives and the world around us. Change is also the presenter of truth in who we really are. Our being becomes more awake to Itself and Its full potential with our successful completion of each change we encounter. If God is moving with us then as we navigate each change together we are drawn closer together.

Experience has shown me that change is often messy and frequently painful, but it is my greatest teacher and my best friend. I have moved from resisting and running from change to openly embracing whatever change comes my way. My wish is that you also come to see change as a friend. I hope that this book can make change less frightening and easier to easier to work through for all who read it.

CHAPTER ELEVEN

FACING CHANGE TODAY AND BEYOND

Progress is impossible without change, and those who cannot change their minds cannot change anything.

George Bernard Shaw

Most people are protecting themselves. They are holding a lot of things in. They are not living honest, truthful, and sincere lives, because if they were to do so, they would have no control. Of course, they don't have control anyway, but they would have no illusion of control, either .

Adyashanti, *The End of Your World*

We have survived the dire predictions for 2012. We didn't see the end of the world, but what lies ahead continues to change rapidly creating even greater uncertainty. Our way forward is an ever greater mystery. People around the world are experiencing change in all aspects of their lives and at an ever-accelerating pace.

This has created confusion for many and poor choices by others. I believe the rise of senseless violence in the last decade is influenced by an inability to manage the change in the lives of these perpetrators. In many of these cases the acts of a single person or group of people seems to not fit their history or character. Something drove them to act violently. If we look more closely to what brought these people to the breaking point what often arises is an inability to handle the changes in their lives. Having an effective way to view and manage change could have mitigated the fear, anxiety and anger that drove these people to carry out unspeakable acts.

As I look at change over the last decade there are some key focal areas that seem to be touching all of us. I would like to talk about some of the more important changes in these key areas and what it seems to be saying to us all.

Money and Finance

For many the financial crisis of 2008 has created dramatic changes in our financial well-being. Median salaries are down, many have lost their homes, jobs have been lost and unemployment is high, and personal assets for most of us have been cut dramatically.

The security of a steady job no longer seems to exist. Many have had to seek training in a new field of work and have had to take a significant reduction in salary, often starting at the bottom. Others have experienced long periods of unemployment, requiring a total restructure of spending habits and a significant tightening of the family budget. While discretionary spending continues, it has been greatly reduced. In short, our decades old sense of financial security and instant gratification in acquiring the things we desire has gone out the window.

This may seem like a gloom and doom story, but there is also a silver lining. Our current economic situation has made many of us reconsider our dependence on things to make us happy. It is shining a light on our long-held lust for possessions and the misguided power and prestige we have believe they bring. It is also highlighting the truth that there is only temporary gratification in acquiring things and this does not add any greater meaning to our lives. Buying a new car, with no substantive savings in the bank, brings little in the way of sustained gratification or meaning. In turning from acquiring we seek non-monetary ways of finding meaning and lasting joy in our lives.

Many of the people I work with have taken the time they spent researching to make purchases and reinvested it in finding more purpose in life. Self-improvement, family, friendships and community are all getting a greater piece of the recaptured time wasted on acquiring things. All have found a greater sense of personal satisfaction, life purpose and meaning, and joy from these efforts. Most are now looking in hindsight at their wasted time and money in acquiring things, wondering how they could have been so misguided internally and externally.

We don't have to look any further than the 60-inch flat screen in our family room to gain an understanding of the external forces distracting us towards spending our way to change. Often television is our escape from the stress of daily life and the changes going on around us. Mixed within these tales of fantasy are an endless procession of ads and commercials for things we don't really need. Buy a new car, get the perfect body makeover, purchase a fix for the fear of aging. It's all there for a price. Unfortunately, the price is the misdirection it takes us from the actual direction that life is taking us towards. Here is a simple litmus test for these ads. Ask yourself, "Will buying this product or service create greater purpose and meaning in my life?" Most often the answer is no. To our credit, or perhaps the influence credit crunch, I see people turning away from and tuning out mass commercial marketing in favor of more meaningful activities.

I am also seeing a tendency to slow down. Acquiring has a frenetic energy, which over stimulates the mind and consumes our energy. Meditation is making a revival and people are looking to personal and spiritual discovery more than ever before. Life is gaining greater meaning, without all of the trappings.

In a way, we are junkies, who are forced to quit because we don't have the money to purchase the next fix. Acquiring is addictive because it provides that momentary high, which never lasts long. We need another purchase to bring back the high. Our economy and personal financial situations have hit rock bottom, and we are now forced into recovery.

As we start to climb off the gerbil wheel of consumption another phenomenon is occurring. The need to produce more and more products is waning resulting in fewer jobs. Those new jobs are now at a much lower wage. As a result we have seen a widening of the socio-economic gap during this period, and it is playing out in our thoughts, attitudes and beliefs. The rich are getting richer, and with that comes their continued lust for acquiring. Six houses are better than three. The new Ferrari is a must. Their stakes escalate and the need for money grows daily down the road to more, now. For those who are making the shift from acquiring to meaning, either voluntarily or by force, there is a growing, averse view of the rich. The envy of the rich has turned to anger or pity. Those who have not made the shift to purpose and meaning are angry at the rich and look to strike back in an effort to create greater equality. Those who have made the shift and are looking to find a community of like minded individuals no longer want to be a associated with the wealthy or want them in their community. The wealthy are often pictured as ego-centric, with little community commitment.

It is very likely that financial reorientation will continue to dominate the next decade. Financial volatility, on a global scale, will send ripples through our societies and will impact our personal lives. Our financial persona will continue to change and evolve. Allowing financial uncertainty in our lives will be critical in navigating these troubled waters. Being proactive, rather than reactive, to financial change will smooth out the bumps in the road and reduce anxiety. Returning to basics, in finances, family, friends and community, will offer restorative medicine to our overall well-being. Change will lead us from financial addiction to non-monetary ways to find purpose and meaning.

Larry and Judy had been forced into early retirement by the down-sizing of both there jobs. While they had small pensions and social security there was just enough to scrape by. Larry and Judy could no longer afford to spend the way they had when they were both employed and it was making them depressed and fearful of the future.

After a year of working low level and paying jobs that did not use there skills or present meaningful work the two were miserable. They came to see me looking for a fix. "How can we get back in the game?" was the answer they were seeking. My first question back to both of them was, "Is this what you really want?". What I was really asking was 'Are you ready to say goodbye to a life-long habit of measuring your satisfaction in life by acquisition.' After several meetings and much soul searching both Larry and Judy came to the conclusion that they wanted more than possessions to define their legacy to their family, community and planet.

It took several months for Larry and Judy to stay open to the exploration of the present. During this time they changed their spending habits and started to set aside a modest reserve in savings. Both volunteered in the community and found new meaning in helping others by using the skills and talents they had honed over years of education and work. Larry worked with entrepreneurs in new business development and Judy used her teaching skills to mentor failing students. While this shift was good in bringing meaning to their lives, it still seemed to lack 'something more' for both of them.

One day Judy stumbled onto an article about senior Americans who had made the decision to move to a foreign country, where the expenses of living were far more reasonable. The more research Larry and Judy did the more excited they became about the idea. They were particularly interested in Ecuador as a potential for their retirement years. They decided to take a trip to Ecuador to explore the possibilities more. Larry and Judy spent two weeks in Ecuador touring various communities that had 'expats', talking with many families who had made the leap, and reflecting on the positives and negatives of such a venture.

On their return both Larry and Judy were excited and perplexed. While they found the communities beautiful and affordable there were also several obstacles. Besides language and a list of social differences, from owning a car or riding a bus as an example, they were most perplexed by the lack of thing in the local shops and markets. Larry and Judy were both used to going to Walmart or Target and finding anything they wanted. This was not the case in Ecuador. The variety and availability of many items they took for granted were not there. In particular there was very little processed food. The key question for Larry and Judy was whether they could let go of the need to have 'everything' available for a better, overall standard of living on their modest retirement.

Larry and Judy had found in their research that many 'expats' had made the leap only to find themselves unable to assimilate into their community and constantly wanting of the things they could no longer get in Ecuador. One big issue was television. Cable was the only available signal and most of the channels provided were in Spanish. Many of the 'expats' made little to no effort to learn the language, limiting their ability to communicate outside the small 'expat' community they lived in. These 'expats' just couldn't do without and decided, at great expense, to return to the U.S.

After considering all of the positives and negatives they had researched Larry and Judy decided to make the move. It took well over a year for them to get settled in Ecuador. Moving was more of a hassle than they expected, making changes to diet and food preparation was more difficult than they originally thought, and learning conversational Spanish was a more arduous process than what they expected after immersion into the culture. Larry and Judy persevered through all of this, driven by a gut instinct that this was the right change for them.

Today Larry and Judy still find their move a work in process, but the most important thing is they are happy. Some lifestyle changes have been easy and some have been harder to assimilate into. What is critical is even the hard changes are worth it for these two retiree's. They no longer are obsessed with and worry about money. They have plenty to live on in Ecuador. More important, they have become more engaged and involved in their community (extending even beyond the expat community and into the native culture) and are far less focused on possessions. Judy is teaching English at the local school twice a week and Larry likes helping out the local, small businesses in learning how to turn a profit. They both volunteer their time but are repaid by patient, ongoing instruction in Spanish by those they work with.

Our world has been slowly torn apart by the ravages of increased consumption. The desire to 'have' has come at significant cost to our environment and the stability of our maturing economy. When our economic health is totally reliant on continued increases in consumption we have jumped down the rabbit hole and entered a fantasy that is not sustainable. Larry and Judy sensed this and then were forced to face the harsh economic reality that was the reaction to blind overconsumption. They chose to make a change. They still are consumers, but at a much lower level than when they lived in the U.S. More important Larry and Judy have found that they can be happy leading a life of meaning and purpose, rather than by acquiring things.

Change and Community

Over the last 100 years the family and community have suffered in an effort to keep up with change. Our accelerated way of living has placed enormous demands on our time, leaving friends and family with the short end of the stick. Global shifts environmentally, politically and economically have lead us away from the basic principles that brought us together. We are seeing significant shifts in how we communicate, travel and have our basic needs met. All these rapid changes have challenged our sense of independence and redefined our sense of interdependence.

Those who govern no longer seem to make sense or are even in touch with reality beyond their own needs, wants and desires. We are fighting wars that we no longer understand or support. We are experiencing senseless violence from increasingly isolated individuals, who have lost all connection to community. We are seeing our economic stability and wellbeing being eroded by greed in a war to 'have' rather than 'have not'. Life as we know it is rapidly changing and it can seem totally out of control.

What do we do now, resist, give up or just go with the flow? There is no one answer, but I believe if we can follow a structure for change we can move in a positive direction. We can give up what no longer serves us. We can look around us to find what makes the most sense for all of us and move in that direction with eyes wide open. We can look within to seek inner guidance and strength to propel us forward. We can look to start managing the change in our lives, rather than having it manage us.

While this must start at the individual level it gains much more power as we find those who share our vision of the way forward and create a collective energy able to support constructive change. We are starting to expand our thinking into a more global consciousness. Rather than allowing accelerated change to continue to tear us apart we are gaining some control over the change process and learning to guide it collectively towards more positive outcomes. We are coming to the realization that if we don't start acting in an interactive way our very existence is threatened.

To have a global impact we must strengthen relationships and community. Coordinated decisions for change is the only way to get to where we need to be. Yet we are now seeing people moving in two different directions.

One is self-protection and isolation. This is an 'every person for their selves' approach. Grab what you can, stockpile, hoard, prepare to weather the storm. Others will perish, but you will survive. The acquisition of things continues to provide a fragile sense of security and safety. Only connect with like-minded people, who share this view of survival, but don't trust anyone because, in the end, they are only concerned about their survival. This path is based in fear and isolation.

The other direction people are taking holds 'we are in this together' and looks to building community for support. Collaboration, cooperation and the strength of relationships are the key to managing any changes that come their way. They find great strength in the collective, realizing that there is no one answer and that sharing ideas will support the creativity needed to overcome all obstacles. This path is inclusive, open and hope based.

I believe the direction of isolation and self-centered survival is flawed, as it fails to follow the process of change that I have outlined. There is an inability to say goodbye to an appetite for acquisition and consumption. This, in a world of limits, forces a concept of winners and losers. An inability to let go of old ways of living stunts the ability to move on in change.

This direction is also limited in its exploration of the present moment. The more we explore the present the more we come to understand that we live in an interdependent world. Sustainability is a community effort that benefits from collective actions. Looking at the news of today, time and again, it is the story of community action that is creating real change. Whether it is the rebuilding of an inner-city slum by its community in a Detroit suburb or the revival of farming within Japan by a group of urban youths, these programs are having an impact.

It seems that our ability to react to change is now a community effort, which supports our mental and emotional, as well as physical, health. Many of the people I have worked with in the last year have indicated fears related to the future. In working together I have encouraged finding community as a way of exploring how to handle the changes they fear. Those who have pursued community have been less fearful, more energized and more positive about the future. Community connection gives us a sense that we can have an impact on larger changes going on in our city, state, nation, and world.

Change and Relationships

The nature of relationships are also changing at an accelerated pace. It is never more evident than in marital relationships. We are experiencing more divorces than at any time in our history. Relationships seem more impermanent than permanent. Why?

Our personal growth, through change, is accelerating each year. What seemed significant last year, or even this month, is no longer true to us. Everyone's thoughts, feelings and beliefs are being challenged and modified constantly. This accelerated personal evolution is not constant for everyone. Some of us grow faster, or in different ways from others, even those closest to us. What brought two people together in a relationship can become what drives people apart in the future. There is nothing right or wrong about this phenomenon, it is just a fact of life. Change has accelerated our evolution, but not at the same rate or way for everyone.

How can a relationship have a better chance to survive in the face of all this change? Through my work with others I see little value in attempting to get one person to just accept, unconditionally, where the other is going. 'I'll change to save our relationship.' is not the answer. In fact, there are no answers to how to keep a relationship together. What keeps us together is beyond logic and the mind. It is an instinctual, inner, organic understanding of who we are and what we are willing to accept.

There are numerous paths in working on relationships, which I will not try to cover in this book on change. I would like to share one critical point that seem facilitate the process of taking relationships through change. Do not hold anything back. I find that the most common issue in relationships is when one person goes through an internal change, but doesn't share it with their partner. This leaves the other person to observe the external changes, but wondering how they came about and what they mean. Not keeping our significant others informed about the personal changes we are going through is a formula for disaster. Whatever personal change we have, large or small, has an effect on a relationship and needs to be revealed, discussed, and worked through.

Andy was encouraged to take a co-dependency class by a friend. He decided to take the course and asked his wife, Cindy, if she would like to attend. Cindy declined. Each week Andy discovered his wounds and lack of self-confidence that came from his family of origin. He started to understand how this developed into co-dependent behaviors, which he now saw as creating problems in his marriage. Andy made the decision to make some changes. Andy, however, decided that because Cindy did not want to attend the co-dependency class she was not interested in what was going on, so he just didn't share with Cindy.

As Andy's behaviors started to change Cindy started to wonder why their relationship was changing. She saw Andy as less dependent on her and seemed to be pulling away. Cindy started to wonder if there was another woman and if Andy was no longer faithful. She became fearful and hurt by her thoughts and started to become distant. Andy assumed that Cindy's change was because he was being less co-dependent and thought this was a change for the good. One day Cindy told Andy that she wanted a divorce. Andy was shocked and sought my help to sort things out.

I had them describe what brought them together and what had seemed to change. As Andy began to explain the changes he was going through, as a result of the co-dependency class, I watched as Cindy's face show shock and then slowly grow in understanding based on new information. The changes she saw in Andy were now in a new light. Cindy almost immediately moved from fear to anger. Why hadn't Andy shared this with her? This was important to their relationship and Cindy felt that Andy was covertly attempting to change their relationship without talking to her about it.

Andy took to the defensive, suggesting that he had offered to have her attend the class with him and she refused. He just felt that Cindy wasn't interested, so there was no need to share. While a new level of clarity had come to the relationship, there was still a significant issue that needed to be addressed. Andy wasn't being open about his changes and Cindy was being left in the dark, to figure it out on her own. With some work Andy got to a point where he was honestly willing to apologize for keeping Cindy in the dark.

This opened the door to a the more important issue, how Andy's changes were impacting the relationship. As I had Andy explain in detail the areas that he felt they were co-dependent and what he was attempting to change, I gave Cindy a chance to express her views and to explain her understanding of Andy's perceptions. In some cases Cindy could understand where they were acting in a co-dependent manner. She then openly shared where she was willing to change. She also challenged some of Andy's perceptions of co-dependency, which resulted in deeper inquiry during our meeting and became part of homework for further inquiry.

Within a short period of time Andy and Cindy found common ground. Both had made some changes. Andy pledged to be open about whatever changes he was going through. Cindy promised the same. They both committed to listening more and not jumping to conclusions. They also agreed to disagree in some areas. They now took there relationship as a work in process that was going to have continual changes that needed to be openly discussed and considered. They had given up the blind belief that they would be together for ever, but were committed, more than ever, to work on making their relationship grow in a way that would serve both of them.

Andy and Cindy had come to the second, big understanding of relationships. They came to understand and accept that relationships are impermanent and subject to change. They realized that the best contributions they could make to their relationship was to be open, honest, willing to listen and consider, and a willingness to seek a common ground. They were also willing to accept that in some cases they would agree to disagree. They saw that these differences would put a strain on their relationship, and could, eventually, lead to them separating. Andy and Cindy were less certain about their future, but also had a greater confidence in where the stood with each other and what it would take to keep the relationship healthy and alive. They felt they had moved from fantasy to reality. Andy and Cindy enrolled together in the next available co-dependency class, and found it to be very healthy for the evolution of their relationship.

A Change From Religion to Spirituality

For millennia others have taught us about God. The thoughts, ideas, beliefs and doctrines have been refined to quantify what God is and what God is not. During this period the consciousness of man, real or perceived, was considered generally to dense to actually know God. So religion became the teacher, the director of actions, and, most importantly, the determinant of salvation. In this consciousness we abdicated our relationship with God to others, the holy ones, the seers, the faithful.

In the last two decades this view of God has changed dramatically. These long-accepted precepts, ingrained in all major religions, are being challenged by an evolution of consciousness and a greater awareness of our own spirituality. Many teachers are now emphasizing that we are awakening to our God essence within. To the degree that traditional religions are resisting this personal awakening, we are seeing a mass exodus of the formerly faithful. Not everyone, but the numbers are growing. Our view of and relationship with God is changing.

I would once again like to quote Sister Joan Chittister from her book, Welcome to the Wisdom of the World:

> "If God is the very origin of our lives and the support of our existence, then God is our companion on the way, the air we breathe, the thoughts we think, the ocean of the Spirit in which we move.
>
> The presence of God is not dependent on ecclesiastical rank of any kind or ilk. The presence of God does not reside in who or what we think we are. Instead, it lodges in what we carry within us.
>
> Only the aggrandizement of the self can block the presence of God within us. Only the consciousness of the omnipresence of God can enable it. If God is everywhere, then the locus of God is both within us and around us at the same time. And if God is not everywhere, how can God possibly be God?"

When asked, "Where is God?" the new answer is, "everywhere and right here", and this, quite frankly, changes everything. It provides a whole new perspective of who we really are, and it puts the burden of life squarely on our shoulders. For those who have taken this path of inquiry the old ways of observing our faith are no longer relevant. A totally new reorientation to spirituality and life is required. The effects, internally and externally, expand beyond thought to feelings, beliefs and actions. This is perhaps the greatest change in what we are becoming.

This shift is impacting all phases of our life. Family, especially parents, may react strongly to this new perspective and Self. Friendships will be challenged as religious beliefs and spiritual beliefs may be at polar opposites. Even marriages can be pushed to the breaking point as one partner undergoes a spiritual shift, while the other remains steadfast in current beliefs. Sustaining our relationships will require honesty, openness, compassion, and patience. Yet when we awaken to this 'presence within' there is no turning back.

While in corporate America I developed a long-term friendship with Kimberly. She and I worked closely together on many legal issues and we often would have lunch together. Kimberly is an individual with high moral values and strong Christian beliefs. She regularly attends and participates in Bible study through her church. On the other hand I am a spiritual mutt, part Christian, part Buddhist, and mostly 'New Thought'.

During our lunches together our conversations began to turn towards our spiritual beliefs. It was very troubling for Kimberly that my view of Jesus was different from hers. Kimberly believes that Jesus is our only way to salvation. I believe that Jesus was awake, enlightened, and one of the greatest spiritual teachers of all time. While we both hold Jesus in high regard, there was a significant difference in perspective with regards to the role of Jesus in our lives. In short, Kimberly believed that I am going to hell, as I had not accepted Jesus as my personal savior.

Kimberly would often quote Bible passages to me in support of her position. I would listen and then give my perspective on the meaning of the passage. To Kimberly the Bible is literal and defines a single path to salvation. For me the Bible speaks in general terms that supports an evolutionary consciousness through inquiry and interpretation. We listened to each other, attempted to take in each person's perspective, but we had to agree that we simply disagreed on Biblical meaning and interpretation.

After weeks of lunchtime discussions about faith, beliefs and spirituality one day Kimberly said to me, "I don't know what else to say. I care for you and your Soul, and I know you are going to hell. It saddens me that you will not accept Jesus as your savior." It brought a tear to my eye to see how much my friend cared for me, and the pain my beliefs were causing her. This difference in spiritual orientation had created a gap in our friendship, but we were also determined to work in other areas to keep our relationship viable. During the next couple years we supported each other in a variety of professional and personal changes in our lives, but when it came to spiritual beliefs we had agreed to disagree.

Whatever our view on spirituality there is a trend for us to take it deeper, make it more personal and to learn to stand for what we believe in. This is the real value of the spiritual renaissance that is going on today. While a great variety of religions and spiritual views remain, there does seem to be a greater openness to listen to and explore the spiritual ideas of others. This can only enhance our spiritual evolution.

I do not have any fixed expectations about our future. I find it better to live in the present moment, and experience life as it unfolds. I believe that our future is not written on some Mayan stone, but is the product of how we deal with change right now. I know is that change is accelerating, and it is our responsibility, to ourselves and the planet, to understand how to acknowledge and deal with change in a more effective and efficient way. That has been my motivation for this book.

CHAPTER TWELVE

TO DIE BEFORE I DIE.

To die before you die is to let go of this life prior to one's physical death, so that any future fears of dying do not get in the way of living.

James Young, *Journal on the Appalachian Trail*

A friend who had been meditating for some time, approached a Zen master recently arrived in this country. He asked the roshi if he might study with him. To which the roshi replied, "Are you prepared to die?" My friend shook his head in bewilderment and said, "I didn't come here to die. I came here to learn Zen." The roshi said, "If you are not willing to die, you are not ready to let go into life. Come back when you are ready to enter directly, excluding nothing."

Stephen and Ondrea Levine,
Who Dies? An Investigation of Conscious Living and Conscious Dying

'To die before you die.' Many stories, fiction and non-fiction, have been written about it. Poets and philosophers muse on it. Soldiers have lived it, and, in many ways, we have all had a glimpse. What does it really mean? Why should we want this experience? What will we learn? These are just a few of the questions around this short statement of truth. One last question might be, "Why include it in this book?"

Well death is definitely a significant change, and to experience death before we die is consistent with what we have discussed in this book about change. Change is about saying goodbye to our 'old self', which precedes a period of limbo before we birth 'who we are becoming'. Quite simply, there is death, a form of resurrection in Spirit, and a new birth. So, as we experience change in our life, we are experiencing a type of death before we die.

How we manage and deal with change during our lives seems to play an important roll in our final encounter with death. There are two reasons I can point to. Effectively dealing with change requires our willingness to stop resisting and to accept what life has to offer. Second, understanding that change is a transformation of 'who we are' will cause the ego to play a lesser role in self-awareness and in how we live our lives. We literally see beyond what the ego defines as 'who we are now' and take a broader view of what existence means at a much Higher Level. Change, then, can help us lose a sense of finality with death and see it as another change we are going through.

THE EXPERIENCE OF NEAR DEATH

My first job in healthcare was as a respiratory therapist. In my position I was part of the cardiac arrest team for the hospital. Over my years as a respiratory therapist I attended hundreds of 'code blues', or cardiac arrests. At first I was puzzled by the outcomes. There were times when we would find the patient with few positive physical indicators for survival and they would bounce back. Other times, the best looking patients at the beginning of the arrest never made it. I quickly came to learn that initial physical sign and most of our efforts were not the final determinant for survival.

Slowly, but surely, I came to understand that cardiac arrest victims were undergoing a dramatic change, and how they moved through this change had the biggest impact on outcome. In talking with many of the survivors they described a variety of different experiences and visions, but they all shared a common theme, "The experience has changed who I am and how I look at life." Near death experiences have left survivors with a total reorientation to how they have lived their lives and how they want to live the rest of their current lives. Consistently I found that these survivors had lost their fear and sense of finality with death. They now saw death as just another change to experience. As I have described in the change model, these survivors have discarded who they had been and are ready to embrace a new way of being.

Ben was a corporate executive who had lived fast and furiously for 56 years. One day, during a particularly stressful time at the office, Ben started to experience chest pains. Ben was admitted to our hospital for tests and underwent a cardiac stress test. The test did not go well and it was terminated early, due to poor indicators. Upon returning to his room Ben had a massive heart attach. His cardiac arrest was extensive and protracted. It took us over 60 minutes to get Ben back and stabilized. There were times when he would come back and then slip away again. All the time I was doing cardiac compressions on his chest when Ben's heart stopped. I was drenched in sweat and exhausted, but I didn't ask for relief as I felt a strong connection to Ben and felt he was fighting to survive.

Later that day, after Ben had stabilized and improved, I was called to discontinue the ventilator that was breathing for him, and remove his breathing tube. This was the first time Ben could speak since the arrest. I was shocked by Ben's attitude. His first statement to me was, "Wow! What an unbelievable experience!" Ben went on to explain how he had watched the whole cardiac arrest from directly over the bed. As the arrest progressed his attention turned to the life he had lived. In the light of his possible death, Ben came to view his life as having been petty, with little meaning. He had acquired power and money, but it held no value during this experience. Ben felt he had a decision to make, accept his death or return and make some meaningful changes. He chose the latter.

Ben went on to have open-heart surgery, so he was in the hospital over 10 days. During that time we had the opportunity to have several, deep conversations. As Ben continued to look at his near-death experience he continued to see it as a special blessing. He took it as the 'wake up call' that he needed to move into a more meaningful life. Ben was determined to not miss this second opportunity. I stayed in contact with Ben after his discharge. Ben made several, significant changes in his life. He quit his executive job, sold his big house, dumped the Cadillac for a Subaru, and went back to school to become a social worker.

What amazed me the most was Ben's absolute determination to change. He had no hesitation or fear. Ben joked on the phone once, "I have already died. What is there left to be afraid of?" Three years later I got an invitation from Ben to attend his graduation with a masters in social work. I asked Ben why social work? He replied, "I spent the first 56 years of my life only concerned about me. That is not enough. That is not how I was meant to live my life. Now I am going to help others." Ben had died before he died.

Many people I worked with in the hospital were not going to survive. It was a moving and instructive time for me to experience with these people their last days. Some struggled and fought, sometimes a horrible death. Others were at peace, exhibiting a philosophical and calm demeanor related to their death. The more I talked with these terminal patients a pattern started to surface. It seemed that those who had experienced and moved through significant changes during their life were better prepared for the end of their lives. Those who had struggled with and fought change at every turn were struggling with the end of their lives. I came to understand that effectively working with change during our lives helps to prepare us for our death. There is less of a tendency to see death as final and scary. Death takes on the mantle of just another change, even though it is a big one.

It seemed to me that the personality of these lifelong change agents was much more flexible and adapting. Don't get me wrong, they didn't want to die, but they were much more accepting of death. Who they were had lost its importance and their attachment to things had long gone. Connections with others and coming to some completion with them was the most important activity left in life. Closure with others seemed to be more important than finalizing or changing their last will and testament.

These lifelong change agents seemed to also hold a much more intimate knowledge and emotional relationship with God. For them, God had always been with them, and they saw God as ready to welcome, rather than judge them. This view was independent of religion and belief. They just seemed to know God differently from others within their faith.

My years as a respiratory therapist became an amazing study in change and death. I have returned many times to the faces and their stories as I have worked to gain a perspective of difficult changes in my own life. It has had a dramatic impact on how I have decided to live out my life. I used to fear death, but now I also see it as change. I know it is a change that I will eventually face, but I hope to experience many more changes before then.

THE ROAD OF A THOUSAND DEATHS

What we do, how we connect with others, the way in which we are productive, our individual source of happiness, all of these qualities are unique to each of us and are constantly changing. There is no, single mold that fits us all. No single path for everyone to walk, and no single map to show us where we are going. Life is a mystery and very few of us find the smooth and easy path right from the start. None of us ever find the perfect path. That is because there is no perfect path. This is just another illusion propagated by the ego.

During our developmental years parents, family and friend try to define our path for us. They can be so convincing, in a positive or negative way. We usually follow without consideration for our own happiness. Often parents would like us to live the dream they were never able to manifest in their lives. The question is whether their dream is really our dream. If we accept their vision for us, will it satisfy that part of us that holds the bigger plan, our Soul.

Based on this coaxing and prodding many of us have developed careers, lifestyles and personas that we are really not comfortable with or motivated by. What do we do? We have to die! Not literally, but for us to make a radical change to a new way of being we have to bring to an end the old way of being. We must die before we die.

What we become may be well thought out or a reaction to what we have accepted as who we are up to this point. So our next shift may move us closer into alignment with what our Soul has in mind, but it may also be just off the mark if we carry forward some of the less troubling trappings of our old way of being. So we die again in change and become again. This process often continues time and again as we traverse the long and winding path in search of our true destiny, who and what we were really meant to be in this life. What can be even more confusing is that as we look back we may become confused by all of the different masks we have worn and sometimes ashamed of these personas in how they presented to the world. This can really complicate the view going forward and sap some of the energy is 'moving on'.

So who we are is not constant, but continually going through deaths and resurrections. We are traveling the road of 1,000 deaths. We start off excited and motivated, make commitments, expend time and energy, and then, just as we seem to hit a peak, there is something inside that says, "This is not quite It!" Our balloon gets a small leak and starts to deflate. Energy and enthusiasm is lost, and we begin to question and become confused. Our confidence wanes and we are filled with doubt. Most important, we are not happy. Without even knowing we start to conspire with life to construct our own demise.

Happiness, contentment, energy and excitement then, become guideposts to the paths we take. When we are hold positive energy, no matter how long it lasts, we are on the right path. When we start to loose that sense of joy, we took a wrong turn. This is not a matter of struggle. Many people I have worked with are struggling, but quite happy. They are on the right path. It just happens to be a little or a lot difficult. We can also be sailing along in life without any difficulty but are miserable with the life we are leading. If the path holds a deep meaning for our Soul then it is never too difficult.

Many times we try to change the trajectory of our path just a little but still cannot find happiness. I have seen many situations where people try to adjust their career or lifestyle by small degrees, thinking they will then be happy only to come to a later realization that they are not. I am not saying it can't work, just that, more often than not, it seems to never deliver real joy.

I worked with a dentist who didn't like all of the issues he was facing with his patients. Too little preventive care and now it was too expensive to fix their teeth properly. Gary decided to go into orthodontia. He said at the time, "These are younger patients, with fewer dental issues, and I can spread out their payments over a couple years." I attempted to get Gary to inquire more deeply into his life as a dentist, but he was sure that his death as a dentist and his birth as an orthodontist was going to make him happy.

Gary spent a considerable amount of time, energy and money in making the shift until he was finally an orthodontist. Two years later Gary returned to see me. Life as an orthodontist was not making him happy. Getting his patients to do what they needed to do to straighten their teeth, especially teenagers, was very taxing. Gary was good at what he did, but he wasn't happy. The mechanics of dentistry was OK, but the work at getting individuals, especially teenagers, to change their habits was debilitating.

We started to inquire more deeply into what he felt called to do. After some work what surfaced was his desire to teach. Gary had felt that he had learned a lot during his years of practice and would like to share that with dental students. After a difficult transition in closing down his practice and finding a position with a dental school, Gary made the move to instructor of dentistry. Gary felt he was on his path.

A year later Gary reappeared. He was struggling. The didactic part of his job was going fine. Gary liked the classroom. But he also had clinical responsibilities for teaching students how to work on real patients. He was back again in the clinical setting he didn't enjoy.

Gary and I went back to the drawing table and really looked deeply into what he enjoyed and didn't enjoy in his current position. After some deep Soul searching Gary felt his real calling was to teaching, but not in dentistry. He came to the realization that there wasn't anything about dentistry that motivated him or gave him joy. It was time to go radical.

After much consideration a pathway for Gary into a high school biology teacher opened up. Gary was a little hesitant, but something in his gut felt right about it. I worked with Gary over the next couple of months as he made the most radical, career change of his working life. It wasn't an easy transition. Gary had to make many adjustments, especially in his lifestyle. After six months at teaching high school biology Gary was very happy. He loved the kids, enjoyed the issues and interactions that high school can bring, and even got a position as the assistant track coach, a passion he had in college.

The road to happiness was not straight for Gary. His original commitment to dentistry had more to do with his family – father was a dentist – and his desire to make a lot of money than following a vocation that moved his Soul. His resistance to all of the time and money he spent on becoming a dentist influenced Gary to make small adjustments, rather than radical change. Gary went through three deaths to get where he wanted to be. Some, including his father, thought that Gary had lost his mind. I know Gary found his Soul.

As I look back on my own life I have held dozens of different positions in that time. From paperboy to counselor the road looks more like a winding trip through the mountains, compared to a run down the interstate. With each death I reflected back on the lessons learned, considered the possibilities going forward, and took time to listen to my Soul. My path has never been perfect, but I am happy. Even with the wrong turns I can now see how the detours helped me to get here. Some deaths came easy, and some deaths were way too hard. In the end, I choose to die before I die, not once but many, many times and I don't regret any of them. Most important, I know there are more deaths on the road ahead and I am ready to take them on.

JIM'S DISCOVERY ON THE APPALACHIAN TRAIL

I would like to close with an interview with my friend, Jim, who chose to hike the Appalachian Trail, in parts, on three different occasions. The interview reflects how this 'time out' that he gave himself set the groundwork for managing change in his life and the absolute commitment to stay awake and aware.

Jim and I are members of a men's group that has met weekly for over four years. We are committed to honestly sharing our lives, supporting each other, and holding each other accountable. We have no agenda but to be present with each other, to listen with intention, and to respond from the heart. It is a road that many men find difficult to take, and I am blessed that I have chosen this path with my other brothers.

One of the commitments we made in our men's group was for each of us to take two full meetings to tell our life story. This was something that Jim had done before, and we agreed to do. It was a difficult task. Each of us had to honestly reflect on our lives, decide on what was important, and to put it together into a cohesive story, which made sense. Each man in our group was encouraged to ask questions and provide insights back to the storyteller. The impact on each of our lives cannot be put into words.

Jim was raised in the farming country of Tennessee. He grew up in a family of simple means, where work put food on the table and everyone pitched in. Jim has worked hard to become educated, make his way in the business world, and to support his family. Jim's journey through life had taken him west, far from his Tennessee roots. In 2006 Jim decided to give himself a time out, to take the opportunity to explore the wilderness of the Appalachian Trail. He decided to make this journey alone, and to see what the trail and nature could teach him and to find out where it might lead him for the rest of his life.

Question: Why did you decide to hike the Appalachian Trail?

Jim: He just smiled and opened up one of three notebooks of writings and pictures from the trail. "Glad you asked. I actually wrote a purpose statement to get clear on my intentions for the trip at the very beginning. Let me read it to you."

> To isolate myself from the world I know so that I may become clear of what other purposes my life shall still give or have. To die before I die, so that my hanging on does not affect those whose time is not the same as mine. That they too can live on their own path and that I perhaps can be a mentor, in some way, for others to approach and accept their own mortality. To transform into another or perhaps tweak my own being to become more present with myself, to show that new quality in the presence of others, and to allow myself to enter the winter of my life with high self esteem and pride for having done my work to earn the right to be an elder and to be available to mentor those wanting mentoring. To cease my condemnation and unnecessary judgments of others and to be willing to grieve the losses and atrocities of others and myself in an attempt to shine light where darkness now exists. To be willing to shine a light, if I must do it alone, where the darkness has caused minimal dampness or has been void for such a period of time that water, rust and mildew is persistent. To develop patience that allows me to take on such tasks and gain strength in knowing that such actions are the only course that will make a difference in the long run.

After reading his purpose statement to me Jim was quiet, looking out the window. A flood of memories and commitments returned and the time between then and now flashed before his eyes. Jim knew from the beginning that the trail was going to be lonely, challenging, filled with insight and awakening, and life changing. He was prepared to face those challenges and changes in his desire to attain a personal transformation to become an elder, but the trail proved to be more daunting than what he expected.

Question: How did you come to choose your trail name, 'Die before I die'?

Jim: "It came from a story that I read in <u>Who Dies,</u> by Steven and Ondrea Levine. In the book they discussed how the Native Americans frequently practiced dying so that it was not so dramatic when it actually happened.

I was taught that dying caused deep grief and that was overwhelming for me as a young child. Levine's story made sense to me. We are so dependent on routine and habits that we are not prepared to die. I decided that each day, as I started on the trail, I would perform a ritual. I reflected on the unimportant aspects of my daily life, I grieved for the things I need to let go, and I gave thanks for having the opportunity to walk on this earth one more day."

Question: How long were you on the trail?

Jim: "I have been on the trail three different times for approximately 900 miles and ten weeks. My gift from the trail was clarity, time alone, and the space to allow me to capture the words of my heart and soul. It gave me rest and perspective that I could not easily achieve in my normal life. Each day was amazing as to what it brought and what it revealed to me. The unexpected became the expected.

As I transitioned from trail to rest stop along the way, my life constantly changed day by day. Different feelings, emotions, thoughts and ideas appeared at each turn of the trail. The trail was challenging at times and inspiring at others. I often sang the old spiritual songs I learned as a child, especially 'I Come to the Garden Alone' (Jim took a few moments and we sang together). This song had great meaning as it gave me the spiritual connection I was seeking, and I came to accept that I entered this world alone and I will leave it alone. What arose was a deep desire to take more responsibility for my life."

Question: What did the trail teach you about change?

Jim: "It is still teaching me that I have very little control over my life. It hurts sometimes to see how much of my life is in change and how drastic each change can be. The unending desire that we will wake up and do whatever is necessary to save our world and what little control I have over that."

Question: How has the trail changed your life?

Jim: "It's a hard question to answer. The trail started something that continues to this very day. The changes that started on the trail just continue to unfold years later. I continue to constantly reflect on personal responsibility, something I rejected most of the first part of my life. I came from a dysfunctional family, were I didn't have to take responsibility for my actions. The trail made me totally responsible, each and every day. I find myself more accepting of what is mine, and less likely to project onto others, making me less critical of others."

Question: Are you continuing to die before you die?

Jim: "Yes, it is still not easy and sometimes painful, but I continue to attempt to die a little each day as it makes my ongoing life more real. Each step helps me cut through the race consciousness I have assimilated. (Jim refers to race consciousness as a collective way of thinking, where we blindly accept the thoughts, beliefs and feelings of a group. Jung referred to this as the collective unconscious.) I believe the daily bombardment of the media and the influence of race consciousness is a constant challenge for the people who choose to walk the path of reality.

I know this is the only way, but I have a tremendous resistance to walking this path alone. There are days when I feel it is a curse to wake up to reality. Life seems simpler for the person who is willing to compromise and fall into a dream, rather than facing the reality of really living on a daily basis. No one, even those closest to me, can help me really face the reality of my life. To really get to my truth I have to face reality on my own. This trail often feels lonely because there seems to be such a small percentage of people who choose to walk this path. Sometimes I say to myself, "Why God do I have to endure the pain of others being asleep."

The trail has also brought so much into my life that I am grateful for. So often we hide the depths of our feelings and I appreciate my gift from the trail to live consciously, to feel deeply. I can't turn off my Soul, I have no control over it. I have made a connection to God that challenges and changes me each and every day. It is tremendously validating when someone acknowledges what I so deeply feel as the truth. I am stubborn so it may take me 300 miles of hiking to realize what others could realize through meditation. But it is the way I choose, and the path I feel I must follow. However we both got there, it is very exciting for me to find that one of my fellow travelers has reached the same location and we have a meeting of the minds.

So the trail continues on and each day I die to a new day. I make no promises about the trail. It will only reveal to you what is yours to awaken to. The trail has changed me forever and I accept its challenge each day that remains before I die. I accept its unknown and the uncertainty that it brings. So I beckon to everyone, "Come hike with me, if only in your heart."

When Jim decided to tackle the Appalachian Trail he had a goal to become an elder. Elders have existed in our tribal cultures for millennia. Elders hold a position of responsibility within many of our religious communities, especially the Quakers. Most traditions have a right of passage to enter into Elderhood. In this transformation they commit to serve the community for the greater good. They humbly seek the truth and take personal responsibility for their actions. By awakening to the changes they face, each and every day, they can share what they have learned with their community.

Jim chose the Appalachian Trail as his right of passage. He walked it alone, and it permanently changed his life. As I have discussed in this book, one of the parts of the process for change is to explore the present. Exploring the present is critical to assist with any successful change, but it can also be a continuous source for ongoing change. Being present to the moment forces us to be responsible for our actions and to see the many paths forward that will help us to constantly evolve. In the present moment change happens, and the more present we are the more we change. Jim accepted the challenge of the trail to stay present. It has helped him to achieve his goal to become and Elder. It has also made him an important, dear friend of mine.

CHAPTER 13

AWAKENING IN CHANGE

. . . we know now that this search for the whole self is no longer resolved through an educational process alone or even the choice of a good career. This search for the whole self is a process of making spiritual choices between the good and the better, the holy and the mundane, the essence of life and the cosmetic. We have built change into our futures, our educational options, our lives. We have come to understand that no life is set in stone anymore. On the contrary, life is a slow-won evolution of the self that raps every level of our lives and touches all its great questions.

Joan Chittister, <u>Following the Path</u>

For many years, a new worldview has been forming intuitively in the hearts and minds of people around the world. Though this emerging picture of our place in the universe has not been fully articulated, it is based on a central perception that we have capacities for a greater life than most of us have realized – a life that seems essentially joined with the evolution of the universe itself. We sense this connection, many believe, because we and the world are unfolding from the same transcendent source and are secretly moved to manifest more and more of our latent divinity.

James Redfield, Michael Murphy, Sylvia Timbers
God and the Evolving Universe

During my lifetime I have learned many lessons from change, and, more important, change has revealed much about myself. I credit change with helping me to glimpse through the door at my true nature and accept my continual process of becoming. Change has provided the stimulus to wake up from a mental stagnation that often masks my interaction with life and impedes my evolutionary progress. Through the changes, good and bad, which I have experienced, I now know that I am capable of anything, and, at the same time, I am in total control of nothing. So change is my conundrum to the truth of who I am, what life is about, and what really is. Like a good Buddhist Koan, change cannot be fully understood, but continues to reveal greater and greater meaning to the life I am living. In short, I have come to accept change as my teacher.

I would like to say that I am some master of change, but that would not be the truth. I am just as susceptible today to fall back into my ego, and its dream of consistency, as ever before. I do find myself more aware of my impermanence, and all it brings to my sense of security, but also my pure sense of wonder. This awareness of impermanence makes me more welcoming of change and less resistant. The tools that I have gathered give me greater confidence that I can work with change, rather than battle against change. So I can say that learning the lessons of change outlined in this book has given my some mastery of change and my periods of lapsing into unconsciousness seem shorter and less frequent. Most of all I am now excited about what is next rather than dreading any shift in my world.

As an example, my deep seated, co-dependent nature for perfection still echo's in my mind on a regular basis. For whatever reason, I have not been able to get to the root of its being within me. Yet change has constantly brought to light my need for perfection and has helped me to understand the futility of this need. I may never be cured, but I am in remission. Some day I hope to peel away the last 'ah ha' to my need for perfection and to finally be free of its gravitational pull. Until then, change is my partner in uncovering the next layer in my quest for the truth behind the mask of perfection.

As we master the process of change we become more awake and aware of the holistic nature the process represents in our very being. Saying Goodbye helps us to discover what is untrue in our lives and self. Exploring the present uncovers the connections we have missed and allows for the unfolding of our transcendent self. Moving on brings a discovery of ever-greater wholeness within and without. Finally, the constant use of inquiry allows us to mine deep and find the golden vein of truth.

Cleaning the Closet

The many things that seem important and immediate in our lives constantly distract us. Each distraction saps our energy and instills confusion as we cling to what is impermanent, rather than release. Change makes us take a hard look at all these distractions, and, in the process, there are some we just let go. In this way change helps us to clean out the clutter and become more focused on what is really meaningful.

At the same time, as we get clearer about what is meaningful, we uncover more distractions. There never seems to be an end to what is in the closet. Yet with each change, each cleaning, we find more energy to move forward with the process of unburdening our lives. The freeing up of the energy committed to distractions accumulates and gives us the needed momentum to tackle the serious inquiry into our true meaning and Higher Self. At the same time, as we hone our skills of inquiry into the value of our distractions, we gain greater skills in tackling the deeper questions of our being and existence. Why are we here? What are we doing? Where are we going? What are our connections? After this, what next?

Over time the distractions start to abate and our natural state of mind becomes clearer. This, in turn, assists us in avoiding future, potential distractions that can draw us back to confusion, delusion, and the dream. What comes with this clarity is a calmness that allows the simplicity of life to come to the fore. Our needs decrease along with the desire for more distractions. A common phrase comes to mind, 'Zenning your life.' As we move to a deeper understanding of 'what we are', within the context of the impermanence of life, then life becomes simpler in a very natural way. Finally, there is some sense of order in the closet!

Connecting the Dots

In change we find out what we don't know, we come to understand what we did not know about ourselves, and we find that there is so much more to be discovered. Change reveals the pristine field of the unknown, and as the unknown is revealed to us there are connections to be made. We see life as an interconnected web spinning out into infinity. Our ability to integrate the new information discovered through change is key to our process of becoming.

It is the integration of new experiences that allows our transcendent self to unfold. By transcendent self, I am referring to our true nature, awakening from the dream of limitation. Our transcendent self know no limits, as it is fully connected with all that the universe offers. Through integration, we connect the dots of our true nature and expand our awareness. This expanded awareness continues to reveal the falsehoods of the ego and its contrived limitations.

As we connect the dots we become more aware of, and open to, synchronicity in our lives. We are alert to even more connections. Our attention is looking for the next puzzle piece that fits the expanded mosaic of our life. Our attention sees and grasps the opportunities as they present. We begin to unleash our minds to a paradigm of 'anything is possible'.

In Search of Wholeness

As Joan Chittister suggests in the quote at the beginning of this chapter, we are on a quest for wholeness, and change is the holy grail of our quest. Without change we cannot see the areas where we are incomplete, we cannot recognize what we take for granted underlying fabric that brings us together in life, and we cannot understand what we *truly* prize within ourselves. God and life is the mystery that everybody wants to understand, but nobody can ever reveal. Yet we can, in our own way, reveal who and what we are. We can become more whole, and end this life with a sense of satisfaction that we had completed this journey.

There are countless stories of saints and common people, who have found and lived their purpose in life, and have faced death with a calm sense of completion. As we hear the recounting of their lives, they did not start out fully aware of their purpose, their calling. Einstein was a clerk before he uncovered the secrets of the universe. Buddha was a prince, then a pauper before becoming a teacher of wisdom. Lincoln lead a difficult childhood and young adulthood, wondering through the Midwest before becoming a lawyer and then President of the United States. Each one faced many twists and turns in life before coming upon their purpose for being. Each faced change with a bold resolve and used change as their teacher and guide. Each was an explorer of the present, who sought out the unknown in their quest for purpose.

Each of us has the same opportunity to find deeper meaning in life, to grasp our true purpose, to find what makes us whole. To quote Joan Chittister again from <u>Following the Path</u>, "It is the coming to the completion of our best selves, it is in following the magnet in our hearts, that we become our whole selves. Then we will have come to fullness of life, to the flowering of our best gifts, to being what we were meant to be, to finding the reason for which we were born."

The Cycle of Evolving with Change

Change facilitates us to become more awake and aware, and, as we become more awake and aware we are better able to face new changes in our life. This is an endless cycle that is integral to our evolution of consciousness and the expanded awareness of our true nature. Through change we are challenged and stretched to our limits and beyond. If we accept and work with change we discover that we are capable of so much more. We awaken to the fact that we *are* so much more.

As we successfully move through change we tap into an infinite energy that accentuates our thoughts, feelings and awareness. We become explorers of the present. We become intimately connected with this essence called God. We wake up to life. The price we pay is the devaluing of our ego and an acceptance that we don't really control anything in life. What we embrace is the unknown, and the wonders change brings. We awaken to the infinite cycle of evolving and becoming, and with each cycle we become more intimate with this thing we call life, with our awareness of God.

It is my hope this book has helped to make you less fearful and more accepting of change in your life. The tools and processes have provided for many a way to make change more manageable, resulting in evolutionary advancement of mind, body and Spirit. Change cannot be controlled, but we can manage it in a way where we can be what we were meant to be in this life, to find and live out our Soul purpose. We can come to better understand the infinite. By managing change we can fully engage in loving our life. We can live in joy, no matter what change comes our way.

A Final Meeting

Jason and I had worked together on multiple occasions managing many significant changes in his life. There had been several relationships that had come and gone, jobs that seemed exciting only to fizzle and end, moves to various parts of the world for exploration and adventure, and it was all encased in a whirlwind of change. Jason had become a change expert and, over time, a change junky. Jason had become comfortable with change and no longer feared it. The question at hand in our last meeting was whether he had come to understand the real meaning of change.

We met at our favorite Starbucks over a couple of latte's to inquire once again into the meaning of the current changes in his life. He had just returned from overseas and was looking to settle for a while in our area. He needed to work, but didn't know what direction he should look to find 'meaningful employment'. I had a hunch is it was something bigger that Jason was seeking, 'a meaningful life'.

Jason: "Well here I am again, knee deep in change with no idea as to where I am heading. I know that I am definitely squarely planted in 'exploring the present' but this time it seems different."

Merl: "Well let's start there. Tell me about how change is different for you this time?"

Jason: "It seems I am really good at 'saying goodbye'. With all of my most recent changes I have no problems or lingering feelings when saying goodbye. I guess I have developed a 'don't look back' attitude when moving through change. Is that bad?"

Merl: "Not necessarily, but consider this. What if we thought of change as our teacher and the change process as our lessons? If you never look back how can you gain the knowledge and insights you were meant to receive from change?"

Jason: "I guess I never truly bought into the idea that change was a teacher. But I get your point, if change is my teacher then I am not a very good student."

Merl: "Well let's start by looking at the facts. Tell me exactly what was happening in your life and why you felt the need to make a change. You know the rules, no stories, look at this with logic and your tools of inquiry. Drill down until you can't go any further." Jason was always a quick study and understood where I was coming from.

Jason: "All right just the facts, get to the root and find the reality in my change. I get it. I was traveling through Europe, staying in youth hostiles and picking up odd jobs to pay the way. I was really in the flow. I had no expectations each day, accepting whatever came in front of me. I was totally in the present moment. Life was fresh, exciting and joyous and I was fearless. It just seemed that whatever direction I went it always seemed to work out. If I needed work it would magically appear. If I needed a ride it always seemed to come along. If I needed a place to stay I always seemed to meet someone who would offer me shelter.

Don't get me wrong. It wasn't perfect. I spent some nights in my sleeping bag outside and in the middle of nowhere. I did miss a few meals, but I wasn't worrying about it. Things always changed, they always got better."

Merl: "OK, what did all of this teach you?"

Jason: "Teach me! Oh, I get it. What was change trying to help me understand? Well . . . I guess it was how to not fear change, but to just accept it when faced with a change in my life. I was riding a river of change. The rapids were exciting and the calm waters restful. Every day just felt really alive and it seemed to fill me with an energy that I had never had before."

Merl: "If that is true, then what made you change the life you have been living?"

Jason: "I guess I haven't really thought about it much. I just had a feeling in my gut that I was done wondering and it was time to reach out for something more."

Merl: "Something more, like what? Take that deeper."

Jason: "I don't know. (Yes, you do) I guess I just wasn't feeling like I was connecting with anyone. You know, really connecting. I loved being in new places and it isn't hard for me to make friends. I guess there were people who it would have been nice to have had a deeper connection with, but I just felt this drive to keep on moving."

Merl: "Let's just stop there and take it deeper. You seemed to be mastering change and that made you feel good. Yet by pushing for more change in your life you seemed to be leaving something behind. What were you leaving behind?"

Jason: "Like I said, some of the people I met that I would have liked to know better. There were some people I felt very close to we seemed to just click. They were hard to leave behind."

Merl: "So it's more than just connecting with people. There were certain people that felt special, that you might have gotten closer to if you hadn't moved on. Take a minute to experience your feelings for these people. Tell me about how you feel about them."

Jason: "I liked them, liked them a lot. We really seemed to be getting along and enjoyed each other's company. We seemed to share things in common. I felt relaxed with these people. We got into deeper conversations and I felt like I knew them a lot better than other people I have met on the road. I felt a kind on kinship with them. We would hug when we parted and that seemed warm and genuine."

Merl: "If these people meant so much to you why did you decide to move on?"

Jason: (silence, looking off, uncomfortable in his seat, pupils dilated, no response for several minutes)

Merl: "It seems like we have hit a hot spot for you. There are no wrong answers here. I like that you are looking at your feelings for these people. To me it means you are emotionally connected, which is a big step. Stick with your feelings. What were you feeling when you decided to move on?" (more silence)

Jason: "I guess I really liked these people and they seemed special to me, but I just didn't want to be tied down by developing deeper relationships on the road. I guess I was a little scared of what I was feeling and just thought it was time to move on."

Merl: "Scared . . . Scared of what?" (a long silence) We had been down the road of inquiry before and Jason is no dummy. He knew he had to incorporate his feelings into his answer. Beyond the logic are feelings, feelings of the heart and feelings of the gut.

Jason: "I was afraid that they would see how shallow I really am and would dump me before I dumped them." Jason's words reflected a mix of anger, sorrow and regret.

Merl: "So let me see if I understand you right. You had a feeling that the people you liked and would have liked to know better would come to the realization that you were a shallow person, without depth, if they got to know you better. Is that right? What sort of signs were you getting that they were turning away from the level of friendship you had established with them?"

Jason: "Well . . . there wasn't anything that I can put my finger on. I just had this feeling in my gut that they would eventually see right through me and break off the friendship."

Merl: "So tell me, what would they see if they could look deeper into who or what Jason really was?"

Jason: "I don't know, I guess they would see a guy who lives on the surface and is incapable of going deeper. You know, really able to open up and to explore a deeper meaning to life and relationships. I think people want more than I am capable of giving."

Merl: "Is that true? Is it really true that you are a shallow person, incapable of honestly sharing your thoughts and feelings with others? I have known you for sometime now Jason and that is not what I see. In fact, I think you are being pretty open and honest right now."

Jason: "So you think I'm not a shallow person?"

Merl: "No, I don't think you are a shallow person at all. In fact I don't believe that there are any shallow people. I believe there are people who are afraid of revealing who they really are because of some mistaken belief that they can't be real. We are all capable of showing our true self. It just takes some courage in taking a first step."

Jason: "Thanks for that. It's good to know that someone sees me different from how I see myself. So you think I am capable of having a deeper, more revealing and intimate relationship with other people?"

Merl: "Yes I do. Tell me, how would you picture that in your life? Close your eyes for a minute and let a picture come into focus of how it would look with you going deeper with others around you."

Jason: after several minutes with his eyes closed and deep in thought.

"It's funny, I picture myself in a small village, surrounded by children, and I am telling them a story. One, small child is setting on my lap and helping me to turn the pages of the book. All the children are laughing and giggling at the story and their parents are standing in the background listening and smiling. We all seem like one big family and I am accepted in the village. One of the elders in the group comes forward and paints a red line across my forehead with a paste in a wooden bowl. He then embraces me and offers me water and bread from the bag he is carrying. I am smiling and thank him before setting back down to finish the story."

Merl: I have found when people have a vision that is so clear and detailed it is coming from their Higher Self and represents a deep, hidden desire that is waiting to manifest. "That is a very vivid vision you are having. How does this vision make you feel in your chest and heart?"

Jason: "I have a very warm and peaceful feeling in my chest. I feel very relaxed and comfortable with these people. We all seem to really know and understand each other. There is no animosity or struggle for power, and everyone seems willing to support one another."

Merl: "Do you have the feeling that you need to move on?"

Jason: "No. . . It feels like I belong in this place."

Merl: "Before you open your eyes take one more long look around you and tell me how you feel in your gut."

Jason: After a couple minutes of looking around his vision, "My gut feels good. I don't have that knot in my stomach that I usually have when I think it is time to move on. I'm not afraid of staying in this place. It seems to have all I need to be happy."

Merl: Open your eyes and take a few minutes to process what you just experienced." After ten minutes of silence Jason turned to me and gave me the smile of the Cheshire Cat from Alice in Wonderland.

Jason: "That was amazing! I never knew this existed within me. I think I know where I am heading. It's funny, I have always had a thought in the back of my mind that said, 'how about the Peace Corps?' but I never gave it any serious consideration. You are a miracle worker!"

Merl: "No, the miracle worker is inside you. I just happened to be here at the right time to help you unlock the door that has kept the miracle worker imprisoned all this time. I think you are moving out of the present and are ready to move on. All of your travels have just been preparation for your next big change. So, what next?"

Jason: "I am off to find out more about the Peace Corps. I think . . . no I know that is where I am headed next. I need to get started with my research. Thanks for all your help."

Jason took the next six months to do his research, make a commitment and get his training. His first stop was a small village in South America. After two years there Jason moved on to Africa helping out in another small village. I got postcards for the first few years, but then they stopped. I don't have an ending to this story, but I will share what I learned. There are changes layered within changes. Some changes are just preparation for bigger changes down the road. What the postcards told me was that Jason allowed change to help him could go deeper in seeking more meaning to his life, and in going deeper he found real joy in his life. I don't think Jason would have ever reached that point without his ability to accept and work with change.

Diving Into the Miracle of Change

I thought I was,
And then I changed.
No longer recognizing
What was, but what is.

I am awake to wonder.
Filled with the power
Of what is.
Revealing the truth of now.

And with a smile
I simply ask,
"What next?"
Diving into the miracle of change.

AUTHORS AND BOOKS THAT HAVE TAUGHT ME ABOUT CHANGE

The End of Your World, Adyashanti, Sounds True, 2008.

Falling into Grace, Adyashanti, Sounds True, 2011.

Transitions, Making Sense of Life's Changes, William Bridges, Da Capo Press, 2004.

Managing Transitions 3rd Edition, William Bridges, Da Capo Press, 2009.

The Way of Transitions, William Bridges, Da Capo Press, 2001.

How to Change Your Life, Ernest Holmes, Science of Mind Publishing, 1999.

The Science of Mind, Ernest Holmes, Putnam Books, 1997.

Loving What Is, Byron Katie, Three Rivers Press, 2002.

The Wisdom of No Escape, Pema Chondron, Shambhala Press, 1991.

Taking the Leap, Pema Chondron, Shambhala Press. 2009.

The Courage to Be Present, Karen Kissel Wegela, Shambhala Press, 2010.

The Art of Uncertainty, Dennis Merritt Jones, Penguin Group, 2011.

Emotionally-Focused Therapy, Leslie Greenberg, American Psychological Association, 2011.

ABOUT THE AUTHOR

Merl Will-Wallace has a bachelors degree in organizational management and a masters degree in mental health counseling. For over twenty years Merl has been a personal and professional coach and counselor in business and private practice. Merl synthesized his approach to change through personal experience, business consulting in change management and his work with a wide range of individuals, helping them to understand and move through change. Merl speaks to large groups about change and conducts seminars and workshops on Working With Change.